CATHOLIC SCHOOL EDUCATION IN THE UNITED STATES

SOURCE BOOKS ON EDUCATION
(Vol. 31)

GARLAND REFERENCE LIBRARY
OF SOCIAL SCIENCE
(Vol. 474)

CATHOLIC SCHOOL EDUCATION
IN THE UNITED STATES
Development and Current Concerns

Mary A. Grant
Thomas C. Hunt

GARLAND PUBLISHING, INC. • NEW YORK & LONDON
1992

Library of Congress Cataloging-in-Publication Data

Grant, Mary A.
    Catholic school education in the United States : development and
current concerns / by Mary A. Grant and Thomas C. Hunt.
    p. cm. — (Garland reference library of social science ; vol. 474.
Source books on education ; vol. 31)
    Includes bibliographical references (p.) and indexes.
    ISBN 0–8240–6342–2 (alk. paper)
    1. Catholic schools—United States—History. 2. Catholic Church—
Education—United States—History. I. Hunt, Thomas C., 1930– .
II. Title. III. Series: Garland reference library of social science ;
v. 474. IV. Series: Garland reference library of social science. Source
books on education ; vol. 31.
LC501.G55 1992
377'.82'73—dc20   92–14907
                                    CIP

Printed on acid-free, 250-year-life paper
Manufactured in the United States of America

DEDICATION and ACKNOWLEDGEMENTS

Mary Grant and Thomas Hunt gratefully and lovingly dedicate this book to their mothers, Bridget Grant and Marion Kinney Hunt. Mrs. Grant died on October 23, 1989; Mrs. Hunt passed away on November 21, 1990. *Requiescant in pace!*

We acknowledge with thanks the help of many people, whose assistance was indispensable in the preparation of this book. In particular, we wish to thank: Professor Hunt's graduate assistants, Ann Wilson, Suzanne Reid, and Donald Inman who helped in a number of ways; David Starkey, of the Word Processing Center of the College of Education at Virginia Tech for printing the text; and Marilyn Norstedt, of Virginia Tech's Newman Library, who guided the indexing process. Finally, we wish to express our gratitude to the Division of Curriculum and Instruction and to the College of Education at Virginia Tech for the support they provided.

Mary A. Grant
St. John's University

Thomas C. Hunt
Virginia Tech

Contents

Foreword

From the early missionaries to this country, Catholic schools have contributed to the public good of this Nation as well as to the mission of the Church.

Quality educational opportunities for all of America's children are of great concern to parents, professional educators and politicians. It is especially timely then that *Catholic School Education in the United States: Development and Current Concerns* presents not only a history of Catholic schools, but also cites their recognized accomplishments and the challenges they face.

The authors have provided public policy-makers as well as educators with an accurate and readable study of Catholic schools which serve more than 2.5 million students today and have educated millions of this country's citizens.

Catholic educators especially will find this publication helpful as we remember our roots. Colleges and universities should adopt it as they prepare the next generation of Catholic school teachers and administrators.

Lourdes Sheehan, RSM, Ed.D.
Secretary for Education
United States Catholic Conference

Introduction

In 1986 the writer served as the coordinating editor for a reference book, *Religious Schools in America: A Selected Bibliography*, which was also published by Garland Publishing. Seventeen of that book's twenty-four chapters were devoted to the K-12 schools of various denominations.

The compilers of the chapter on Catholic schools included more than three hundred entries in their selection. The chapter was limited, in their words, to an "intentional contemporary slant," both because of the importance of the Second Vatican Council and to the "enormous literature on Catholic schools." Due to that enormity and to limitations imposed by space, references were listed under selected subject headings rather than annotating individual entries.

At the time, the writer conceived the idea of a reference book devoted solely to Catholic schools. Following the publication of two sister volumes, *Religious Colleges and Universities* (1988), and *Religion Seminaries* (1989), a contract with Garland Publishing was signed to produce such a text. The writer was fortunate to be able to enlist the aid in this project of Ms. Mary A. Grant, Director of the Health Education Resource Center, College of Pharmacy and Allied Health Professions, St. John's University, New York, who had most effectively compiled the chapters on Catholic colleges and universities, and on Catholic seminaries, for the aforementioned 1988 and 1989 reference works.

This book has nine chapters. Following an initial overview chapter, there are eight chapters arranged chronologically beginning with colonial times and concluding with 1991. Each of the nine chapters starts with a brief prose description. The writer is responsible for the first eight of these; Karen Ristau of St. Thomas University authored Chapter Nine. Mary Grant assembled the second half of each chapter, which features annotated bibliographic entries.

This book is intended to be a resource for those interested in Catholic schools -- in the past and/or present, whether scholar, student, policy-maker, or interested citizen. These schools have made, and continue to make, major contributions to American society in a myriad of ways. It is the writer's most sincere hope that this work will increase the knowledge and respect for that contribution, albeit in a minor way.

Thomas C. Hunt
Blacksburg, Virginia

Catholic School Education in the United States

CHAPTER 1
An Overview

In 1988-89 there were 7,505 Catholic elementary schools and 1,362 secondary schools in the United States, constituting a total of 8,867, a considerable decline from the figure of 13,292 in 1965.[1] Likewise, during that same period, Catholic K-12 enrollment underwent a reduction of approximately fifty-five percent, from a high point of 5,601,000 in 1964 to 2,551,000 in 1988-89.[2] These numbers are but a manifestation of changes which were occurring in the Catholic Church in the United States.

It is the purpose of this first chapter to provide a brief overview of Catholic schooling (K-12) in the United States, focusing on the nature, purposes, and goals of those schools. In the process, I will endeavor not to treat issues which will be dealt with in subsequent chapters, other than in a most rudimentary fashion. To a considerable extent, one's view of those ends is influenced by how one perceives the Catholic Church itself and its function in society and role in relation to eternity.

The Mission of the Church and Its Schools

Historically, the "traditionalist" view of the Church's mission served as the undergirding for the nature and purpose of its schools. God sent His Son, Christ, to redeem the world. Christ founded the Church to carry on his work of salvation. The

Church's three-fold task was to teach, sanctify, and govern. One of the first questions the Catechism asked of the youthful Catholic was "Why did God make me?" The correct response was, "He made me to know, love and serve Him in this world and so be happy with Him in the next." The supremacy of the supernatural and the eternal to the natural and the temporal was clear.

The conventional wisdom was, then, that Catholic schools were to exist primarily for the supernatural and eternal. They were to be agents of the Church in its salvific mission. As such, the right of the Church to establish and maintain such schools was basic to its fundamental mission, and a right that both preceded and superseded the rights of parent and civil authority.

The Recent Dilemma

There has been, in the United States, corresponding with the Second Vatican Council (Vatican II) in the 1960s, a disintegration of the sense of mission described above. This phenomenon has been evident in a number of ways, e.g., by the challenges from lay and clerical Catholics to the Church's teaching on birth control and abortion, by the departure of priests and nuns in large numbers from their religious states, and by loss of consensus on the nature and purpose of Catholic schools. The decline in Catholic schools has been due to some extent by fiscal pressure, but it has been brought about in the main due to a loss of a widely-shared sense of purpose and agreement about the importance, indeed indispensability, of Catholic schools on the part of Catholics, clerical as well as lay. The income level of Catholics in this era far exceeds that of their forebearers, who were willing to sacrifice to support their schools. It is this change in attitude which in the main accounted for the decline in Catholic school attendance from 1965 on.

Currently, Catholic schools face a number of challenges. The two which appear to be most critical are identity and financing (see Chapter Nine). Other issues, such as staffing, leadership, governance, and support also exist. The "National Congress on Catholic Schools for the 21st Century," held in November of 1991 under the sponsorship of the National Catholic Educational Association, was called to provide leadership in addressing these concerns.

Endnotes

1. Frederick H. Brigham, Jr., *United States Catholic Elementary and Secondary Schools 1988-89: A Statistical Report on Schools, Enrollment, and Staffing.* Washington, D.C.: National Catholic Educational Association, 1989, p. 24.

2. Ibid.

Bibliographic Entries

1. Blum, Virgil C. *Freedom of Choice in Education.* Rev. ed. Glen Rock, NJ: Deus Books-Paulist Press, 1963.

    Supports the claim that tax funds should be provided for education of children in church-related schools. Connects the central issue of federal aid to education to the freedom of religion and provides the arguments to prove that the constitutional guarantee of freedom of religion gives parents the right to place their children in the school of their choice. Details a tax credit plan that is concerned with both public and independent schools. Examines positive effects that would occur including preservation of the fundamental liberties of all Americans, and the improvement of the quality of education in both public and independent schools.

2. Buetow, Harold A. *The Catholic School: Its Roots, Identity, and Future.* New York: Crossroad Publishing Company, 1988.

    Treats fully the question of identity and viability of Catholic schools examining both opponents' and proponents' views. Studies the purpose, the history and philosophy of Catholic schools and presents evidence not only that Catholic schools have contributed to God and country, but they have demonstrated the worth of religion in education and the benefit of religion in personal growth and formation. Concludes that a Catholic school will not remain Catholic for long without attention to its identity, and if the Catholic school identity is properly reflected upon, understood, and implemented by Catholic educators, then Catholic schools should be welcomed everywhere.

3. Campbell, James F. "Through Childhood to Adolescence: Developing Moral Values." *Priest* 30 (September 1974): 38-44.

    Discusses the stages of moral development from infancy to maturity and helps parents and educators to understand moral behavior that is appropriate to each age level. Finds that moral maturity allows the learner to move freely from self to God.

4. Campbell, Paul E. "The Heritage of Catholic Education." *The Homiletic and Pastoral Review* 44 (June 1944): 683-87.

    Summarizes the principles that guide Christian teachers and reminds them of their heritage of two thousand years of Christian education. Reflects on the objects of true education stressing spiritual aims while seeking after academic proficiency, professional excellence or vocational competence. Upholds Christian education's primary purpose of fitting students for life in time and eternity.

5. *Christian Education of Youth.* Encyclical Letter of His Holiness Pius XI. With a Discussion Club Outline by Rev. Gerald C. Tracy, S. J. New York: Paulist Press, 1940.

    Presents the authoritative position of the Church on Christian educational theory and practice. Charts the course for Catholic educators touching on all aspects of Christian education: its importance, its activity, the Church's right in education, the rights of the family and state, the alignment of temporal power with the spiritual, sex instruction and co-education, the educational environment, and the obligation of parents. States the duty of the state in a nation of different beliefs to leave free scope to the Church and family, while giving them the assistance that justice demands.

6. Conrad, John F. "A Theological Rationale for Catholic Schools." *Notre Dame Journal of Education* 3 (Winter 1973): 310-17.

    Argues that the philosophy that keeps Catholic schools in existence must be fused with the theology that keeps the philosophy valid. Focuses upon pastoral theology as the motivation or foundation for the existence of Catholic schools and discusses such pastoral concerns as providing opportunity for a Christian value formation and for effective methods to create an atmosphere of faith-culture in which the morality of the gospel becomes a foundation for relevant living and fulfillment. Reflects that dogmatic foundations of Catholic schooling begin with the essentials of faith but the expression of it goes beyond the Baltimore Catechism.

7. Conwell, Mother Francis Regis. "A Panoramic View of Objectives." *The Catholic Educational Review* 54 (October 1956): 449-58.

    Meditates on the noble work of Christian education reflecting on the formation of the intellect, the will and the heart. Supports the treatise with the words of Pius XI who stressed that education is concerned with the whole man.

8. Cushing, Richard Cardinal. *The Mission of the Teacher.* Boston: St. Paul Editions, 1962.

    Records the addresses given by Cardinal Cushing to various groups of Catholic educators over a period of two decades. Exhorts Catholic teachers to form in their students the perfect image of Jesus Christ and to realize that through them the Church will fulfil her social mission in the world. Declares that no school is more devoted to American principles, institutions and traditions than the Catholic school.

9. Dulles, Avery. *The Communication of Faith and Its Content.* Washington, DC: National Catholic Educational Association, 1985.

Examines the nature of religious knowledge and faith and clarifies the three functions of religious education: the apologetic, expository and nurturing. Asserts that religion is distinguished from all other subjects because it focuses attention on God, the absolute transcendent. Advocates a symbolic approach to God based on the Christian symbols found in the Bible and the traditions of the Christian community. Relates that the believer deepens his or her faith through assent of mind and heart to the truth revealed by God in divinely given signs and symbols, the central symbol being the figure of Jesus Christ.

10. Dwyer, John F. "The Contribution of Catholic Theology to Certain Aspects of the Catholic Theory of Education." Ph.D. dissertation. Fordham University, 1952.

Researches how Catholic theology contributes to the Catholic theory of education which integrates principles derived from revelation with those derived from reason. Recognizes the need for a knowledge of the bases of education which depend on revelation through theology, and investigates by philosophical procedures the teaching of Catholic theology relevant to the nature of the pupil, the goals of education, the right to educate, the nature of education, and the means of education. Examines the Papal documents and concludes that they give evidence that the Holy See has acted consistently with the teaching of Catholic theology in its decisions and pronouncements on Catholic education.

11. Faerber, Louis J., ed. *The Emerging Objectives of Catholic Education.* Dayton, Ohio: School of Education, University of Dayton, 1970.

Recounts the proceedings of a workshop in which teachers and administrators of elementary and secondary Catholic schools reexamined the role of Catholic schools in the modern world and found new emphases to educational objectives after the Vatican II Council. Describes the seminar on secondary education which starts with the premise that the philosophy of Catholic education remains very much the same today as it always was; that is, to provide the best possible means for developing good Christians. Summarizes the attitudes and objectives of the seminar on elementary education noting that Catholic education is broader than Catholic schooling and that quality rather than quantity should be stressed.

Contains items 324, 353, 354

12. Gilbert, John (R). "Teaching Values in the Catholic School." *Origins* 6 (May 5, 1977): 736-60.

Believes that the values in a Catholic elementary school must be exemplified by its community of teachers and the teaching of Christian values by the way the curriculum is carried out. Explains that the faculty must be a community of mature Christians who understand moral development as a growth process. Exhorts teachers to help students, according to their ability and level of maturity, to grow towards a complete living of the gospel. Addresses the marking system, authority and value development, and social concerns and value development.

13. Hamilton, Clinton D. "Theory of the Roman Catholic Church in the Support and Control of Education, With Special Reference to the United States." Ph.D. dissertation. Florida State University, 1965.

Ascertains from statements and decrees issued by Church Councils or encyclicals, and from decrees of the Popes what the theoretical position of the Roman Catholic Church is with regard to the support and control of education, especially in the United States. Examines the Church's position in the milieu of the debate on separation of Church and State. Shows that the original aim of the Church in America in building and in supporting her own school system was broadened to include the goal of receiving federal aid to support Catholic schools.

14. Henle, Robert J. "American Principles and Religious Schools." *Catholic Mind* 54 (June 1956): 301-09.

    Looks at the principle of the separation of Church and State and the principle of religious liberty, combining them in the discussion. Warns that an unbalanced and extreme application of the separation of Church and State can lead to religious discrimination and destroy the meaning of religious liberty. Documents the above principles through Supreme Court decisions, and also the principle that the family is the basic unit of society with a primary right to educate its children. Addresses the role of the State as the caretaker of the common welfare and the protector of religious liberty. Contends that the same principles should apply to both indirect and direct educational aid which is in itself intended for the general welfare.

15. Jordan, Edward B. "Catholic Education: Its Philosophy and Background." *Essays on Catholic Education in the United States*, pp. 3-24. Edited by Roy J. Deferrari. Washington, DC: The Catholic University of America Press, 1942.

    Provides a summary of the contributions of the Fathers of the Church in their writings on educational philosophy. Notes that Catholic thought on the aims, goals, purposes, and values in education have been consistent through the centuries and any modifications introduced affected secondary objectives. Indicates the need for more scholarly presentations of the Catholic position on educational questions which can come from men and women well trained in Catholic philosophy and the methods of scientific research. States the need for a restatement of Catholic educational philosophy in the twentieth century.

    Contains items 73, 79, 137, 229

16. Lannie, Vincent P. "Church and School Triumphant: The Sources of American Catholic Educational Historiography." *History of Education Quarterly* 16 (Summer 1976): 131-45.

    Traces the development of the written history of the American Catholic Schools, citing specific works and the authors who wrote them. Includes James A. Burns, John Gilmary Shea, Isaac Hecker, Orestes Brownson, John O'Kane Murray, Bernard J. Meiring, Charles I. White, James R. Bayley, William Byrne and Andrew Lambing. Shows how the history of Catholic education is linked with that of the Church in America, and expresses the theme of triumph and the compatibility of Catholicism with Americanism.

17. Lazerson, Marvin. "Understanding American Catholic Educational History." *History of Education Quarterly* 17 (Fall 1977): 297-317.

    Contends there are complexities and subtleties about American Catholicism that make the study of its historiography a complicated one. Notes the same concerning Catholic education but finds some insights into why and how the Catholic school system developed in an essay by Robert D. Cross, "The Origins of the Catholic Parochial Schools in America." (item 102). Interprets the issues in American Catholicism and public education that were related to the development of the Catholic parochial school system through the nineteenth century and into the twentieth century. Explains that the organization and standardization of Catholic schools in the twentieth century are based on public school norms.

18. Lee, James Michael. *The Purpose of Catholic Schooling.* Washington, DC: National Catholic Educational Association, 1968.

    Analyzes the ultimate purpose and proximate purpose of Catholic schooling and describes a third type of purpose as that of the particular school level. Describes the intellectualist position and the moralist position, giving the strengths and weaknesses of each point of view. Declares that on every level, the Catholic school is a deliberate conscious apostolate of the Church.

19. Leen, Edward. *What is Education?* New York: Sheed and Ward, 1944.

Expounds on the meaning and object of education and the principal work of the educator which is to use all the means offered by art, science, literature and revelation so that human living is in harmony with God. Reflects on the work of the school in the process of education and states that the Church is the chief educational institution assisting its members to attain full Christian personality. Declares the theory of the Church that man can achieve his full and proper development only in and through society.

20. McBride, Alfred (A). "The Nature of the Church and Its Educational Mission." *Notre Dame Journal of Education* 3 (Winter 1973): 293-96.

States that any theory to back up new and better ways of financing and renewed efforts towards quality Catholic education is a consideration of the nature of the Church and its educational mission. Believes that it is religious experience and considers the element of religious experience which is exterior expression, publicly expressed in words, community and organization. Addresses each of these experiences reflecting on the purpose of institutionalizing which is to sustain the life and vision of the community and its mission. Identifies the mission of the Church from which comes its educational mission.

21. McCluskey, Neil G. "The Catholic Obligation to Educate." *Catholic Lawyer* 4 (Summer 1958): 238-43.

Explores the obligation to educate from which flows the right to educate, a right upon which Catholics insist in order to establish schools in which their children can be taught Christian values. Delineates the problem of religion in public schools and concludes that character education in the public schools is necessarily circumscribed by the secular order.

22. McCluskey, Neil G. *Catholic Viewpoint on Education.* Garden City, NY: Hanover House-Doubleday & Company, Inc., 1959.

Explains the Catholic position on various aspects of education in America. Outlines the history of American schooling with the development of private and public education and the rise of the Catholic school system. Discusses the evolution of the secular public school which could not provide for the moral side of a Catholic child's education and demonstrates the valuable contributions that private education has made to American society. Makes a clear statement on the Church's position regarding parental rights in the courts, governmental aid to nonpublic education, but also reminds Catholics of their civic obligation of moral and material support of the public schools.

23. McDermott, Edwin J. *Distinctive Qualities of the Catholic School.* Washington, DC: National Catholic Educational Association, 1985.

Expands on the characteristics of the Catholic schools that make them different. Asserts that Jesus Christ is the cornerstone and His teaching is a guide for reaching the fullness of human potential. Describes the Catholic schools as a community of learners and believers with a common vision of the meaning of life. Regards parents as the primary educators of their children and examines the role of the Church, the Catholic teachers, and Catholic administrators in Catholic schools. Finds the state is served well by the Catholic schools which prepare citizens to function effectively in society.

24. McGrath, Sister M. Bernard. "The Compatibility of Catholic Schools and Democratic Standards." Ph.D. dissertation. The Catholic University of America, 1948.

Develops the concept of democracy historically and philosophically, discussing the two concepts prevalent in society, the Christian one based on the belief in the brotherhood of man under the Fatherhood of God and the concept based on the evolutionary doctrine which sees man as a creature of matter only, but above the animal world. Analyzes the Catholic philosophy of education, investigates the curricula and procedures at elementary, secondary and higher education. Concludes that Catholic educational principles based on supernatural values, the curricula and educational procedures of Catholic schools are not only compatible with democracy but its surest guarantee.

25. McKeough, Michael J. "Education's Need for Philosophy." *The American Catholic Philosophical Association Proceedings For the Year of 1954* 28 (April 20-21, 1954): 239-42.

Speaks for all American youth in public as well as Catholic schools in discussing the need for a concept of philosophy as an objective, unified body of knowledge. Declares that Catholic educators have an obligation to communicate to fellow educators, through the printed and spoken word, a sound philosophy based on scholastic principles.

26. McLaughlin, Sister Raymond. *The Liberty of Choice: Freedom and Justice in Education.* Collegeville, MN: The Liturgical Press, 1979.

Deals with the inability of the United States to allow private schools to have a substantial share in the public funds and to face the issue of implementing the primary rights of parents to educate their children. Traces the history of American schools which were private and religiously oriented for three hundred years following the early beginnings in America. Shows that the other Western democracies have implemented the parents' right to choose freely the type of education they desire for their children and have satisfied the demands of distributive justice. Advocates the voucher system as the most equitable and simplest way for the United States to do the same.

27. Manno, Bruno V. "The Ministry of Catholic Education." *New Catholic World* 224 (March-April 1981): 52-55.

Reflects upon the nature of ministry, discusses its purpose, and explores the basic educational orientations and religious metaphors found in the learning experiences that shape the curriculum. Identifies the ministry of education with the mystery symbol of the Trinity: creating, parabling, and hallowing. Concludes with an assessment of the minister, the moral agent who applies norms to particular situations. Reports the result of research that suggests that men and women define their identity differently: women through attachment, affinity and bonding; men by means of detachment and separation.

28. Mullaney, James V. "The Natural Law, the Family and Education." *Catholic Education: A Book of Readings.* pp. 90-102. Edited by Walter B. Kolesnik and Edward J. Power. New York: McGraw-Hill Book Company, 1965.

Relates the natural law to education with emphasis on the family, the student, the teacher and the state. Understands education in three distinct senses: 1) the sum total of all the life-long processes through which a person is led to fulfillment; 2) every type of formation undertaken with regard to young people; 3) the specific task of intellectual formation by elementary and secondary schools, and by colleges and universities. Considers alternatives that will provide for the rights of the family, the student and the state in resolving the problem of religious education.

29. Murray, John Courtney. "The School and Christian Freedom." *National Catholic Educational Proceedings, 1951* 48 (August, 1951): 63-68.

Reflects on the meaning of Christian freedom and on the teaching of the idea of Christian freedom in the school while respecting the personal and social living that takes place within its walls. Sees the Catholic school as a City of freedom where there is order, discipline, obedience, but where there also must be enterprise, initiative and responsibility. Examines democracy as a depository for man's freedom but finds that it has become an idol rather than a servant. Exhorts Christian people to take the concept of American freedom and make it the soul of a renewed people.

30. National Conference of Catholic Bishops. *To Teach As Jesus Did: A Pastoral Message on Catholic Education.* Washington, DC: U.S. Catholic Conference, 1972.

    Articulates the educational ministry of the Christian community which is to carry on the mission of Jesus Christ entrusted to the Church. Discusses the dictum to teach as Jesus did and considers the forms that ministry takes in the education of adults and the education of youth.

31. O'Brien, Kevin J. *The Proximate Aim of Education: A Study of the Proper and Immediate End of Education.* Milwaukee, WI: Bruce Publishing Company, 1958.

    Considers that man as a free agent and self-directed should be brought gradually to the recognition of the proper ends of human activity. Looks at the formation of the true and perfect Christian as constituting the proper and immediate end of education, which involves the development of all the powers of the human person, natural and supernatural. Develops the implications of the proper end of education with regard to educational theory, moral formation of the child, the school, the curriculum, the teacher, and the parents.

32. *Papal Teachings: Education.* Selected and arranged by the Benedictine Monks of Solesmes. Translated by Rev. Aldo Rebeschini, Coll. Propaganda Fide. Boston: St. Paul Editions, 1960.

Presents in chronological order the Papal documents on the spiritual formation of Christians and particularly, on the education of youth from Pius VII to Pius XII. Follows the alphabetical index with an analytical one which briefly summarizes a line of thought and indicates the relative texts. Illustrates that the Catholic school plays an essential role in the education of youth, achieving a positive training and formation of the physical, intellectual, moral and religious nature of the young.

33. Papillon, Cassian Edmund. "A Catholic Philosophy of Curriculum." *The Catholic Educational Review* 44 (June 1946): 329-34.

Examines the concept of curriculum in each of its two broad aspects: the choice of experiences that are to affect the education of children, and the order or sequence in which these experiences are to be presented to the students. Observes that any curriculum can have aims that are also Catholic but contrasts the Catholic philosophy of curriculum which subordinates all the factors in life to a man's spiritual end, and the naturalistic philosophy of curriculum which makes the curriculum an end in itself, thus causing differences both in content and sequence of the curriculum.

34. Pegis, Anton C. "Catholic Education and American Society." *National Catholic Educational Association Bulletin* 50 (August 1953): 52-58.

Believes that Catholic educators must not only restate their belief in Catholic principles but must manifest them as Catholic teachers living in the present. Understands the Thomistic doctrine that man has spiritual and physical dependence upon a temporal existence in order to complete himself as a human person. Urges Catholic educators to help the student to bring truth to the world in which he lives, and to build an American society that is truly human and spiritual. Emphasizes that Catholic education includes both the salvation and perfection of the person in time and unites its own citizens with their fellow American citizens.

35. Phelan, Gerald B. "The Problem of Communication Between Catholic and Non-Catholic Educators and Philosophers." *Catholic Education: A Book of Readings* (item 28), pp. 154-62.

Discusses the problem of communication and regards it as a practical one based on understanding rather than agreement. Points out that Catholic philosophers and educators must understand and appreciate the positions and principles of non-Catholic philosophers and educators. Tells Catholics it is essential to set forth their own stand on philosophical and educational issues clearly and with complete scholarship. Encourages honest, fair-minded, and well-informed discussions and recommends the start of a dialogue by reading and discussing Pius XI's encyclical letter, *Christian Education of Youth.*

36. *A Primer on Educational Governance in the Catholic Church by the Governance Task Force of the Department of Chief Administrators of Catholic Education and the Boards Department of the NCEA, the National Association of Boards of Education.* Edited by J. Stephen O'Brien, National Catholic Educational Association, 1987.

Provides a detailed explanation of the structures for governance of the Church's educational ministries on the elementary and secondary levels. Analyzes where authority is vested, how it is distributed and used throughout the educational programs and distinguishes between authority and power. Includes an appendix of samples of Board constitutions, as well as a glossary of terms.

37. Redden, John D. and Francis A. Ryan. *A Catholic Philosophy of Education.* Milwaukee, WI: The Bruce Publishing Company, 1956 (revised edition).

Covers the principles of Catholic education drawn from scholastic philosophy which accepts the supernatural way of life and way of thought. Describes and evaluates the false principles of other philosophies of education: naturalism, socialism, communism, and experimentalism. Shows that Catholic education embraces man as a whole, developing and disciplining the powers of the body and soul.

38. Ryan, J. Joseph. "An Operative Concept of Christian Education From the Papal Encyclicals of the Past Century." Ph.D. dissertation. Fordham University, 1952.

Demonstrates unchanging tradition of papal thought on Christian education and considers the total operative concept from the point of view of the individual in himself, in the family, in society, and as a member of the Mystical Body of Christ. Reflects on individual principles of the educative process which are working within the whole fabric of Christian education; namely, the Christian meaning of liberty, love, social justice, social charity, social authority, common good, and human solidarity in Christ.

39. Ryan, John Julian. "The Idea of a Catholic School." *National Catholic Educational Association Bulletin* 43 (February 1947): 11-28.

Considers the same general end of all Catholic schools and exhorts administrators to keep in mind the fundamental principles governing all Catholic education. Discusses the papal interpretation of Catholic education and its final object. States that Christian education must be professional and examines the principles of professional training. Asks questions concerning the Catholic school, whether or not it is what it should be.

40. Shelton, Charles. "The Adolescent, Social Justice, and the Catholic School: A Psychological Perspective." *The Living Light* 17 (Fall 1980): 223-33.

Examines the difficulties in social justice education at the secondary level and addresses the jump from personal moral decision making to that of a complicated political and economic world. Considers the psychological processes that underlie an adolescent's perception and internalization of social justice. Looks at findings of prosocial behavior and social justice research and declares that Catholic secondary educators must fuse positive behavior in the context of the gospel. Provides strategies for creating a climate for social justice education in the secondary school.

41. Traviss, Mary Peter. *Student Moral Development in the Catholic School.* Washington, DC: National Catholic Educational Association, 1985.

Understands that the concept of moral education is broader than moral development and embodies an awareness of one's values; presupposes a moral atmosphere and modeling adults. Discusses a variety of educational approaches to moral education including values classification and examines the climate and atmosphere of the classroom in a Catholic school. Indicates the characteristics of an effective moral teacher and considers effective teaching strategies focusing on problems arising from the experience of the student. Explains the formational levels of the Christian conscience.

42. Winning, Thomas J. "The Positive Value of Catholic Education." *Catholic Mind* 74 (October 1976): 9-13.

Addresses Catholic education as an essential expression of the mission of Christ preparing the young to be mature and responsible Christians who make a positive contribution to society. Explains that Catholic schools concern themselves with teaching not only academic subjects but with guidance, sex education, social and community subjects. Asserts that Catholic education offers positive Christian positions, nurturing, encouraging and supporting Faith which is a free and personal decision. Urges parents to play active, supportive roles in the life of the school.

CHAPTER 2
Colonial Times to 1840

Catholic schools existed in Florida and Louisiana as early as the seventeenth century. Franciscans, Jesuits and Capuchins joined lay teachers, who were predominant overall, in pre-nineteenth century schools. There were secondary schools, the first one founded in St. Augustine, Florida in 1606, as well as primary schools. The lines between secondary schools and colleges were often blurred.

Catholic educational institutions were sometimes racially integrated as in New Orleans. There also were black religious orders and separate schools for free blacks, mainly in Louisiana.

The Church's educational efforts in colonial times were not limited to the deep south, however. Catholic schools were established in Connecticut, Illinois, Michigan, Maryland, the Louisiana Territory, New York, Pennsylvania, Maine, California and in the Southwest, under French or Spanish jurisdiction. Some were day schools, others were exclusively for boarders, and yet others were combined. Schools were often segregated by gender, with some coeducation. Missionary zeal, the conversion of nations, was one of the reasons for their establishment. Like their counterparts in Congregationalist New England, religion was a major factor for their existence and in their operation.

Conflicts occurred, especially in colonies under English (Protestant) rule. Some of these conflicts endured into the national period. Tensions, as evident in the turmoil in New York City in the early nineteenth century, presaged subsequent strife between the Church and civil society, Protestant or secular, over the control of schooling. Another form of conflict between the Church and civil authority occurred in South Carolina, where Bishop England opened a school for free blacks in 1835 in Charleston, an action deemed imprudent.

In the 1830's, the nation was to witness the creation of the state-supported, state-regulated common school movement under the leadership of Horace Mann in Massachusetts. This movement would ring in a new era for Catholic as well as public schools. The colonial periods of "Transplantation," and the national era of "Formative Foundations," as referred to by Buetow, for Catholic schools had ended.[1] New challenges lay ahead.

Endnotes

1. Harold A. Buetow, *Of Singular Benefit: The Story of Catholic Education in the United Statees*. New York: MacMillan, 1970, p. VII.

Bibliographic Entries

43. Balmain, Alexander F. "The History of Catholic Education in the Diocese of Brooklyn." Ph.D. dissertation. Fordham University, 1935.

Traces the origin and development of Catholic education in Brooklyn, New York, which began in 1828 when three Sisters of Charity opened the first Catholic school in the basement of St. James Church, the first Catholic church in the Diocese. Describes the foundation built by Brooklyn's first bishop, John Loughlin, and the achievements of Bishop McDonnell in developing Catholic schools. Explains the contributions of the Franciscan Brothers, the teaching Sisterhoods, and the College of St. John's, now St. John's University. Records the founding of minor and major semi-

naries, the expansion of Catholic grade schools and the beginnings of free diocesan high schools under Bishop Malloy.

44. Browne, Henry J. "Public Support of Catholic Education in
New York, 1825-1842: Some New Aspects." *Historical Records and Studies* 41 (1953): 14-41.

Examines the conditions that hindered New York's
Bishop John Dubois from obtaining state aid for Catholic
schools during the years 1825 to 1840 and discusses how Catholics were divided in 1840 when the Coadjutor Bishop of
New York, John Hughes, became the chief Catholic figure in
the cause of public support for Catholic education. Explains
Dubois' unsuccessful negotiations with the Public School Society which sought exclusive control over the education of the
children of the poor and describes how two Catholic papers
agitated the issue, spearheading the Catholic campaign led by
laymen and clergy. Recounts Bishop Hughes' role in unifying
his people and taking control over the situation.

45. Buetow, Harold A. "Historical Perspectives on Catholic
Teachers in the United States." *Notre Dame Journal of Education* 3 (Summer 1972): 171-82.

Researches the contributions of lay and religious teachers
in Catholic schools to the Church and to America and states
that teachers in the early periods were almost exclusively lay.
Covers the history of religious communities engaged in education, beginning with the Franciscans and Jesuits during the
colonial times and surveys the organization of religious communities of American origin devoted to Catholic education.
Describes the poor economic status and the arduous conditions experienced by lay and religious during the westward
movement and recounts the strong leadership exerted by
American bishops in educational matters. Concludes with a
list from historical records of some of the contributions of
Catholic school teachers.

46. Buetow, Harold A. *A History of United States Catholic Schooling*. Washington, DC: National Catholic Educational Association, 1985.

> Reflects on United States Catholic schooling as a phenomenon that has made many tremendous contributions to the country and extols the religious, clergy, and lay Catholic teachers who sacrificed to the point of heroism. Observes that the laity took on the responsibilities of Catholic schools in the early 19th century and were willing to undergo double taxation. Traces the history of Catholic schools in the United States from the colonial period of transplantation through the early and later national periods, into the twentieth century and the contemporary period from Sputnik on. Discusses the family, Church, and State as secondary agents of education. Concludes that history shows Catholic schooling in the United States is worth fighting for and requires the same heroism and sacrifice as that of the past.

47. Buetow, Harold A. *Of Singular Benefit: The Story of Catholic Education in the United States*. New York: The Macmillan Company, 1970.

> Develops a detailed chronological study of Catholic education in America, beginning with the colonial period of the Spanish and French missions and the English colonies. Continues through the formative years to 1828, the transition years to 1884, and sets the growth years to 1917 with the maturation of the Catholic schools by 1957. Presents conclusions, trends and prospects in 1970 and relates the history of Catholic education to the intellectual, social, economic, and political history of America, examining the past in order to see today's "innovations" in proper perspective. Sets forth the contributions of Catholic education to America and advocates continuation of Catholic education based on tradition.

48. Burns, James A., Bernard J. Kohlbrenner, and John B. Peterson. *A History of Catholic Education in the United States:*

A Textbook for Normal Schools and Teachers' Colleges. New York: Benziger Brothers, 1937.

Covers the general field of the history of Catholic education in the United States, including philosophy and principles, methods and administration and curriculum. Sees it in relation to the growth of the Church and the evolution of public education. Begins with the Old World heritage of Catholic education, the story of the mission schools, the colonial era and into the beginning of the organized Church. Continues with the changing society in the mid-nineteenth century and the expansion of Catholic education, describing the relationship between Catholic schools and the state or civil authority.

49. Burns, James A. *The Principles, Origin and Establishment of the Catholic School System in the United States.* New York: Arno Press and the New York Times, 1969. Reprint of the 1912 edition, Benziger Brothers. (American Education: Its Men Ideas and Institutions, Teachers College, Columbia University Series.)

Records the history of the Catholic school movement in the United States from the earliest beginnings to the immigration period which began about 1840. Describes the mission schools and the colonial schools in the French possessions, Maryland and Pennsylvania, and looks at the characteristics of these early schools. Shows the influences of the American Revolution, the early teaching religious communities, and the hierarchy.

50. Butler, Loretta Myrtle. "A History of Catholic Elementary Education For Negroes in the Diocese of Lafayette, Louisiana." Ph.D. dissertation. Catholic University of America, 1963.

Traces the development of Catholic education for the Negro from 1700 to 1960 in the Diocese of Lafayette, an agricultural area with a French Catholic tradition and discusses the chief obstacles to educational progress including economic deprivation, racial discrimination and lack of qualified personnel. Details the history of eighteen Catholic schools for black children and notes the contribution of the Negro religious communities of women, the Holy Family Sisters, and the Blessed Sacrament Sisters in providing education for the Negro in Lafayette.

51. Connors, Edward M. "Church-State Relationships in Education in the State of New York." Ph.D. dissertation. The Catholic University of America, 1951.

   Investigates the educational relations between Church and New York State through the nineteenth century and into the twentieth century. Views the trend in public education from sectarianism to secularism, ensuing from the controversies surrounding the granting of funds to religious schools and the permitting of Bible reading in the public schools. Relates in Chapter One how the Public School Society between 1825 and 1840 became the dominant educational organization in New York City, obtaining a monopoly over the common school fund. Explains the petition to the School Board by Bishop Dubois in 1834 on behalf of Catholic interests, its rejection, and the Bishop's failure to pursue it.

52. Costello, William J. "The Chronological Development of the Catholic Secondary School in the Archdiocese of Philadelphia." Ed.D. dissertation. Temple University, 1957.

   Covers a period of one hundred forty-nine years from 1806 to 1955 in the development of Philadelphia's Catholic high schools examining the philosophy, aim and purpose of the schools studied. Reflects that 1805 to 1850 was the least productive period but records successful attempts to establish Catholic secondary schools during the second half of the nineteenth century. Believes that the basic fundamental philosophy of Catholic education must remain constant.

53. Dalton, M. Arthemise. "The History and Development of the Catholic Secondary School System in the Archdiocese of De-

troit 1701-1961." Ed.D. dissertation. Wayne State University, 1962.

Describes the early history as individual efforts by clergy, laymen and religious communities to provide Catholic schools and explains that the period from 1829 to 1933 was the era of coordinating the Catholic educational system beginning with the creation of American dioceses. Examines the philosophy and aims, as well as the political, economic, cultural, educational and religious factors which influenced the growth of the system. Regards the Church councils and the religious communities as the prime forces in stabilizing and coordinating Catholic secondary education.

54. Day, Edward. "How the Catholic Schools Began." *The Ligourian*, 50, Summer 1962, pp. 9-12.

Surveys the background of Catholic schools, explaining the Church's supervision of Catholic education since the early Spanish and French colonies and its going underground during the eighteenth century. Cites the founding of particular Catholic schools, crediting the efforts of clergy and missionaries to establish quality parochial schools with teaching sisters. Discusses the problem of support and Archbishop John Hughes' battle with the New York Public School Society. States that the failure to find a balanced religious policy in public schools has done much to perpetuate Catholic education.

55. Dolan, Jay P. "Schools." *The American Catholic Experience: A History from Colonial Times to the Present.* New York: Doubleday and Company, 1985, pp. 262-93.

Renders an account of Catholic schooling which began in a church basement or a log cabin and then developed in distinctive ways in different regional areas. Describes the evolvement of schools in New York, Cincinnati and the Midwest, Washington and the frontier regions and notes that Boston and New England Catholic schools were local parish initiatives rather than any concerted efforts by their bishops. Explains the major factors for the Catholic commitment to a separate school system in the nineteenth century and addresses the emergence of the Indian mission school, giving the report of a typical school day on an Indian reservation. Discusses teacher education and concludes that the Catholic school had a major influence in shaping the American Catholic ethos.

56. Donohue, Francis J. "Financial Support for Early Catholic Schools." *The Catholic Educational Review* 40 (April 1942): 199-216.

    Discovers types of sources from which funds for Catholic education were received before the mid-nineteenth century. Finds that donations and legacies, fairs and social events, and state-authorized lotteries contributed to the financial support of schools and in many states direct aid was granted to Catholic schools. Details sources and amounts given or raised for specific educational purposes. Explores the policy of state and federal aid prior to 1840 and the foreign aid contributed through the Society for the Propagation of the Faith and the Leopoldine Association.

57. Donohue, Francis J. "Textbooks for Catholic Schools Prior to 1840." *The Catholic School Journal*, 40, March 1940, pp. 65-68.

    Finds that for the most part the few available textbooks in Catholic schools prior to the American Revolution were by European authors and printed in Europe. Reports that books were published to satisfy local needs for the parochial school at Philadelphia, for the Sulpician college of St. Mary's at Baltimore and for the parochial schools established in Detroit by Father Gabriel Richard. Identifies the textbooks printed and notes that the catechism in its various forms was the most commonly used, sometimes the only textbook used into the nineteenth century. Observes that mathematical, geographical and natural philosophy textbooks that seemed the least bigoted to the Church were used in Catholic academies and colleges.

58. Faherty, William Barnaby with Elizabeth Kolmer, Dolorita Maria Dougherty and Edward J. Sudckum. *From One Generation to the Next -- 160 Years of Catholic Education in Saint Louis.* Saint Louis, MO: Catholic School Office, 1978.

Develops the history of Catholic education in St. Louis whose beginnings were guided by four major figures: Louis W. V. DuBourg, Bishop of Louisiana Territory; Joseph Rosati, first Bishop of St. Louis; Mother Philipine Duchesne, Religious of the Sacred Heart from France; and Peter Verhaegen who founded the first Catholic medical school in America. Discusses the trends in nineteenth century American education describing the anti-Catholicism of nativists, the historical view of the public schools as Protestant institutions and notes the limited vision of some Church leaders that put American Catholics on the defensive. Continues with the expansion of the St. Louis Catholic school system under Archbishop John J. Glennon and examines the integration and innovation years to post-Vatican II.

59. Fitzpatrick, Edward A. "Catholic Education in Colonial America." *Catholic School Journal*, 58, October 1958, pp. 26-29.

Outlines the history of Catholic education in the colonies and finds that there was only sporadic educational activity since there was no effective organization of the Church during that time. Describes the religious and specifically anti-Catholic climate in which Catholics were without status and were restricted by colonial penal laws. Provides a chronological list of the milestones in Catholic education in colonial America.

60. Friesenhahn, Mary Clarence. "Catholic Secondary Education in the Province of San Antonio: Its Development and Present Status." Ph.D. dissertation. Catholic University of America, 1930.

Studies in the first part the historical growth of Catholic secondary education in Texas and Oklahoma and analyzes in the second half the organization of the Catholic secondary schools explaining the reasons for the slow progress of secondary education in Texas compared with that of other states; particular difficulties and hardships attendant upon its colonization; the vastness of its territory; and the barbarous nature of the Indians roaming overs its plains. Indicates that the increase in the number of secondary schools resulted from the growth and expansion of religious communities already there.

61. Gabert, Glen (E.) Jr. *In Hoc Signo? A Brief History of Catholic Parochial Education in America.* Port Washington, NY: Kennikat Press, 1973.

Studies the history of the American Catholic school system continuing through the eras of the English, the Irish and German Catholics and into the twentieth century. Analyzes the influence of the official writings of the Church on the development of Catholic parochial education, finding that statements of the American hierarchy seemed to have been more significant than papal documents and that other factors such as ethnicity had more effect on the rise of the system.

62. Goebel, Edmund J. "A Study of Catholic Secondary Education During the Colonial Period Up to the First Plenary Council of Baltimore, 1852." Ph.D. dissertation. Catholic University of America, 1937.

Investigates Catholic institutions on the secondary level for boys and girls from the founding of the classical school in St. Augustine in 1606 to the First Plenary Council in Baltimore. Analyzes the character of specific schools considering curriculum, teachers, general regulations and characteristics. Defines secondary education as intermediate between the elementary and college but not synonymous with the high school as known today. Divides the study into three parts covering the Colonial period; the formative years, 1789-1829; and the period of expansion, 1829-1852.

63. Guilday, Peter. "Catholic Education and Social Welfare." *The Life and Times of John England First Bishop of Charleston (1786-1842)*, Vol. II. New York: The America Press, 1927, pp. 133-72.

   Researches the efforts of Bishop England to establish religious communities of women in the Diocese of Charleston in order to provide for the education of youth and describes the activities of the two groups of Sisters who came to the diocese, the Sisters of Mercy and the Ursulines. Discusses the slavery issue and Bishop England's opening of a school for the free Negroes of Charleston in 1835 which was considered most imprudent. Includes many letters written by Bishop England regarding his schools and the teaching communities, as well as his address to the Georgia Convention in 1835 summarizing the educational work of the Charleston Diocese.

64. Heffernan, Arthur J. "A History of Catholic Education in Connecticut." Ph.D. dissertation. The Catholic University of America, 1936.

   Studies the heritage of Catholic schooling in Connecticut from the organization of the first Catholic Sunday school in 1829 to the establishment of the diocesan system in the 1930's. Focuses mainly on the history and growth of the elementary schools, but contains a chapter on Connecticut's Catholic secondary schools which were parish responsibilities and did not develop as well. Relates the growth of Catholicism in the state during the immigration era, the anti-Catholic views and feelings, especially in schools which were Puritan in teaching and teachers. Shows how the accomplishments of the Catholic schools earned the respect and admiration of a once Calvinistic state.

65. Hunt, Thomas C. and Norlene M. Kunkel. "Catholic Schools: The Nation's Largest Alternative School System." *Religious Schooling in America*. Edited by James C. Carper and Thomas C. Hunt. Birmingham, AL: Religious Education Press, 1984, pp. 1-34.

Presents the story of American Catholic schools from the beginning, touching on issues faced during the era of America's first Bishop, John Carroll, and New York's Archbishop Hughes. Describes the growth of the system during the immigration periods, the importance of the ethnic factor and the support given to Catholic schools in the pronouncements of the Vatican and the American bishops. Continues into the twentieth century, an era in which Catholic schools were more secure and respected. Explains that during the period after the Second Vatican Council heavy criticism of the schools came from within the Church. Describes the impact of the American bishops' proclamation during the 1970's to "Teach as Jesus Did" and concludes with consideration of the different challenges of the 1980's and beyond.

66. Kaiser, M. Laurina. "The Development of the Concept and Function of the Catholic Elementary School in the American Parish." Ph.D. dissertation. The Catholic University of America, 1955.

Traces the attitude of the American Catholic Bishops on the concept, function, and necessity of a Catholic school in the American parish through the educational legislation of the provincial and plenary councils, diocesan synods and statements of Bishops in their pastoral letters. Tells of Bishop Carroll's hope that a separate Catholic school system in America would not be necessary and describes the early mission schools as laying the foundation for the parish school.

67. Klinkhamer, Marie Carolyn. "Historical Reason For Inception of Parochial School System." *The Catholic Educational Review* 52 (January-December 1954): 73-94.

Examines the reasons for the Catholic parochial school system in the United States and reduces them to three possible hypotheses: 1) the roots might be found in the European experience, but the parish school in Europe was not the same as the Catholic school introduced into the United States in 1789; 2) the coming of many religious communities to the

United States gave an impetus to the formation of parish schools; 3) the situations in the United States demanded that the Catholic hierarchy meet them with their own educational answers. Discusses the early bishops' alarm over anti-Catholic influences and an anti-Catholic crusade in the 1820's and their efforts to counter them.

68. Leary, Mary Ancilla. "The History of Catholic Education in the Diocese of Albany." Ph.D. dissertation. The Catholic University of America, 1957.

 Traces the growth and development of Catholic education in the Diocese of Albany on all levels of instruction from the first half of the seventeenth century to the mid-twentieth century. Describes the establishment and history of individual elementary and secondary schools, private and parochial. Explains the important role played by the religious and lay teachers in the school system and notes the opening of many schools with the aim of preserving not only the Faith, but the national language of the particular parish.

69. M. A. C. "Education in Louisiana in French Colonial Days." *American Catholic Quarterly Review* 11 (July 1886): 396-418.

 Gives an account of the efforts of Father Bienville to establish a settlement in Louisiana in 1718 and to provide educational facilities and teachers which would assure permanence in the Colony. States that the first boys' school was established with the first teacher, Father Cecil, a Capuchin monk. Describes the coming of the Ursuline nuns from Rouen, France, in 1727 and details their educational and charitable works. Assesses their beneficial influence on girls and young women, recording the continued support given to them and to education by Governor O'Reilly, an Irishman who was an officer of the highest rank in the Spanish armies and who had quelled an insurrection in Louisiana in 1769 after it had come under Spanish rule.

70. M. A. C. "Education in New Orleans in Spanish Colonial Days." *American Catholic Quarterly Review* 12 (April 1887): 253-77.

Recounts the early history of New Orleans and the favorable attitude towards education particularly during the reign of Governor Miro. Reports eight schools with 400 French-speaking scholars in 1788 besides the generally attended Ursuline schools and the Spanish schools. Demonstrates Miro's support of the nuns and their educational efforts.

71. McCluskey, Neil G., ed. *Catholic Education in America: A Documentary History.* New York: Columbia University, 1964.

Traces the growth and development of the American Catholic School System resulting from the issuance of official documents beginning with the letters of Bishop John Carroll in 1792 to the statement of the American Hierarchy in 1950 on the philosophy of Christian education. Introduces the historical letters and pronouncements with an explanation of the educational dilemmas that these documents confronted. Points out the accomplishments resulting from the drive for universal Catholic education in America, but also gives some "less than beneficent" outcomes such as clerical domination of the schools and confusion of the academic mandate and the pastoral charge.

Contains items 118, 119, 167

72. McNally, Michael J. "The Church, Black Catholic Women Religious in Antebellum Period." *Negro History Bulletin* 44 (January-March 1981): 19-20.

Contains a short account of the founding of two communities of black religious, the Oblate Sisters of Providence, established in the Caribbean, whose purpose was to educate black children and who admitted the first American black into their community in 1830; and the Congregation of the Holy Family in 1842 in New Orleans who cared for the abandoned and taught catechism to black children. Gives a brief explanation of the hostile climate in the South toward Catholicism, the wretched conditions, and shortage of priests, and recognizes the "...faith, perseverance, and sacrificial courage displayed by these Antebellum black Catholic women."

73. McNally, William P. "The Secondary School." *Essays on Catholic Education.* (item 15), pp. 118-40.

Presents the story of Catholic secondary education during the early history of America and during the early years of the new republic. Explains the parish high schools, the central high school and the universal secondary education concluding with a commentary on teachers and the lack of properly trained religious teachers for secondary education. Records that the Jesuit Manor schools of Maryland were academies founded to prepare students to enter the college of St. Omer in France; and states that the Latin school established in Boston in 1635 is generally considered to be the forerunner of the American high school. Recounts the work of the Sulpicians and Jesuits who labored successfully in the West during the first quarter of the nineteenth century and helped to further the growth of secondary education.

74. Mahoney, Charles J. "The Relation of the State to Religious Education in Early New York 1633-1825." Ph.D. dissertation. The Catholic University of America, 1941.

Investigates the relation and attitude of the state toward curriculum, support and control of the religious school in New York as evidenced from legislation enacted and the political and religious influences that swayed such legislation. Brings the study from the early colonial era to 1825 when the ordinance of the common council of New York City excluded religious schools, departing from the established tradition of long standing. Assesses the historical significance of this action and its far-reaching effects within the state.

75. Maria Alma, Sister. *Standard Bearers*. New York: P. J. Kenedy & Sons, 1928, c1929.

> Considers civil educational legislation, both federal and state, in each district of the United States before 1850 and the work of Catholic Sisterhoods according to diocese and their place in the history of Catholic education from the earliest times until 1850. Surveys education in colonial times examining school legislation and the educational ventures of the missionaries and Sisters. Provides a history of the foundations of Catholic Religious in the United States.

76. Martire, Harriette A. "A History of Catholic Parochial Elementary Education in the Archdiocese of New York." Ph.D. dissertation. Fordham University, 1955.

> Provides a study of Catholic elementary education in New York from 1800 to 1954 but limits it to parish schools. Gives a brief account of the geographic, economic, social and political background of New York State and a history of the Catholic Church in New York State to 1808 when it became a diocese. Examines Catholic elementary education prior to 1842 and during the administrations of Archbishops Hughes, McCloskey, Corrigan, Farley, Hays, and Spellman. States that the history of the Archdiocesan parochial schools is similar to the educational endeavors of many other dioceses in the United States.

77. Mary Christina, Sister. "Early American Convent Schools." *The Catholic Educational Review* 39 (January 1941): 30-35.

> Describes the aim of the early Catholic academies to develop the ideal Christian woman preparing her for her duty as wife and mother. Gives an account of the course of study, the pursuit of cultural accomplishments and the rules and regulations and provides a typical curriculum offered by Mount Benedict Academy of Charleston, Massachusetts, in 1834, the year that the school was burned by a bigoted mob.

78. Mary Janet, Sister. "Foundations of Catholic Secondary Schools." *Catholic Secondary Education: A National Survey.* Washington, DC: National Catholic Welfare Conference, 1949, pp. 3-10.

   Chronicles the history of Catholic secondary education in America citing the classical and preparatory seminary founded in 1606 in St. Augustine, Florida, as possibly the beginning and the Ursuline Academy founded in 1727 in New Orleans as the first Catholic school for girls in the United States. Records that Catholic education has its lasting foundation in the English-speaking colonies, mainly in Maryland and Pennsylvania, and gives Georgetown as the oldest Catholic high school for boys in the United States. Continues the chronology explaining the indefinite line within the yearly schools on the elementary, secondary and college levels, and discusses the rise of the Catholic high schools after the Third Plenary Council of Baltimore in 1884.

79. Mary Vere, Sister. "The Elementary School." *Essays on Catholic Education.* (item 15), pp. 97-117.

   Describes the history of the elementary school in the United States from the Catholic colonial elementary schools to the problems and trends of the 1940's. States that the first Catholic elementary school was established in Maryland in 1640 and that the first parochial school at St. Mary's Church in Philadelphia is considered the mother-school of all parochial schools in the English colonies. Remarks that there was comparative security and freedom for Catholics in the Maryland and Pennsylvania colonies and claims that Catholic elementary education kept pace for the most part with the growth of the Church. Describes the period of immigration as the time of rapid growth of the Church and parochial elementary schools. Reviews the decrees of the Plenary Councils to raise the standards and efficiency of the schools and to address the preparation of teachers.

80. Maynard, Theodore. "The Educational Effort." *The Story of Catholicism*. New York: Macmillan Company, 1941.

Provides an historical commentary on Catholic education in America beginning with the arrival of the Jesuits in Maryland and the opening of schools in New Mexico and Florida by the Franciscans. Notes the direction toward higher education at the end of the eighteenth century because of the need to educate seminarians for the priesthood. Continues the historical development of Catholic schools with the founding of the first parochial school by Elizabeth Seton, Bible reading in public schools and an account of the school controversy involving Archbishops Ireland, McQuaid, Corrigan and Satolli, the Apostolic Delegate, and which ended through the intervention of Pope Leo XIII.

81. Melville, Annabelle M. "Angels in the Valley." *Elizabeth Bayley Seton 1774-1821*. New York: Charles Scribner's Sons, 1951, pp. 208-227.

Tells the story of Mother Seton's educational work at St. Joseph's School at Emmitsburg, Maryland, describing its organization and management, her personal care of the pupils and her work and concern for her religious community, the Sisters of Charity. Attempts to give a clear picture from archival research of the "free school" and distinguishes between the day pupils and the boarders. Notes the evidence that indicates boys were not included. Reflects that Mother Seton made an invaluable contribution to nineteenth-century education but suggests that the claim that she was the "foundress of the parochial school system" in the United States is open to debate.

82. Montay, Mary Innocenta. "The History of Catholic Secondary Education in the Archdiocese of Chicago." Ph.D. dissertation. The Catholic University of America, 1953.

Describes chronologically the history of Catholic high schools in Chicago individually and according to type rather than as a system. Provides a background of early education in Illinois from 1673 to 1843 and of education under Diocesan organization. States that until 1857 the Chicago Archdiocese was coextensive with the boundaries of the State of Illinois.

83. National Conference of Catholic Bishops. "Christian Education," Pastoral Letter to the Laity, issued October 17, 1829, First Provincial Council of Baltimore. *Pastoral Letters of the United States Catholic Bishops, Volume I 1792-1940*. Edited by Hugh J. Nolan. Washington, DC: United States Catholic Conference, 1984, pp. 38-41.

Exhorts Catholic parents to attend to the education of their children teaching them first to seek the kingdom of God and His justice and to place them at school where teachers will cultivate the seed they have sown. Urges them, if their means and opportunities permit, to commit their children to the care of those who have been placed over the seminaries and female religious institutions.

84. Newton, Robert R. "The Evolution of the New York Archdiocesan School System 1800-1967." Ph.D. dissertation. Boston College, 1982.

Covers the educational system of the New York Archdiocese from its beginnings at St. Peter's Church in 1800 to its emergence as the most extensive in the country during the era of Francis Cardinal Spellman and into the mid-1960's. Relates the struggles of New York's third Bishop, John Dubois, with the Public School Society and his efforts to recruit religious teachers to staff his schools. Examines the leadership of Archbishop Hughes, the continued growth through the administrations of John Cardinal McCloskey and Archbishop Michael Corrigan who reaffirmed the directive of the Baltimore Councils to provide a Catholic school in every parish. Describes Cardinal Spellman in the mid-twentieth century as the "Cardinal of Education."

85. Obreza, John Edward. "Philadelphia's Parochial School System: An Adjunct to "The Only 'The' Church"." In "Philadelphia Parochial School System from 1830-1920: Growth and Bureaucratization." Ph.D. dissertation. Temple University, 1979, pp. 1-24.

Contends that the histories of the American Catholic Church and her parochial school systems during the nineteenth century are incomplete since they reflect the clerical view and tell little about Catholic life among lay Catholics. Asserts that these accounts do not test the Catholic membership's reaction to the parochial school system; they simply make historical assertions. Believes these histories need to be synthesized and extended to reveal how Catholics in the urban Church responded to parochial schools. Describes nineteenth century Catholic schooling in America and the reasons for its existence and maintains there are unexamined aspects. Looks at Philadelphia as a model case in Catholic institutional history.

86. O'Brien, Mary Agnes. "History and Development of Catholic Secondary Education in the Archdiocese of New York." Ph.D. dissertation. Columbia University, 1949.

Outlines the history of Catholicism in New York during the colonial and early national period until 1830 citing the attempts to establish secondary schools. Describes the permanent foundation, growth and expansion of Catholic secondary education in New York between 1833 and 1925 when European and American religious communities were the mainstay in educational efforts. Details the account of five pioneer communities who established secondary education before the Civil War laying the foundation for the future high school system: Sisters of Charity, Ladies of the Sacred Heart, Ursuline Nuns, the Jesuits, and Brothers of the Christian Schools. Evaluates contemporary Catholic secondary education which had developed rapidly during the first quarter of the twentieth century.

87. Paré, George. "Education." In *The Catholic Church in Detroit, 1701-1888*. Detroit: Wayne State University Press, 1983, c1951, pp. 615-55.

   Deals with the story of Catholic education in Detroit documenting the educational endeavors of Father Gabriel Richard who was active from 1805 onward in getting public support for education. Adduces that Father Richard's activities were concerned principally with the education of girls and discusses the Act of 1817, "An act to establish the Catholepistemiad or University of Michigania," with Father Richard as Vice-president. Relates that the Poor Clares were the pioneers of Catholic education after Detroit became a diocese in 1827 and tells the story of the various religious communities who came to teach there. Comments that the Sisters crowned the efforts of the struggling immigrant groups who managed to obtain buildings and lay teachers to teach the essential Catholic education to their children.

88. Perko, F. Michael. "The Educational Evangelicals: Protestant and Catholic Missionary Societies' Influences on Midwestern School Formation, 1830-1860." Paper presented at the Annual Meeting of the American Educational Research Association (Montreal, Canada, April 11-15, 1983).

   Demonstrates how two Protestant and three Catholic missionary societies contributed to the development of American schooling. Addresses the importance of the Catholic groups: the Leopoldine Association of Vienna, the Association for the Propagation of the Faith of Lyons and Paris, and the Ludwig Missionsverein of Munich in providing funds to promote Catholic growth in the United States. Shows how they aided the development of Catholic schools by funding parishes, especially those with German immigrants, and minority groups such as blacks and native Americans. Assesses the negative contributions, encouraging mutual suspicion and distrust by Catholics and Protestants, and the fostering of two parallel systems of public and parochial schooling.

89. Purcell, Richard J. "Irish Educational Contribution to Early New Jersey." *The Catholic Educational Review* 41 (May 1943): 273-87.

   Identifies the Irish teachers who settled in New Jersey before 1700 to the mid-nineteenth century describing their sectarian and educational backgrounds and relating the educational legacy they left to New Jersey. Tells of the contributions of the Catholic teachers who were in the minority since Roman Catholics were barely tolerated. Explains the "Irish Celtic" movement about 1820 which gave impetus to the beginnings of Catholic life and education.

90. Redden, John (D). "The Beginnings of Catholic Education in Maine." *The Catholic Educational Review* 37 (October 1939): 509-16.

   Gives an account of the religious and educational work of Jesuits in Maine among the Abnaki Indians from 1612 to 1738. Chronicles the missionary activity of the first Jesuits particularly Father Rasle whose Christianizing and civilizing influence on the Indians was opposed by the English who persecuted him and eventually killed him. Describes how the Abnakis fought for the colonies against the British and after the war presented Father Rasle's crucifix to Bishop John Carroll requesting that he send them another missionary to guide and to instruct them.

91. Reilly, M. Patricia Ann. "The Administration of Parish Schools in the Archdiocese of New York 1800-1900." *Historical Records and Studies* 44 (1956): 45-83.

   Researches how parish schools in the New York Archdiocese were administered in the nineteenth century noting that Catholic lay trustees were responsible for hiring teachers, inspecting classrooms and financing the school. Records that St. Peter's Free School was established in 1800, six years prior to the opening of the first school by the Free School Society of New York. Relates the history of the parish schools during the tenure of each bishop.

92. Sullivan, Daniel C. "Catholic Elementary Education Prior to 1853." In "A History of Catholic Elementary Education in the Archdiocese of Newark, New Jersey." Ph.D. dissertation. Fordham University, 1942, pp. 62-111.

    Discusses Catholic education in New Jersey during the years before and after the War for Independence, the difficulties encountered and the atmosphere of anti-Catholicism that prevailed. Cites a law passed in 1704 prohibiting Catholics from establishing schools or employing Catholic tutors in order to prevent "the growth of Popery." States that Catholics were in a better position to profess their faith after the ratification of the Constitution of the United States and, although the growth of Catholic schools up to 1853 was slow, the foundation was laid for future development. Explains the significant part played by Rev. Bernard McQuaid, later Bishop of Rochester, in the founding of parish elementary schools that continued into the 1940's.

93. V. M. "Early Catholic Secondary Education in Philadelphia." *Records of the American Catholic Historical Society* 59 (September 1948): 157-180.

    Consists of two chapters with the first chapter giving an historical background of the development of Catholic education in Philadelphia and the second chapter recording the beginnings of Catholic secondary education in Philadelphia, 1806-1850. Relates the story of individual institutions and tells of the educational efforts of Philadelphia's bishops. Notes that nine schools for boys and five for girls were established. Finds Catholic secondary education from 1806 to 1850 made slow progress because of financial difficulties, the evils of trusteeism, the small number of students, and the lack of religious teachers.

CHAPTER 3
The Era of the Councils
1840-1884

Tensions Begin

In his "Pastoral Letter" of 1792, Bishop John Carroll of Baltimore had instructed Catholic parents in the importance of the lifelong benefits of a Catholic education, dedicated to the service of God and to the benefit of the nation.[1] Subsequent Provincial Councils of Baltimore, in 1829, 1833, and 1837, also made reference to the importance of Catholic education.[2] It was in the fourth such Council, held in 1840, that the Bishops referred to specific troubles Catholics were having with the public schools over issues related to the Protestant influence in the system itself, and in its practices, such as devotional Bible-reading, and curricular materials.[3]

New York City: Conflicts Intensify

Other conflicts between Catholics and Protestants erupted in the 1840s, which spilled over into the schools. New York City, for instance, was the scene of what Diane Ravitch has termed a "great school war."[4] There the aggressive bishop, John Hughes, unsuccessfully sought funds for Catholic children from the allegedly nonsectarian, philanthropic Free School Society due to what he termed an "intolerable" situation for Catholics as regards the orientation of the Society's schools and their textbooks.[5] One result of the struggle was the establishment of a separate system of Catholic parochial schools, established to teach the Catholic faith *"in its entirety."*[6]

Immigration and Nativism

Catholics comprised about one percent of the nation's population in 1800.[7] Immigration increased the numbers of Catholics, which in turn was accompanied by acts of anti-Catholicism, including the burning of Catholic-owned buildings in the 1840s. In a period in which Nativism was influential, it was inevitable that the hostilities were reflected in the schools and their practices. As the state governments began to be more active in the conduct of schooling under the auspices of the common school movement, spearheaded by Horace Mann in Massachusetts, Catholic opposition to these schools, viewed as "pan-Protestant," increased.

Between 1821 and 1850 almost 2½ million Europeans emigrated to the United States, with over 1.7 million arriving in the decade of the 1840s.[8] More than a million of the total were Irish, with 780,719 coming during the 1840s.[9] Unable, in the main, to achieve religious neutrality in the public schools, these impoverished immigrants generally followed the lead of their bishops and erected and supported parish elementary schools for their children.

Official Church Pronouncements

Though some lay Catholics had as a goal religious neutrality on the part of the public schools, the official Catholic policy, as enunciated in the organs of the Church, e.g., in the First Plenary Council of Baltimore, called for the establishment and support of Catholic schools for Catholic children.[10] German Catholic bishops, utilizing the appeal of the preservation of culture, were outspoken in their conviction of the need for Catholic schools to preserve the faith and other customs of their flocks.[11] Pastors were enjoined under pain of sin to found schools in their parishes;[12] parents were warned of the "unwise system" of public schooling, which would produce a "generation of religious indifferentists," who would be dangerous to "religious principles...."[13]

The Bishops returned to Baltimore in 1866. In the Second Plenary Council they reaffirmed the pre-eminence of religious teaching in education and reminded Catholic parents of their duty to follow the Church's teaching in educational matters.[14]

Catholics' ranks were swelled by immigration from 1851-1870. A total of 1,349,897 Irish, almost all Catholic, and 1,739,135 Germans, many of whom were Catholic, landed in the United States, making up about 64 percent of the immigrants during those two decades.[15] Partially as a result of this immigration, Catholic school enrollment grew. In 1875, with fifty-seven of the nation's sixty-two dioceses responding (the only large sees missing were Brooklyn and Newark), the Catholic population had grown to 5,761,242 with 1,444 parish schools in operation.[16]

As Catholics grew in numbers, their efforts to obtain tax monies for their schools increased.[17] Basically, Catholic policy-makers argued that education belonged by right to parents. It was the responsibility of the civil state to assist the parents to fulfill their God-given duty, not usurp it. Catholic parents were to meet their divinely-imposed obligation by following the teaching of the Church, which called for attendance at Catholic schools.

The Catholic campaign for funds alarmed American nativists. They rejected the Catholic arguments, and pushed the public schools as necessary for the survival of American democracy. Some of the nativist efforts, as in the political "Know-Nothing" party, were virulently, and sometimes violently, anti-Catholic.

Throughout the 1860s and into the 1870s, individual Catholic bishops lent their support to the Catholic school movement. Not all of the bishops joined in this crusade, however; nor were all of the laity heeding their bishops' mandates. Then, in 1875, a call was issued by some American prelates for a formal document of support from the Vatican, "...to impress upon the faithful the seriousness of the matter and to strengthen their own authority in persuading pastors to build parish schools."[18] The report was issued by the Congregation of the Propagation of the Faith, the arm of the Catholic Church in charge of worldwide missionary activities, since the Catholic Church in the United States had missionary status at that time. It was directed to the American hierarchy. Basically, the Congregation adjudged public schools as the source of "evils of the greatest kind," called on Catholic authorities to build Catholic schools, and on the laity to support, maintain and have their children attend them.[19] It was left to the judgement of the Bishops to decide when the danger of perversion of the faith was sufficiently remote to permit attendance at public schools. Catholic parents were reminded of their solemn charge to protect and strengthen the faith of their children, upon which their eternal destiny depended.[20]

The Congregation's statement was interpreted as a victory for those bishops who were ardent advocates of Catholic schools.[21] Increasingly, Catholic opposition to the public schools shifted from its Protestant orientation to its secular, or as it was sometimes called, "godless" nature, occasionally viewed as influenced by the ideas of Darwin and Spencer.[22] Indeed, one writer urged Protestants to "Fight, therefore, Protestants, no longer us, but the public enemy."[23]

The Third Plenary Council of Baltimore

The overriding concern of the prelates as the Council approached was, as the Catholic historian Peter Guilday has observed, the presence in and fate of Catholic children in the public schools.[24] It was in this climate that the Bishops were called to assemble again in Baltimore for the epochal Third Plenary Council, held in 1884. The impetus for the Council itself, and much of its agenda, had emanated from the Vatican, which sought to control the growing church in the United States.[25]

Addressing educational issues, the Bishops maintained that the survival of civilization depended on morality, which in turn rested on religion. The three agencies of home, church, and school each had to play a part in this drama for its success; however, attainment of this goal was impossible when public policy excluded religion from its rightful role.[26] The banishment of religion from the schools of Europe, being accomplished by the enemies of Christianity, should awaken Americans both to the fact that the secular state could not teach religion, and that they send their children to "denominational schools, where religion can have its rightful place and influence."[27]

Turning their attention directly to the Catholic laity, the Bishops urged the faithful to assist in the multiplication, and then perfection, of Catholic schools so they would be available in their finest form to every Catholic child in the nation.[28] Not content with exhortations, the Bishops set forth two decrees which were to guide Catholic policy on educational matters in the United States for decades:

I.   That near every church a parish school, where one does not yet exist, is to be built and maintained in perpetuum within two years of the promulgation of this council, unless the bishop should decide that because of serious difficulties a delay may be granted.

IV.   That all Catholic parents are bound to send their children to the parish school, unless it is evident that a sufficient training in religion is given either in their own homes, or in other Catholic schools; or when because of a sufficient reason, approved by the bishop, with all due precautions and safeguards, it is licit to send them to other schools. What constitutes a Catholic school is left to the decision of the bishop.[29]

It is clear from these decrees that neither the pastor nor the people of the parish were free to decide whether to erect or support parish schools, to the delight of the conservative Catholics that choice resided only with the bishop.[30] Pastors were enjoined with the supervisory responsibility for these schools, but were reminded to observe the agreements made with the religious orders of some who had, by this time, taken over the instructional duties in the schools.[31] (The customary pattern that was established was one order per parish school; if the parish were ethnic, e.g., German, then the teaching order would be of that ethnic group.)

The prominence of the school issue in the minds of the Catholic leaders as the conciliar era drew to a close was evident. Two assessments, written more than eighty years apart, attest to the crucial role the schools were seen to play in matters of faith. These views serve also as a summary of the Catholic Church's position at that time on the school question. Writing a year before the

Council in 1883, James Cardinal Gibbons of Baltimore (the nation's sole Cardinal at the time), penned:

> It may safely be asserted that the future status of Catholicity in the United States is to be determined by the success or failure of our day-schools.[32]

Almost a century later in 1964, Mary Perkins Ryan, the lay critic of contemporary Catholic schooling, wrote:

> ...in the midst of a predominately Protestant society, hostile both to Catholicism as such and to the traditionally Catholic immigrant groups, the Church established a school system of her own and attempted to establish a parochial life which would keep Catholics away from harmful influences, enabling them to preserve their faith and some semblance of a Catholic pattern of life.[33]

Endnotes

1. John Carroll, "Pastoral Letter," in Neil G. McCluskey (ed.), *Catholic Education in America: A Documentary History*. New York: Teachers College Press, Columbia University, 1964, p. 48.

2. "Pastoral Letter," First Provincial Council of Baltimore (1829) in McCluskey, ed., *Ibid.*, pp. 52-53; "Pastoral Letter," Second Provincial Council of Baltimore (1833), in McCluskey, ed. *Ibid.*, p. 56; and "Pastoral Letter," Third Provincial Council of Baltimore (1837), in McCluskey, ed., *Ibid.*, p. 56.

3. "Pastoral Letter," Fourth Provincial Council of Baltimore (1840), in McCluskey, ed., *Ibid.*, p. 58.

4. Diane Ravitch, *The Great School Wars: New York City, 1805-1973*. New York: Basic Books, 1973, pp. 46-76.

5. John Hassard, *Life of Archbishop Hughes*. New York: Arno Press, 1969, pp. 229-31.

6. James A. Burns, *Catholic Education: A Study of Conditions*. New York: Longmans, Green and Co., 1915, p. 15.

7. H. Daniel-Rops, *The Church in an Age of Revolution*, 2 vols. Garden City, New York: Doubleday and Co., Inc., 1967, II, p. 173.

8. *Report on the Population of the United States of the Eleventh Census 1890*. Vol. I, Part I. Washington, D.C.: Government Printing Office, 1895, p. lxxx.

9. *Ibid.*

10. "Pastoral Letter," First Plenary Council of Baltimore (1852), in McCluskey, ed., *Ibid.*, pp. 79-81.

11. "Pastoral Letter," First Provincial Council of Cincinnati (1855), in James A. Burns and Bernard J. Kohlbrenner, *A History of Catholic Education in the United States*. New York: Benziger Brothers, 1937, p. 138.

12. "Pastoral Letter," Second Provincial Council of Cincinnati (1858), in Burns, *The Growth and Development of the Catholic School System in the United States*. New York: Benziger Brothers, 1912, p. 186.

13. "Pastoral Letter," Third Provincial Council of Cincinnati (1861), in Thomas J. Jenkins, *The Judges of Faith: Christian versus Godless Schools*. Baltimore: John Murphy and Co., 1886, p. 34.

14. "Pastoral Letter," *Second Plenary Council of Baltimore* (1866), in McCluskey, ed., *Catholic Education in America*, pp. 82-83, and in Peter Guilday, ed., *The National Pastorals of the American Hierarchy 1792-1919*. Westminster, MD: The Newman Press, 1954, p. 206.

15. *Report on the Population of the United States at the Eleventh Census 1890*. Vol. I, Part I. Washington, D.C.: Government Printing Office, 1895, p. lxxx.

16. *Sadliers' Catholic Directory, Almanac, and Ordo, for the Year of Our Lord 1875*. New York: D. J. Sadlier and Co., 1875, p. 22.

17. R. Freeman Butts, *The American Tradition in Religion and Education*. Boston: The Beacon Press, 1950, p. 141.

18. McCluskey, ed., *Catholic Education in America*, p. 121.

19. "Instruction of the Congregation of the Propaganda de Fide" (1875), in McCluskey, ed., *Ibid.*, p. 121.

20. *Ibid.*, p. 122.

21. James Conway, "The Rights and Duties of the Church in Regard to Education," *The American Catholic Quarterly Review* IX (October 1884): 669.

22. See, for instance, "The Catholics of the Nineteenth Century," *Catholic World* XI (July 1870): 436-41; "Are Our Public Schools Free?", *Catholic World* XVIII (October 1873): 9; and "The School Question," *Catholic World* XI (April 1870): 98-100, 104.

23. "The School Question," *Catholic World* XI (April 1870): 106.

24. Guilday, *A History of the Councils of Baltimore* (1791-1884). New York: The Macmillan Company, 1932, p. 237.

25. Thomas T. McAvoy, *The Great Crises in American Catholic History, 1895-1900*. Chicago: Henry Regnery Company, 1957, pp. 28-29; McAvoy, "Leo XIII and America," in Edward T. Gargan, ed., *Leo XIII and the Modern World*. New York: Sheed and Ward, 1961, p. 165.

26. "The Pastoral Letter of the Third Plenary Council of Baltimore," in Guilday, ed., *The National Pastorals of the American Hierarchy, 1792-1919*, p. 245.

27. *Ibid.*, p. 246.

28. *Ibid.*, p. 246-47.

29. "Decrees of the Third Plenary Council of Baltimore," in McCluskey, ed., *Catholic Education in America*, pp. 93-94.

30. Francis P. Cassidy, "Catholic Education in the Third Plenary Council of Baltimore," *The Catholic Historical Review* XXXIV, Part I (October 1948): 305.

31. Cassidy, "Catholic Education in the Third Plenary Council of Baltimore," *The Catholic Historical Review* XXXIV, Part II (January 1949): 430.

32. In Jenkins, *The Judges of Faith: Christian versus Godless Schools*, p. 122.

33. Mary Perkins Ryan, *Are Parochial Schools the Answer?* New York: Guild Press, 1964, p. 39.

Bibliographic Entries

94. Abonyi, Malvina Hauk. "The Role of Ethnic Church Schools in the History of Education in the United States: The Detroit Experience, 1850-1920." Ed.D. dissertation. Wayne State University, 1987.

    Provides an historical overview of ethnic church schools in the United States and focuses on selected schools outlining the contributions of these schools to the history of education and of bilingual education in Detroit. Examines the Polish church schools and the history of the Felician Sisters, the largest Polish teaching order in the area. Recounts the story of other ethnic Catholic schools and finds that the Catholic Church adopted guidelines observed by public schools without sacrificing either religion or ethnicity. Believes that the role of ethnic church schools in the maintenance of language and culture deserves to be documented.

95. Agatha, Mother M. "Catholic Education and the Indian." *Essays on Catholic Education in the United States.* (item 15), pp. 523-53.

    Surveys the history of Catholic schools for Indian children beginning with the first schools opened in 1493 by Franciscan priests. Discusses the work of the Jesuits and the development of the California Indian Missions under the Franciscans and Father Junipero Serra. Continues the story of the missions throughout the territories, discussing the treaties made by the United States government and the concerns of the Catholic bishops for the Indian Missions which they felt suffered great injustices. Reports the work of Father Gabriel Richard in Detroit, the Benedictine Fathers in the Dakotas, and the Sisters for Indians and Colored People, a Congregation founded by Katherine Drexel.

96. Angelus, Brother Gabriel. *The Christian Brothers in the United States 1848-1948: A Century of Catholic Education.* New York: The Declan X. McMullen Company, 1948.

Divides this one-volume history of the Brothers of the Christian Schools into eight books, beginning in book one with the origins and expansion of the Congregation founded in 1680 in France and dedicated to the education of young men. Details in book two the story of the pioneer foundations in the United States in Baltimore, New York and St. Louis. Examines the work of the Christian Brothers in elementary and secondary education throughout the states from the east to the west coast in books three and five. Devotes the remaining books to the Community's work in higher education, to the social welfare of youth, and to the expansion of its novitiates and houses of study.

97. Austin, Brother Matthias. "Origin of Teaching Brotherhoods in the Archdiocese of New York." *The Catholic Educational Review* 60 (September 1962): 377-85.

Reveals the difficulties and misunderstandings Bishop John Hughes encountered in his efforts to obtain Brothers for the educational development of young boys in his diocese during the 1840s. Tells of the arrival of the Brothers of the Christian Schools in 1848 to teach in St. Vincent's parish which undertook the Brothers' support. Finds that negotiations with the pastor of the parish for their work and upkeep were an important change in policy, since prior to the Brothers' arrival the Bishop took care of all arrangements for bringing religious teachers (Sisters) into the diocese.

98. Bollig, Richard Joseph. "History of Catholic Education in Kansas 1836-1932." Ph.D. dissertation. The Catholic University of America, 1933.

   Chronicles the history of Catholic schools of Kansas beginning with the establishment of the first school in 1836 and describes the Catholic Indian schools before 1866; the schools in the Vicariate Apostolic Kansas Territory from 1857 to 1877; and the schools in the three dioceses of Leavenworth, Concordia, and Wichita from 1887 to 1932. Gives an historical perspective of the role that Catholic schools played in the development of the territory of Kansas.

99. Brewer, Eileen Mary. *Nuns and the Education of American Catholic Women, 1860-1920.* Chicago: Loyola University Press, 1987.

   Looks at the role nuns played in the intellectual, emotional and religious formation of young American Catholic women in convent schools in the Midwest between 1860 and 1920. Describes the organization and development of these academies which differed from the Catholic high school for girls established mainly after 1900. Depicts a typical convent education detailing the academic, social and religious life within selected academies which prepared girls for either convent life or motherhood. Evaluates the far-reaching effects of convent school graduates who carried values they learned from the Sisters to the wider Catholic community and helped shape Catholic faith and piety in America.

100. Burns, James A. *The Growth and Development of the Catholic School System in the United States.* New York: Arno Press and the New York Times, 1969. Reprint of the 1912 edition, Benziger Brothers. (American Education: Its Men, Ideas and Institutions, Teachers College, Columbia University Series).

Continues the narrative of the Catholic School movement in the United States during the immigration period from about 1840 to 1866 when a new era in American Catholic education began with the Second Plenary Council in Baltimore. Describes the evolution of the diocese and the influences of the religious teaching orders in the mid-nineteenth century. Reviews the problems and movements within the system towards the end of the century and chronicles the formation of the Catholic Educational Association in 1904.

101. Cassidy, Francis P. "Catholic Education in the Third Plenary Council of Baltimore." *The Catholic Historical Review* Part I, 34 (October 1948): 257-305; Part II, 34 (January 1949): 414-36.

Examines the regulations on Catholic education in the United States promulgated by the American bishops at the Third Plenary Council convened in November 1884 at Baltimore. Shows how changes in religious, social, and educational aspects of American life and conflict between sciences and religion affected the conciliar deliberations. Notes that the American prelates prevailed upon Vatican authorities to have a new draft of the agenda drawn up with their active participation. Details the various documents on clerical education and parochial schools explaining the participation of various bishops in the preparation of the Schema. Concludes that this is a culmination of educational legislation initiated in all other previous provincial and plenary councils.

102. Cross, Robert D. "Origins of the Catholic Parochial Schools in America." *The American Benedictine Review* 16 (1965): 194-209.

Addresses the reasons why parochial schools were the Catholic answer to the school problem by the end of the nineteenth century. Traces the attitude of bishops and priests towards education explaining why it did not evoke strong Catholic responses until the Fourth Provincial Council in 1840. Proposes that the growth of parochial schools was due more to religious orders and immigrant groups and finds that the German Catholic leadership took the lead in defending the foreign language parochial school. Describes the attitudes of some Catholics in the late nineteenth century concerning the importance of formal education and parochial schools and reviews Archbishop Ireland's efforts to develop an alternate mode of education to both the public and the parochial school.

103. Dever, Daniel J. "Catholic Schools of Hawaii." *Educational Perspectives* 20 (Winter 1981): 31-35.

Divides the story of Catholic schools in Hawaii into three phases: the first phase under the monarchy when the minority of Catholics were permitted to teach their own beliefs in a separate system of public schools supported by government aid; the second phase in which the growth of Catholic education began in 1859 when the Sacred Heart Fathers brought religious teachers to Hawaii from Europe and America; and the third phase from 1941 forward when Hawaii was raised from a missionary status to a diocese. Describes the expansion of Catholic education from the mid-1940's to the mid-1960's and reflects on the years following the Vatican Council, noting that the Sacred Heart Fathers relied on lay teachers to lay the foundation for Catholic schools in the mid-nineteenth century and that is maintained today by lay teachers.

104. Eakin, Myrtle Sue. "How Can We Get a School Here? The Church and Parochial Education." In "The Black Struggle for Education in Louisiana 1877-1930's." Ph.D. dissertation. University of Southwestern Louisiana, 1980, pp. 40-63.

Depicts the black church as the center for educational and religious efforts and for all social activities of blacks noting that the Baptist denomination was the most popular. Tells of building schools during and after Reconstruction, the struggle to survive and experiences of individual blacks. Describes the establishment of Catholic schools in New Orleans, the first area in Louisiana where Catholic schools for blacks were established. Explains the nature of the Catholic organizational structure noting it did not allow for blacks to develop their own leadership as did the Negro Baptist churches. Observes that Catholic schools usually had better educated teachers, especially when they were members of a religious community.

105. "The Educational Question." *The School Question: Catholics and Education.* New York: The Catholic Publication Society, 1876, pp. 33-47.

Refutes the anti-Catholic tract issued by the American and Foreign Christian Union Office called Bible House in New York City. Exposes the anti-Catholic bias in secular education setting forth the reasons for Catholics to educate their own children.

106. Evans, John Whitney. "Catholics and the Blair Education Bill." *The Catholic Historical Review* 46 (October 1960): 273-98.

Reports on the bill for federal support of education proposed by Senator Henry William Blair of New Hampshire during the 1880s detailing the debates which brought to light political, sectional and social issues. Explains the bill which would provide a ten-year program of federal aid to the schools to help surmount the serious illiteracy problem in the nation. Points out three factors that were major elements in the milieu of the country -- the question of the State's right to educate, Protestant influence in state-supported schools, and creeping secularism in the schools. Discusses Catholic opposition to the bill which was defeated on constitutional and fiscal grounds in the Senate and on sectional issues in the House.

107. Fell, Marie Leonore. "Bishop Hughes and the Common School Controversy." M.A. dissertation. The Catholic University of America, 1936.

Researches the story of Bishop Hughes' conflict with the Public School Society in 1840 when the Bishop asked for a share of the common school fund in the name of New York Catholics. Discusses each phase of the two-year controversy detailing the history of the common school fund, the Public School Society and the early Catholic school system. Examines the adversarial relationship of Bishop Hughes with the Public School Society which asserted that a share of the common school fund for sectarian schools was unconstitutional and inexpedient. Reports the final outcome as a compromise and disappointment to both sides with the passing of the Act of 1842 after which the Public School Society lost its monopoly and Hughes established his own system of schools on a firmer basis.

108. Flynn, Austin. "The School Controversy in New York 1840-1842 and Its Effect on the Formulation of Catholic Elementary School Policy." Ph.D. dissertation. The University of Notre Dame, 1962.

Investigates the New York school controversy of 1840 and analyzes its significance despite failure to obtain financial aid for Catholic schools. Notes that up to 1825 denominational schools were included in the distribution of public funds for education. Recounts the determination of Bishop Hughes to establish an independent Catholic school system and set policy concerning the control of school property, the employment and supervision of teachers, and the publication of textbooks. Reflects that many other dioceses began to expand their own school policy and comments that the decade following the controversy marked the beginning of the Catholic elementary school system in the United States.

109. Gallagher, Marie Patrice. "The History of Catholic Elementary Education in the Diocese of Buffalo, 1847-1944." Ph.D. dissertation. The Catholic University of America, 1945.

Develops the progression of Catholic elementary schools in the Diocese of Buffalo beginning with the episcopates of Bishop John Timon and Bishop Stephen V. Ryan who laid the foundations for a strong parochial school system. Continues through the bishoprics of five successive prelates who furthered the system's growth and development and concludes with a discussion of the administration and supervision of the schools explaining the organization of the diocesan school system. Recounts the appointment of the first diocesan Superintendent of Schools in 1900 noting that schools were under a Board of Examiners prior to that time.

110. Gill, Mary E. and John S. Goff. "Edmund Francis Dunne and the Public School Controversy, 1875." *The Journal of Arizona History* 25 (1984): 369-84.

Tells the story of Edmund Francis Dunne, Chief Justice of the Arizona Territorial Supreme Court, who delivered a speech in 1875 in response to an uproar evoked by a group of Catholics who refused to attend a ball given to raise money for a public school. Explains that as a consequence Edmund Dunne was no longer a highly regarded Chief Justice with a promising judicial career. Discusses the Catholics' position as described by Dunne and the subsequent battle between him and the Arizona newspapers. States that President Grant removed him from office on December 11, 1875, and "the jurist's enemies rejoiced." Remarks that it was the first time a school issue in national politics entered into the appointment or removal of a federal office holder.

111. Gleason, Philip. "Baltimore III and Education." *U.S. Catholic Historian* 4 (1985): 273-313.

Analyzes the 1884 proceedings of the Plenary Council of the American Catholic Church with a commentary on the essay by Bishops William D. Borders, Daniel E. Pilarczlyk and William E. McManus who are reflecting on the Council a century later. Explores the thinking of the American hierarchy that went into the Council's actions which were a major milestone in the development of Catholic schools. Reassesses the impact of the Council on Catholic education.

112. Guilday, Peter. *A History of the Councils of Baltimore (1791-1884)*. New York: The Macmillan Company, 1932.

Presents a narrative of the development of canonical legislation promulgated at the eleven Baltimore Councils from 1791 when Bishop John Carroll met with a small group of priests to 1884 when Archbishop James Gibbons presided at the Third Plenary Council attended by a hierarchy of over seventy archbishops and bishops. Summarizes the mind of the bishops on Catholic education at each conciliar assembly and states that formal legislation on the elementary school begins with the decree of the Council of 1829. Relates that the Instruction from Propaganda in Rome in 1875, urging American bishops to establish a Catholic educational system, formed the basis of the legislation of the Third Plenary Council of 1884 which insisted on parochial schools wherever they could be supported.

113. Jones, William H. "The History of Catholic Education in the State of Colorado." Ph.D. dissertation. The Catholic University of America, 1955.

Contains a history of Catholic schools within the state of Colorado as they were founded and developed under the direction of five bishops: the early organization under Bishop Joseph P. Machebeuf, 1850 to 1889; further growth under Bishop Nicholas C. Matz, 1889 to 1917; greater expansion under Bishop John Henry Tihen, 1917 to 1931; educational developments under Archbishop Urban J. Vehr, 1931 to 1955; progress in the Diocese of Pueblo under Bishop Joseph C. Willging, 1941 to 1955. Includes a description of the early Catholic educational activities of the Catholic missionaries in the territory of Colorado from 1541 to 1850.

114. Kuhr, Nancy Jane Newton. "Catholic Parochial Schools in the Austin Diocese: Background, Development Since 1849 and Present Status." Ph.D. dissertation. The University of Texas at Austin, 1974.

Divides this study into two parts: 1) a history of the development and contribution of Catholic parochial schools in Central Texas and 2) a study of contemporary conditions in the Diocese of Austin. Records the story of the Texas parochial schools prior to statehood including the Spanish mission schools, the schools established during the Mexican control of Texas and the English-speaking schools after Texas became a republic. Continues the history of the schools during the nineteenth century and from 1900 to 1948 when the Diocese of Austin was created citing the reasons for the rapid growth of Catholic schools between 1849 and 1909. Claims that the decline of the schools in the 1970s is a result of the loss of moral training and the changes in the Church since the Second Vatican Council.

115. Kunkel, Norlene M. "Christian Free Schools: A Nineteenth-Century Plan." *Notre Dame Journal of Education* 7 (Spring 1976): 18-27.

Analyzes the educational philosophy of Bernard McQuaid, the first Bishop of Rochester, New York, which was encompassed in his lectures to persuade Protestants to establish other denominational school systems along with the Catholic schools. Studies McQuaid's arguments on the public school violation of American liberties and his unmodified convictions on Catholic education. Discusses the Bishop's refutation of an editorial in a Cleveland paper which claimed there were "contradictions" in his position and the position of Archbishop Hughes of New York. Observes that, although the crusade failed to convince Americans of the need for Christian Free Schools, Bishop McQuaid campaigned for strong legislation concerning the establishment of Catholic schools at the Plenary Council in 1884.

116. Lannie, Vincent P. "The Emergence of Catholic Education in America." *Notre Dame Journal of Education* 3 (Winter 1973): 297-309.

Examines the various factors and elements in a Protestant culture that caused Catholics to develop a religious, cultural and social separatism and to become more determined to safeguard their religious beliefs and ethnic identity bringing about the gradual development of the parochial school system. Describes the Protestants' fear and distrust of Catholic immigrants and the defensive mentality adopted by Catholic churchmen. Describes the areas of disagreement and the punishments meted out to Catholic children in public schools who refused to recite the Protestant version of the Bible. Addresses the shift of emphasis concerning Catholic discontent with the public schools in the 1850s and 1860s and the vision that emerged of every Catholic child in a Catholic school.

117. Luetmer, Nora. "The History of Catholic Education in the Present Diocese of St. Cloud, Minnesota, 1855-1965." Ph.D. dissertation. University of Minnesota, 1970.

Studies the Catholic elementary and secondary schools in the diocese of St. Cloud beginning from 1855 with the early schools and continuing through the years 1870 to 1915 presenting the historical background of each parish or church-supported school, the separate public school system and church-state conflicts. Shows the impact of the Catholic immigrant groups and the schools they established. Examines the role of the abbots and bishops in influencing education and attributes time in history, personal background and prevailing ideas to the way they exercised authority. Describes the organization and administration, and the formation of diocesan policy which began after the Diocese of St. Cloud was established in 1889.

118. McCluskey, Neil G., ed. "Instruction of the Congregation of Propaganda de Fide (1975)." *Catholic Education in America: A Documentary History*. (item 71), pp. 121-26.

Embodies eight points of instruction concerning Catholic children attending public schools. Directs American bishops to exhort their people not to attend public schools and to make every effort towards establishing Catholic schools. Advises Catholic parents to provide the necessary Christian training and instruction if circumstances warrant sending their children to the public schools. Reminds Catholics of the dangers of perversion and tells bishops, parish priests and missionaries in the United States to heed the decrees of the Plenary Councils of Baltimore to establish schools in connection with parish churches.

119. McCluskey, Neil G., ed. "Petition of the Catholics of New York For a Portion of the Common-School Fund (1840)." In *Catholic Education in America: A Documentary History.* (item 71), pp. 65-77.

Presents the request sent to the New York City Board of Aldermen by New York Catholics in which they expose the misrepresentations and pretensions of the Public School Society to exclude all sectarianism from the public schools. Introduces the letter with an explanation of the Public Schools Society which was the most powerful educational organization in New York. Asks for a share in the common fund for eight Catholic schools asking for consideration as citizens of the commonwealth and as willing to fulfill the conditions of the law so far as religious teaching is proscribed during school hours.

120. McDonnell, James Michael. "Orestes A. Brownson and Nineteenth-Century Catholic Education." Ph.D. dissertation. University of Notre Dame, 1975.

Reinterprets the views of Orestes Brownson, the controversial educator and publicist, on Catholic education and on the school question. Believes that Catholic bishops misconstrued Brownson's criticism of Catholic schools and scholars misinterpreted much of his writings while ignoring those of the late 1860s and 1870s. Shows how these essays reveal the prominent role Brownson played in advancing the Catholic position on the school question and in reforming Catholic schools.

121. McNeil, Teresa Baksh. "A History of Catholic School Education in San Diego County, California, from 1850 to 1936." Ed.D. dissertation. University of San Diego, 1986.

Traces Catholic school education in San Diego from the founding of Mission San Diego de Alcala in 1769 by Junipero Serra and points out that until the mid-nineteenth century Catholic education focused mainly on the training and conversion of the local Indian. Describes the slow evolution of Catholic education in San Diego County relating it to life and events of the times. Recounts the role of Father Anthony Ubach, a native of Barcelona, who arrived in 1866 and provided not only religious but also educational leadership bringing to San Diego the Sisters of St. Joseph of Carondelet who opened the first Catholic school in the area. Gives an account of each religious community that came to San Diego and of the thirteen schools established.

122. Mahan, Harold E. "'Most Pleasant School of Wisdom': Martin J. Kerney and a Catholic Vision of History." *The Maryland Historian* 15 (1984): 19-26.

Identifies Martin J. Kerney as a Baltimore educator, editor, legislator and amateur historian of the mid-nineteenth century who, perceiving a need for textbooks suited for parochial schools, wrote and edited numerous grammar school works on science, rhetoric, mathematics and history. Cites *Catechism of the History of the United States* (1850) and *The First-Class Book of History* (1850) as two of his most important historical works for elementary pupils. Analyzes Kerney's interpretations of European and American history and how they related to his perspective on the Catholic condition and destiny in the United States. Quotes Kerney who saw the relevance of history for the present and future as "the most pleasant school of wisdom."

123. Mary Rosalie, Sister. "Music in Early American Catholic Schools." *The Catholic Educational Review* 60 (December 1962): 577-87.

Compares the national influences that were evidenced in the kind and quality of sacred song found in the academies and parochial schools in mid-nineteenth century America, citing the German and French contributions as well as those of the Franciscans who brought their musical heritage from Spain. Explains that Religious Sisters did all they could to learn music and to teach it along with secular subjects and religious instruction. Tells of the influence of Bishop Flaget of Bardstown, Kentucky, in promoting church music and the efforts of Sir John Singenberger who founded *Caecilia* in 1874, a publication devoted to the betterment of Catholic church and school music. Notes the "ornamental branches" of music and art taught in the female academies such as Mother Seton's school in Emmitsburg, Maryland.

124. Mattice, Howard Leroy. "The Growth and Development of Roman Catholic Education in New York City: 1842-1875." Ed.D. dissertation. New York University, 1978.

Deals with the problems encountered by the New York City Catholic school system between 1842 and 1875 as it competed with the public schools for pupils and public funds. Describes the background of the school law of 1842 which denied public funds to sectarian schools and prohibited sectarian teaching in the public schools and presents the divergent views held by the Catholic leaders and the public school advocates. Explains the appropriations provided by New York State for the education of destitute children, including those in Catholic institutions and the public furor that was raised which resulted in a repeal of the law. Contends that the primary motivating factor for developing the Catholic school system in New York was the preservation of the faith of Catholic children.

125. Meiring, Bernard Julius. *Educational Aspects of the Legislation of the Councils of Baltimore 1829-1884.* New York: Arno Press, 1978.

Examines all the Councils of Baltimore and the factors which caused the American Catholic hierarchy to decide upon a separate, privately supported school system as the only alternative to the common school system which had many of its principles in direct conflict with the philosophy of the Catholic Church. Analyzes the legislation enacted by the Bishops and follows its successful implementation. Includes the entire educational section of the decrees of the Second Plenary Council with the English translation as well as those of the Third Plenary Council.

126. Parsons, Jackie. *The Educational Movement of the Blackfeet Indians 1840-1979.* Browning, Montana: Blackfeet Heritage Program, 1980.

Begins the educational history of the Blackfeet Indians with a description of the Mission schools recording that the Jesuit priests were allowed to stay as catechists in 1840 but opened their first Mission, St. Peter's, in 1859 in Montana. Describes the moving of the Reservation by the government in 1874 and the establishment of the permanent Mission, Holy Family, in 1890. Interviews some senior Blackfeet members who attended these early schools considered most important since the Black Robes (Jesuits) were the ones who led the way for the government to initiate different types of schools. Continues the educational history explaining the various kinds of schools and notes that of the many schools that once existed, only four schools are operating today.

127. Peterson, Susan C. "Doing 'Women's Work': The Grey Nuns at Fort Totten Indian Reservation, 1874-1900." *North Dakota History* 52 (1985): 18-25.

Recounts the story of St. Michael's Mission boarding school that opened among Devils Lake Sioux Indians in 1875 and combined the three "R"s with training in manual or industrial skills for boys and domestic arts for girls. Describes the problems and difficulties encountered by the Grey Nuns who were agents of President Grant's "Peace Policy" which attempted to assimilate Indians into white society. Describes the attacks in the 1880's on the awarding of government contracts to religious denominations working with Indian children which resulted in the phasing out of contract schools on reservations in favor of government-operated boarding schools making the Grey Nuns government employees.

128. Power, Edward John. "Brownson's Attitude Towards Catholic Education." *Records of the American Catholic Historical Society* 63 (June 1952): 110-28.

Analyzes the writings of Orestes Brownson concerning Catholic education which he believed every Catholic should favor although he felt that Catholic schools tended to depart from the standards he considered true to the fulfillment of the Church's mission on earth and to human progress. States that Brownson believed Catholic education's ideal of perfection was in the past though he conceded the Catholic clergy and laity were sincere in their desires. Says Brownson believed that the Church should become truly American; then the true American character and influence would become part of the school. Discusses Brownson's criticism of Catholic higher education and considers him to be principally a journalist whose contentions seldom deviated from the theoretical.

129. St. Henry, Sister M. "Nativism in Pennsylvania With Particular Regard To Its Effect On Politics and Education -- 1840-1860." *Records of the American Catholic Historical Society* 47 (March 1936): 5-47.

Explores the causes and effects of Nativism in Pennsylvania directed against Catholics in the 1840s and 1850s explaining the discriminatory and prejudicial practices of the Nativists who were against foreigners in general, and Catholics of foreign birth in particular. Relates the rise of the Native American Party in 1835 which organized against Bishop Kenrick who had petitioned the Board of Controllers of the public schools to allow Catholic children the liberty of using the Catholic version of the Bible. Describes the riots in Philadelphia and their effects including the Bishop's decision to suspend public worship and his having to flee the city. Relates the efforts made toward restoring peace and recounts the rise of the Nativists' "Know-Nothing" party in 1854 and its demise in 1856.

130. Sanders, James W. "Boston Catholics and the School Question, 1825-1907." *Building the American Catholic City: Parishes and Institutions.* Edited by Brian C. Mitchell. New York: Garland Publishing, Inc., 1988, pp. 151-83. (The Heritage of American Catholicism.)

   Discusses the effects of the burning of the Ursuline Convent and boarding school in Charlestown in 1834, as well as the anti-Irish riot on Broad Street in Boston, on Horace Mann who concluded that the remedy was a common school for all children, and on the Catholic Bishop, Benedict Fenwick, who believed that a separate school system for Catholics must be created. Explains that all educational growth after 1846 was initiated at the parish level since the building of churches was a priority of Bishop Fenwick's successors. Describes the lot of the Irish immigrants and discusses the reasons why they were not devoted to a Catholic school and their desire to achieve Yankee respectability.

131. Sanders, James W. *The Education of An Urban Minority: Catholics in Chicago, 1833-1965.* New York: Oxford University Press, 1977.

   Researches the Catholic education system in Chicago spanning a century and a third and describes and analyzes the growth of the Catholic school system within the general social, political, and economic climate in Chicago, and in relationship with the public schools. Considers the history of the city's Catholic education in three phases: 1) from the beginnings to the 1920s, a period of immigration, poverty, and hostility towards Catholicism; 2) into the 1920s, a period of transition and promise; and 3) from the 1930s to the 1960s, an era of success, racial crisis, and profound changes in the Church.

Describes the reconciling of national parishes and the establishment of a school system effective in Americanizing many immigrant children.

132. Sohn, Frederick H. "The Evolution of Catholic Education in the Diocese of Rochester, New York, 1868 to 1970." Ed.D. dissertation. Indiana University, 1972.

Examines the evolution of Catholic education in the Diocese of Rochester from its origin in 1868 to 1970 describing the men and events that were dominant in influencing this evolution. Discusses national and regional developments before 1868 and explores the Bishop McQuaid era from 1868 to 1909. Explains the Bishop's plan for Christian Free Schools and his furthering of Catholic schools within the Rochester Diocese. Studies the consolidation and expansion of the parochial school system under Bishop Hickey from 1909 to 1928 and continues into and beyond the depression years. Confronts the growth and change and the questioning of goals during the 1950s and the new directions of the 1960s.

133. Sullivan, Mary Xaveria. "The History of Catholic Secondary Education in the Archdiocese of Boston." Ph.D. dissertation. The Catholic University of America, 1946.

Treats the historical background of Catholic education in Boston describing the times and character of the people. Discusses the anti-Catholic spirit that prevailed, including the Eliot School Controversy caused when a Catholic pupil was whipped severely for refusing to read the Ten Commandments in the Protestant version. Characterizes the years from 1854 to 1907 as the formative period of parochial high schools in the Boston Archdiocese noting that Boston had a reputation among Church officials for inactivity in the number of parishes having schools. Regards the period from 1890 to 1906 as the turning point in Catholic educational achievement as a result of the legislation of the Third Plenary Council. Deals with the schools established, teachers, curriculum, and administration in parochial secondary education from 1907 to 1944.

134. Walch, Timothy. "Catholic School Books and American Values: The Nineteenth Century Experience." *Religious Education* 73 (September-October 1978): 582-91.

> Explores the content of American Catholic education in the nineteenth century by examining the textbooks used in both parochial and public schools and finds that the themes were similar: the educational value of nature, social values and behavior, and patriotism and superiority of the United States, but not the same. Discusses texts published by Catholic publishing houses and gives examples of stories that, although containing themes also found in public school texts, have an added or different emphasis. Points out that Catholic schoolbooks differed in the perspective on the American past by recalling the involvement and contributions of Catholics to the history of America.

135. Walch, Timothy. *The Diverse Origins of American Catholic Tradition: Chicago, Milwaukee, and the Nation.* New York: Garland Publishing, Inc., 1988. (The Heritage of American Catholicism).

> Shows that the different circumstances and educational problems faced by the individual dioceses in the American Church made for a difference in Catholic schooling during the nineteenth century. Emphasizes the parochial school movement in Chicago and Milwaukee and points out the error in Burns' history of American Catholic education in which the experiences of Catholic schools in each diocese are seen as the same. Explains this as being more apologetic than history. Refutes three myths concerning the origins and development of Catholic parochial education: 1) Catholics as a whole responded to the campaign for parish schools. 2) Catholic school curriculum was foreign to the American way. 3) Bishops were united in their support for parish schools.

136. Weisz, Howard Ralph. *Irish-American and Italian-American Educational Views and Activities, 1870-1900: A Comparison.* New York: Arno Press, 1976, c1970.

Explains how many Irish-Americans advocated public schools but anti-Catholicism, Protestant teaching and secularization in the common school, as well as Church legislation on education, turned them towards support of Catholic schools. Explores the arguments of the Irish who opposed public schools and their demands for public subsidy of the parochial schools. Studies the difference in the Italian experience since the Italian immigrants found well-established schools when they arrived in the 1880s. Recounts how most Italian-American children attended public schools and observes how complicated are the questions involving American ethnic groups. Claims that scholars have shown greater interest in the schools' problem with the immigrants more often than they have with the immigrants' problems with the schools.

CHAPTER 4
Catholic Schools and "Americanism"
1884 - 1925

In the latter years of the 19th century, immigration continued unabated. In some parts of the nation "Americanism" or citizenship education, founded on natural moral premises, replaced the Protestant base for public schooling. In this context moral education was divorced from religious education (which belonged to home and church), and became a function of the citizenship-oriented public school system.[1] The trend in public education toward centralization, bureaucratization, and systematization was closely tied to this development.[2] Table 1 reveals that the sources of immigration changed as the 20th century began. While the statistics contained in Table 1 do not reveal the religious affiliation of these immigrants, Buetow notes that the Catholic population of the United States increased almost threefold (from 6,143,222 in 1880 to 17,735,553 in 1920).[3]

Table 1
American Immigration, 1861-1920

Period	Total	Northwest Europe		South and East Europe	
		Number	*Percent*	*Number*	*Percent*
1861-1870	2,314,824	2,031,624	87.8	33,628	1.4
1871-1880	2,812,191	2,070,373	73.6	201,889	7.2
1881-1890	5,246,613	3,778,633	72.0	958,413	18.3
1891-1900	3,687,564	1,643,492	44.6	1,915,486	51.9
1901-1910	8,795,386	1,910,035	21.7	6,225,981	70.8
1911-1920	5,735,811	997,438	17.4	3,379,126	58.9

Source: R. Freeman Butts and Lawrence A. Cremin,
A History of Education in American Culture (New
York: Holt, Rinehart and Winston, 1953), p. 308.

The mix of ethnicity and schooling, especially when compounded with religion, is complex indeed. There were basic attitudinal differences toward Catholic schools among and within Catholic ethnic groups. Some were more inclined to be "Americanized," and endorsed the public schools; others were quite steadfast in their adherence to old-world customs, which included a reliance on ethnic parish schools; and yet still others supported Catholic schools as part of their version of "Americanism."

Catholic Educational Policy and the Control of Schooling in the Late 1800s

The state of Wisconsin witnessed two "case studies" which serve to illustrate the two major positions Catholic educational policy took in regard to the so-called "religiously neutral" school and to the relative rights of parents, church, and civil authority in the late 19th century. The first struggle was embodied in what became known as the Edgerton Bible decision, in which the Supreme Court of Wisconsin ruled that devotional Bible-reading in schools, accompanied by religious exercises, even though voluntary, constituted sectarian instruction, made the school a place of worship, and consequently violated Wisconsin's Constitution.[4] This ruling, the first of its kind by a state supreme court, judicially severed traditional Protestant practices from public schooling. Catholics, whose educational goal was a "religiously neutral" public school, rejoiced in the case's outcome.

To those Catholics who held that education was basically a parental God-given responsibility, for Catholic parents one to be carried out in accord with the official teachings of the Church, a "religiously-neutral" school fell far short of the ideal. The proper role of the state, this view held, was to assist parents in carrying out this responsibility. As a temporal, human entity, the state could only instruct, not educate, because to educate involved a moral component, which the state, as a civil unit, could not possess. Often buttressed by ethnic values, this more conservative approach regularly clashed with adherents of the growing public school system. In Wisconsin, the battle involved the ill-fated Bennett Law, which placed church-affiliated schools under civil control. It was repealed in 1891, subsequent to a bitter election campaign which resulted in the defeat of Governor William Dempster Hoard, a staunch advocate of the Law. As a result, church-operated schools in Wisconsin were free to exist and function with substantial autonomy, but without fiscal support from the state which church leaders originally had sought.[5]

Papal Teaching on "Mixed Matters," including Education

In the Catholic view, education, like marriage, was a "mixed matter," i.e., one in which church, family and state had a role. Vatican pronouncements on church and state, especially by Pope Leo XIII, played a role in the growing American controversy over the place of Catholic schools, without and within the Catholic Church. Official utterances, including papal encyclicals, while they did not exert as much influence over lay Catholics as was formerly believed, forcefully championed Catholic schools. That teaching merits a brief view at this point.

Centuries before, in "Unam Sanctam," Pope Boniface VIII had written of the superiority of the spiritual sword, wielded by the Church, to the temporal one, brandished by civil authority in those areas where each jurisdiction played a part.[6] This teaching had been reaffirmed by Pope Pius IX in 1864 in his controversial

"Syllabus of Errors." It was this doctrine on which Leo XIII based much of his instruction to the world's Catholic bishops and members. In a series of encyclicals (offical letters on matters of faith or morals calling for internal assent on the part of Catholics), Leo set forth the Church's position vis-a-vis the civil state. Catholics were told that the right to rule came from God, and that they were bound to dissent from laws which were at variance with the law of God. Civil authorities were exhorted to work in "friendly agreement" with the Church.[7] Civil states were called on to worship God, to acknowledge the true faith of Christ, which was to be found in the Catholic Church, and to allow the superior authority of the Church full sway in those areas the Church considered to be its field -- one of which was education.[8] The Pope also directed the civil authorities to place the eternal welfare of their citizens ahead of all other considerations when enacting legislation.[9]

Dissension among the Church's Leaders and Followers

Disagreement over the priority and function of Catholic schools in the Church in the United States had existed since their inception among all ranks of Catholics -- bishops, priests, and laity. The Vatican-authored *Instruction* of 1875 did not settle the contention, as was its aim. The urging of the Third Plenary Council of Baltimore notwithstanding, from which was adopted the motto "Every Catholic child in a Catholic school," was never close to fulfillment. For example, in 1884 there were 6,613 Catholic parishes, 2,532 of which had schools. Three years later in 1887 there were 6,910 parishes with 2,697 schools.[10] Despite the occasional castigation of public schools as "godless,"[11] and the imposition of canonical penalties on parents who failed to heed the Church's directives on attendance, such as denial of the Sacraments, the noted Jesuit educator Neil McCluskey observed that this ideal was to remain "distant" throughout this period.[12]

The laity were not alone in their uncertainty about the necessity of Catholic schooling; that sentiment also existed among the clergy. There were dissenting priests, such as the liberal Father

Edward McGlynn, a suspended clergyman from the New York
Archdiocese, who spoke out on behalf of the public schools and
appealed to the nation to "Show no favor to any rival system."[13]
The nation's bishops reflected lack of confidence as well, most
notably in the Archbishop of St. Paul, John Ireland. His struggle
with his fellow bishops, Bernard McQuaid of Rochester, NY;
Michael Corrigan of New York City; and Frederick Katzer of
Milwaukee merits mention at this juncture.

The controversy over Catholic schools had been simmering
for several decades within the Catholic Church in the United
States when Archbishop Ireland addressed the annual meeting of
the National Education Association (NEA) in 1890. Basically,
Ireland granted the civil authority the right to make instruction
compulsory, a right his opponents denied, called for cooperation
between church and state in education for the good of the people,
and praised the public schools, "The free school of America --
withered be the hand raised in its destruction." He concluded his
controversial address with a call for a "Christian state school."[14]

Wisconsin's bishops, all German-born, were livid. Led by
Frederick Katzer, Archbishop of Milwaukee, at the time engaged
in a grim struggle for their schools over the Bennett Law, they
lashed out at Ireland. They were joined by other conservative
prelates, most notably McQuaid and Corrigan. Complaints against
Ireland were forwarded to the Vatican.[15] Ireland defended his
speech to Cardinal Gibbons of Baltimore, calling his NEA plat-
form "a grand opportunity" to dispel the notion that the Catholic
Church was opposed to "the education of the people," and to advance the concept of a Christian school supported by the state, as
was present in his "Faribault Plan."[16]

The opposition to Ireland was so severe that Gibbons, the
nation's only cardinal and certainly its leading prelate, wrote Pope
Leo XIII in December of 1890 explaining that Americans were
proud of their public schools; that some American bishops had
accused the schools of being havens of immorality (Katzer had
described them as being a "union of devils") and thus had contributed to the polarized situation; and concluded with an appeal
to the Pope not to condemn Ireland for his views because such an
act would have a "disastrous effect" on the Church in this country.[17] The Pope heeded Gibbons' advice; a confrontation was

avoided for the moment, but was to arise on a national scale again in the very near future.

The Papal Legate Visits

In January of 1890 Pope Leo XIII had written yet another encyclical, which addressed the topic of Christians as citizens. In this authoritative letter, the Pope wrote that parents have "exclusive authority in the education of their children," and have been divinely commanded to exercise this responsibility by choosing schools which imbued their children with the principles of Christian morality, and "absolutely oppose their children frequenting schools where they are exposed to the fatal poison of impiety." Leo pointed to those Catholics as most entitled to praise "who, at the expense of much money and more zeal, have erected schools for the education of their children...[18] Conservative Catholic prelates, such as Corrigan, Katzer, and McQuaid relied on this papal teaching to advance their position.

That the "school question," as it was popularly known, drew the Vatican's attention was apparent with the appointment by the Pope of a personal legate, Archbishop Francis Satolli, to the American bishops. In May of 1892 the Vatican had ruled that cooperation with public schools, such as in Archbishop Ireland's Faribault Plan, can be allowed ("tolerari potest"). Debate then centered on the meaning of "tolerari potest." Did it mean toleration, permission, or approval?[19] The Pope sent Satolli to the United States in November, and the Archbishop presented his Fourteen Points to the Catholic bishops in November. Fundamentally, the Proposals called for the support of Catholic schools and accepting attendance at public schools "with a safe conscience," if the danger of loss of faith was remote in the eyes of the local bishop.[20]

The Strife Continues

Still the controversy raged. Archbishop McQuaid, for instance, thinking that the Propositions would adversely affect the Catholic school system, wrote Corrigan that "We are all in a nice pickle, thanks to Leo XIII and his delegate."[21] The American Catholic world had also been treated to a series of pamphlets written by the Reverend Thomas Bouquillon, who argued the "liberal" Catholic position, and the Jesuit, Rene Holaind, who espoused the "conservative" cause.[22]

Pope Leo's Letter Ends the Friction

Finally, in May of 1893 the public dissension was ended. Pope Leo XIII wrote to Cardinal Gibbons at the latter's request, stating that Catholic schools were to be "most sedulously promoted," leaving to the local bishop's judgment "when it is lawful, and when it is unlawful to attend the public schools...."[23]

Cahenslyism and "Americanism"

Much of the drive for Catholic schools emanated from the desire to preserve ethnic heritage. The public school was sometimes viewed, indeed even used, as an instrument to "Americanize" the children of immigrants. As such, the public school was seen as the enemy not only of faith but of the entire culture and traditions of ethnic groups.

The movement spearheaded by Peter Cahensly, which became known as Cahenslyism, opposed the assimilation of Catholics into the mainstream of American life. Among its major tenets was the position that Catholic parishes and dioceses be established along lines of national origin, rather than by territory, each to be headed by pastors and bishops respectively of that nationality.[24]

The alleged heresy of "Americanism" attests further to the tensions that existed within the Church and between the Church and the civil state at this time. Again Pope Leo intervened to quell the internal dissension in the Church. He condemned the errors in an encyclical on "Americanism," *viz.,* calling on the Church to adapt itself to modern civilization, show indulgence to modern theories and methods, de-emphasize religious vows, and give greater scope for the action of the Holy Spirit on the individual soul.[25] The Pontiff specified that the name "Americanism" had been attached to these doctrines, but that his denunciation of them did not imply a condemnation of the American people. American Catholic "liberal" leaders, such as John Ireland, who had been advocating cooperation with this nation's institutions, immediately accepted the papal teaching, at the same time denying that they had ever espoused the doctrines condemned.[26]

Catholic Schools at the Turn of the Century: An Established System

School attendance statistics at the turn of the century reveal that schooling occurred predominantly at the elementary level. High schools attracted a small percentage of the 14- to 18-year-old age group. In 1898, for instance, of 100 students in educational institutions, ninety-five were in elementary schools, four in secondary, and one in a post-secondary school.[27] Two years later, in 1900, approximately 10 percent of the high school age population was attending high school.[28] (Secondary enrollments reached about 5 million at the end of the 1920s; elementary schools enrolled approximately 97 percent of the 6-to-13 year olds by the 1920s.)[29] The comprehensive high school, as it exists today, is reflected in the *Cardinal Principles Report* of the National Education Association (NEA), issued in 1918.[30] The *Report* shows the evolution in the kinds of activities secondary schools engaged in. Catholic schools were to undergo parallel changes in the future. The structure of the Catholic Church, with the relative autonomy of the pastor, and with the pastor serving as head of all of the activities of the parish, including the school and the collection and disbursement of funds, militated against a centralized system with an inter-parish high school. The pastors, Burns notes, were not convinced of either the need or desirability for high schools.[31] Thus, despite the activities of the Catholic Educational Association and its Advisory Board, only a few inter-parochial high schools, e.g., Roman Catholic High School in Philadelphia, had been established.[32] The majority of Catholic secondary education resided with the religious orders. Table 2 documents the substantial Catholic commitment to elementary schools from 1880 to 1920, institutions which were supported and conducted by Catholic parishes under the headship of the pastor.

Table 2
Catholic Parochial School Growth in the U.S., 1880-1920

Year	Catholic Population	Parochial Schools	Pupil Enrollment
1880	6,143,222	2,246	405,234
1890	8,277,039	3,194	633,238
1900	10,129,677	3,811	854,523
1910	14,347,027	4,845	1,127,251
1920	17,735,553	5,852	1,701,219

Source: Cited in Harold A. Buetow, *Of Singular Benefit: The Story of U.S. Catholic Education* (New York: The Macmillan Company, 1970), p. 179.

World War I and Its Aftermath

The entry of the United States into World War I was followed, especially after the war, by anti-foreign outbreaks. Much of the enmity was directed against anything German. For instance, the teaching of German was banned in American high schools. Catholic schools, especially in the midwest, were heavily German.

The schools, as socializing agents, were asked to take steps to instill patriotism in their charges. The *Cardinal Principles Report* of 1918, referred to earlier, called for an expansion of the schools' role in society, made necessary the *Report* claimed, due to the loss of influence of home and church.[33]

The anti-foreign, protectionist sentiment extended far beyond the schools, dominating society. For example, following the war the Congress rejected membership in the League of Nations and passed restrictive immigration legislation. Several state legislatures attempted to enact sterilization measures for the "unfit."

This is the social context in which two educational measures were passed by the legislatures of Nebraska and Oregon respectively. These laws led to court challenges which ultimately reached the Supreme Court of the United States for adjudication.

In Nebraska, the legislature had passed a law which prohibited the teaching of subjects in any language other than English, and which delayed the teaching of a foreign language until the ninth grade. Meyer, a teacher in a Lutheran school, taught German to a fifth grade boy.

The Nebraska Supreme Court, while allowing the teaching of "dead" languages, e.g., Latin, prior to the ninth grade, upheld the statute. The United States Supreme Court, however, overturned the Nebraska Court's decision. The nation's highest tribunal recognized that the state had rights in the curriculum but stated those rights were not unlimited. In this instance, the Court ruled that Meyer was being denied his rights guaranteed him in the due process clause of the Fourteenth Amendment. The State of Nebraska had not demonstrated that the knowledge of the German language was inimical to the safety and welfare of the United States or of Nebraska as it had claimed, so it did not have the authority to interfere with Meyer's work as a teacher.[34]

Two years later the Court addressed an even more important issue -- the right of private schools to exist. Following a favorable referendum, the State of Oregon, with the active support of the Ku Klux Klan,[35] enacted legislation which required youngsters between the ages of eight and sixteen to attend public school, based on the assumptions that private schools were divisive and that public schools were necessary to guarantee good citizenship. The defendants, the Society of Sisters (of the Holy Names of Jesus and Mary) and Hill Military Academy contested the legislation. They argued that the intent of the law was the destruction of private and parochial schools. These schools, they insisted, had a beneficial influence on society. The State of Oregon maintained that liberty existed primarily for the good of society, which was served by public school attendance.

The Court overturned the legislation, again under the Fourteenth Amendment, in the process denying the divisiveness claim of Oregon. Additionally, the Court stated that parents have the right to send their children to private and church-related schools, providing those schools offer secular as well as religious education. Finally, the Court declared that the "child is not the mere creature of the state."[36]

These two decisions of the Supreme Court attest to the climate which existed in the nation after World War I. They end an era of considerable growth and turmoil for Catholic schools, within and without the Church.

Endnotes

1. Among the leaders in articulating this position was William Torrey Harris. See, for instance, Selwyn K. Troen, *The Public and the Schools: Shaping the St. Louis System, 1838-1920.* Columbia: University of Missouri Press, 1975. Also consult Neil G. McCluskey, *Public Schools and Moral Education: The Influence of Horace Mann, William Torrey Harris, and John Dewey.* Westport, Conn.: Greenwood Publishers, 1975; and Thomas C. Hunt, "Public Schools and Moral Education: An American Dilemma," *Religious Education* 74 (July-August, 1979): 350-72 for further treatment of this evolution.

2. See, particularly, David B. Tyack, *The One Best System: A History of American Urban Education.* Cambridge, Mass.: Harvard University Press, 1974; and Tyack and Elisabeth Hansot, *Managers of Virtue: Public School Leadership in America, 1820-1980.* New York: Basic Books, 1982.

3. Harold A. Buetow, *Of Singular Benefit: The Story of U.S. Catholic Education.* New York: The Macmillan Company, 1970, p. 179.

4. See Thomas C. Hunt, "The Edgerton Bible Decision: The End of an Era," *The Catholic Historical Review* 67 (October 1981): 589-619.

5. Consult Thomas C. Hunt, "The Bennett Law of 1890: Focus of Conflict between Church and State," *Journal of Church and State* 23 (Winter 1981): 69-94.

6. John F. Clarkson, et al., eds., *The Church Teaches: Documents of the Church in English Translation.* St. Louis: B. Herder Book Co., 1955, pp. 73-74.

7. Pope Leo XIII, "Diuturnum" ("On Civil Government"), in Gerald F. Yates, ed., *Papal Thought on the State.* New York: Appleton-Century-Crofts, Inc., 1958, pp. 2-3, 8.

8. Pope Leo XIII, "Immortal Dei" ("The Christian Constitution of States"), in John A. Ryan, ed., *The State and the Church*. New York: The Macmillan Company, 1922, pp. 4-24.

9. Pope Leo XIII, "Libertas Humana" ("Human Liberty"), in Joseph Husslein, ed., *Social Wellsprings*, I. Milwaukee: The Bruce Publishing Co., 1940, pp. 117-34.

10. James A. Burns and Bernard J. Kohlbrenner, *A History of Catholic Education in the United States*. New York: Benziger Brothers, 1937, p. 144.

11. See, for instance, Michael J. Muller, *Public School Education*. New York: D. J. Sadlier and Co., 1872; and Thomas J. Jenkins, *The Judges of Faith: Christian versus Godless Schools*. Baltimore: John Murphy and Co., 1886.

12. Neil G. McCluskey, "America and the Catholic School," in McCluskey, ed., *Catholic Education in America: A Documentary History*. New York: Teachers College Press, 1964, p. 25.

13. Cited in Anson Phelps Stokes, *Church and State in the United States*, II. New York: Harper Brothers, 1950, p. 653.

14. Archbishop John Ireland, "State Schools and Parish Schools -- Is Union Between Them Impossible?," *National Education Journal of Proceedings and Addresses*. Session of the Year 1890, held at St. Paul, Minnesota. Topeka: Kansas Publishing House, Clifford C. Baker, 1890, pp. 179-85.

15. McCluskey, ed., *Catholic Education in America*, p. 141.

16. John Ireland, "Clarification to Cardinal Gibbons," in *Ibid.*, pp. 142-48.

17. "Cardinal Gibbons' Report to Pope Leo XIII, December 30, 1890," translated from the French by the Reverend P. H. Conway, O. P., in Daniel Reilly, *The School Controversy, 1891-1893*. New York: Arno Press and the New York Times, 1969, p. 233. Originally published at Washington, D.C.: The Catholic University of America Press, 1944.

18. Pope Leo XIII, "Sapientiae Christianae" ("On the Chief Duties of Christians as Citizens"), in Husslein, ed., *Social Wellsprings*, I, p. 162.

19. McCluskey, ed., *Catholic Education in America*, p. 151.

20. "Archbishop Satolli's Fourteen Propositions for the Settling of the School Question," in McCluskey, ed., *Ibid.*, pp. 151-60.

21. Quoted in McCluskey, *Ibid.*, p. 161.

22. Bouquillon's first publication was "Education: To Whom Does It Belong?"; Holaind's response was entitled "The Parent First." For a more thorough discussion of the controversy, consult Reilly, *The School Question, 1891-1893*.

23. Cited in Reilly, *Ibid.*, pp. 228-29.

24. Cahenslyism is treated in a number of sources that deal with American Catholic history. See, particularly, Colman J. Barry, *The Catholic Church and German Americans*. Milwaukee: Bruce Publishing Co., 1953. Cahensly himself was the author of the Lucerne (Switzerland) Memorial in 1890, which he subsequently presented to Pope Leo. The Memorial, which emanated from a meeting of the St. Raphael Society in Lucerne, expressed concern over the loss of Catholic immigrants to the faith. The establishment of national churches in the United States was one of the Memorial's recommendations, designed to protect the immigrants' faith. On this topic consult Gerald Shaughnessy, *Has the Immigrant Kept the Faith*? New York: Arno Press, 1969.

25. John Tracy Ellis, *American Catholicism*. Chicago: The University of Chicago Press, 1956, pp. 118-19. For a thorough study of the Americanism controversy consult Thomas T. McAvoy, *The Americanism Heresy in Roman Catholicism 1895-1900*. Notre Dame, IN: University of Notre Dame Press, 1963. The English text of the encyclical may be found in *The Great Encyclical Letters of Pope Leo XIII*, ed. John Wynne. New York: Benziger Brothers, 1903, pp. 441-53.

26. McAvoy, *A History of the Catholic Church in the United States*. Notre Dame, IN: University of Notre Dame Press, 1969, pp. 333-35.

27. Tyack, *The One Best System: A History of American Urban Education*, p. 66.

28. Neil G. McCluskey, *Catholic Viewpoint on Education*. Garden City, NY: Hanover House, 1959, p. 99.

29. R. Freeman Butts, *Public Education in the United States: From Revolution to Reform*. New York: Holt, Rinehart, and Winston, 1978, p. 310.

30. For an account of the post-*Cardinal Principles Report* attendance growth of the public high school, see *Ibid.*, pp. 318-21, and Edward A. Krug, *The Shaping of the American High School 1920-1941*. Madison: The University of Wisconsin Press, 1972, p. 42.

31. James A. Burns, "Catholic Secondary Schools," *American Catholic Quarterly* XXVI (July 1901): 497.

32. Buetow, *Of Singular Benefit*, pp. 182-84.

33. National Education Association, *Cardinal Principles of Secondary Education*. Washington, D.C.: Government Printing Office, 1981, pp. 10-11.

34. *Meyer* v. *Nebraska*. 262 U.S. 390 (1923).

35. Robert L. Church and Michael W. Sedlak, *Education in the United States: An Interpretive History*. New York: The Free Press, 1976, pp. 359-61.

36. *Pierce* v. *Society of Sisters*. 268 U.S. 510 (1925).

Bibliographic Entries

137. Agatha, Mother M. "Catholic Education and the Negro."
Essays on Catholic Education in the United States. (item 15),
pp. 500-22.

Traces the history of the Catholic Church's efforts to educate Negroes in America from its beginnings to the 1940s,
chronicling the work of Catholic bishops, laity and religious
congregations. Explains the declarations of the Plenary
Councils which dealt with the care of the Negroes, the appointment of "The Commission for Catholic Missions Among
the Colored People and the Indians," and the appointment of
Father John Burke in 1907 to the post of Director General for
the Colored Missions of the United States. Develops the story
of Mother Katherine M. Drexel, a founder of the Sisters of the
Blessed Sacrament for Indians and Colored People, and outlines her system of Catholic Negro education.

138. Archdeacon, John Philip. "The Week-Day Religious School."
Ph.D. dissertation. The Catholic University of America, 1927.

Investigates the extent and character of the Catholic elementary week-day religious school defining the term in two
ways: religious instruction given to Catholic public school
children outside regular school hours and apart from the
public school building; and religious instruction provided
during released time within the regular school day. Traces the
historical development, activities, curricula, and methods in
Catholic week-day religious schools. Points out that the philosophy underlying this type of school is not in complete
conformity with Catholic views of religious education which
is "religion at work," applied to all areas of life and correlated
with all other subjects.

139. Barger, Robert N. *John Lancaster Spalding: Catholic Educator and Social Emissary.* New York: Garland Publishing, Inc.,
1988.

Provides an historical and philosophical analysis and synthesis of Archbishop Spalding's social and educational thought and actions. Examines his educational theories which, although considered to be rooted in the idealist intellectual aristocratic tradition, in operation leaned toward progressivism. Discusses his leadership at the Council of Baltimore in 1884 and his advocacy of parochial schools. Describes Archbishop Ireland's Faribault plan to eliminate a dual system of schools and Archbishop Spalding's exception to it. Reviews his work in founding the Catholic University of America and his authorship of the Baltimore Catechism. Assesses his contribution to parochial education while Bishop of the Peoria Diocese.

140. Boffa, Conrad Humbert. "Canonical Provisions for Catholic Schools (Elementary and Intermediate)." J.C.D. dissertation. The Catholic University of America, 1939.

Divides the study of elementary and intermediate schools as treated in the Code of Canon Law into two parts: 1) an historical account which contains five chapters on the development of ecclesiastical legislation affecting Catholic education up to the promulgation of the Code; and 2) a commentary of the various canons relating to schools and to education. Addresses the roles of family, Church, and state with regard to the control of schools and considers attendance at non-public schools by Catholic youth; the right of the Church to have its own system of schools; the exclusive authority of the Church in matters of religious instruction and morality and the obligations of the local Ordinaries.

141. Bollig, Richard Joseph. "History of Catholic Education in Kansas 1836-1932." (item 98).

142. Browne, Henry J. "New York's Catholic Heritage in Secondary Education." *The Catholic Educational Review* 50 (May 1952): 330-37.

Introduces historical facts and background of the foundations of Catholic secondary education in New York and explains how separation of the secondary from the elementary
and collegiate levels came about. Notes the growth of a
number of private secondary schools in New York and tells
of the beginnings of the Catholic central high school movement in 1926. Regards Bishop John L. Spalding as a valuable
part of New York's heritage since he worked as an assistant
at St. Michael's Church and was the first director of its parochial schools. Challenges the Catholic high schools citing the
Bishop's words, "The test of a school is what it does for the
inferior students -- the dull, the listless, and the unresponsive;
for students of exceptional powers will educate themselves...."

143. Bryce, Mary Charles. "The Influence of the Catechism of the
Third Plenary Council of Baltimore on Widely Used Elementary Religion Text Books from Its Composition in 1885 to Its
1941 Revision." Ph.D. dissertation. The Catholic University
of America, 1970.

Researches the historical origins and effects of the Baltimore Catechism in order to determine its influence on religious education in the United States and on other religion
manuals. Presents the development of the modern catechism
in an historical overview and describes the development of
catechisms in the United States up to the Third Plenary
Council. Explores the origin, sources, and early history of the
Baltimore Catechism which was embedded in the literary form
of the catechism genre. Examines the influence of the Baltimore Catechism on manuals published up to 1918 and manuals published between 1918 and 1941. Explains that it made
its own mark on catechism history.

144. Buetow, Harold A. *Of Singular Benefit: The Story of Catholic
Education in the United States.* (item 47).

145. Carmody, Charles J. "American Catholic Religious Education: From 1776 to the Eve of Vatican II." *Listening* 11
(Spring 1976): 142-60.

Examines the development of Roman Catholic catechesis in the United States focusing on its theory, persons and materials. Explains the influence of the Sulpician method by the 1890s with a three-fold emphasis on explanation, enrichment, and advanced instruction. Describes the progressive traditionalism period from 1900 to 1915 during which time the (National) Catholic Educational Association, founded in 1803, focused on religious education, and American publishers produced many materials for use in the teaching of religion. Reviews the changing tradition from 1916 to 1930 with greater emphasis on offering authentic religious experiences. Explores the newer catechetical trends from 1930 to 1959 with the "Christo-centric" approach.

146. Costello, William J. "The Chronological Development of the Catholic Secondary School in the Archdiocese of Philadelphia." (item 52).

147. Drayer, Adam M. "A History of Catholic Secondary Education in the Diocese of Scranton, Pennsylvania." Ph.D. dissertation. Fordham University, 1953.

Tells of the beginnings and growth of the Catholic secondary school system in the Scranton Diocese progressing from two schools in 1868 to twenty-six in 1956. Provides data concerning the national, religious and economic background of Catholics in Scranton and outlines the growth of Catholicism both in Scranton and in the state of Pennsylvania. Presents the histories of the individual schools detailing their development and sets forth specific conditions and practices in the Catholic secondary schools as found in 1951. Concludes with suggestions for further development.

148. Drouin, Edmond G. "The United States Supreme Court and Religious Freedom in American Education in Its Decisions Affecting Church-Related Elementary and Secondary Schools During the First Three Quarters of the Twentieth Century." Ph.D. dissertation. The Catholic University of America, 1980.

Focuses on the role of the Supreme Court in redefining the issue of religious freedom in the relationships between government and private church-related schools during the twentieth century. Presents an historical investigation of eighteen decisions of the Supreme Court from 1908 to 1977 discussing the major thrusts during each decade: constitutional rights and Indian Mission schools at the beginning of the twentieth century; fundamental rights and church-related schools during the twenties; tax-funded auxiliary services and church-related schools in the thirties through the sixties; issues of government regulations and funding during the seventies. Analyzes the judicial perception of religion and church, society and state, education and schooling, and the judicial interpretation of the Constitution through the twentieth century.

149. Dunney, Joseph A. *The Parish School: Its Aims, Procedure, and Problems*. New York: The Macmillan Company, 1921.

Surveys all aspects of the local parochial school at the beginning of the 1920s presenting each chapter as a discourse on a particular topic such as: organization and cooperation, principals and teachers, grading, discipline, teaching religion, departmental instruction in the intermediate grades, a foreign language in the seventh grade, and commercial classes in the upper grades. Includes an appendix on the priest and education.

150. Durkin, Mary Antonia. "The Preparation of the Religious Teacher: A Foundational Study." Ph.D. dissertation. The Catholic University of America, 1926.

Discusses the religious and professional preparation of the Catholic teacher and presents proposals for the organization of a novitiate normal school built on Catholic principles of philosophy and the nature of religious life. Surveys the state system of teacher training and the Church's system of teacher training in the United States. Describes the qualifications and the qualities of the ideal teacher and the aims and methods of novitiate training. Reports on a suggested curricula presented to twenty-three novitiates and ten colleges and summarizes the responses with a commentary. Regards their schools as the American Catholics' contribution to the welfare of their country and sees the Catholic teacher as a contributor to the achievement of this ideal.

151. Egan, Maurice Francis. "A Catholic on the School Question." *The North American Review* 414 (1891): 637-40.

Reflects on the way the ordinary non-Catholic views the Catholic Church's problem with the American system of common education and the extraordinary non-Catholic who vaguely believes that individual Catholics may be reasonable but will "close ranks behind mitres and crosiers." Answers the non-Catholic's questions as to why the Catholic parent keeps his children out of public schools showing that Catholic laymen have a profound interest in the question of education. Asserts that no thoughtful, conscientious Catholic could accept entirely secular education for his children and expounds on what Catholics want in their Church, their prelates, and their schools.

152. Engles, Leo James. "A Study of Catholic Education in Oklahoma With Special Emphasis on the Diocese of Oklahoma City and Tulsa (1875-1970)." Ed.D. dissertation. The University of Tulsa, 1971.

Details the educational activities of the Catholic Church in Oklahoma from the time the area was known as Indian Territory to 1971. Describes the work of Father Isidore Robot and other Benedictines who made an agreement with the Indians in 1876 to build a monastery, churches and schools. Continues the story of educational expansion from 1886 to 1907 under the leadership of Father Ignatius Jean discussing the schools that were built for Indian, white and Negro children. Describes the growth of elementary and higher education from 1907 to 1969 and provides the results of a survey on attitudes toward Catholic education in Tulsa, Oklahoma, conducted for the Diocesan Board of Education in 1970.

153. Faherty, William Barnaby with Elizabeth Kolmer, Dolorita
Maria Dougherty and Edward J. Sudckum. *From One Gener-
ation to the Next -- 160 Years of Catholic Education in Saint
Louis.* (item 58).

154. Gabert, Glen (E.) Jr. *In Hoc Signo? A Brief History of Catholic Parochial Education in America.* (item 61).

155. Gallagher, Marie Patrice. "The History of Catholic Elementary Education in the Diocese of Buffalo, 1847-1944." (item
109).

156. Grover, Mary Anne. "Preparing Teachers for Homestead Parochial Schools, 1888-1921." *Pennsylvania Heritage* 9 (Fall
1983): 14-18.

Interviews retired parochial school teachers who taught in
the Catholic schools of Homestead, Pennsylvania, an urban
industrial area in the late nineteenth and early twentieth centuries. Relates their recollections that depict how these Catholic Sisters became educated as teachers earning a degree on
Saturdays, after school hours, and in the summers. Relates
how the rapid population growth due to immigration and in-
dustrialization caused extraordinarily high parochial school
enrollments with the Sisters sometimes teaching over a hundred pupils in a classroom. Tells of teacher evaluation by the
school principal and a supervisor of the Religious Community. Finds that each of the Sisters interviewed would live every minute of her early work all over again.

157. Harris, Xavier James. "The Development of the Theory of
Religious Instruction in American Catholic Secondary
Schools After 1920." Ph.D. dissertation. University of Notre
Dame, 1962.

Attempts to perceive the theory underlying religious instruction as expressed by leaders in American Catholic secondary education relating this theory to the special areas of
religious instruction. Covers forty years from 1920 to 1960 divided into four distinct phases of development. Explains the

1920s as the decade when high school religion became one of the chief concerns of educators and discusses the Notre Dame survey in 1924 which brought out the weaknesses of the religion program and offered suggestions for improvement. Describes the efforts to vitalize the teaching of religion in the 1930s, to meet the needs of adolescents in the 1940s, and to construct a core curriculum integrated by the study of religion in the 1950s.

158. Hunt, Thomas C. "The Bennett Law of 1890: Focus of Conflict Between Church and State in Education." *Journal of Church and State* 23 (Winter 1981): 69-93.

Examines the background of the issues, the controversy, and the repeal in 1890 of legislation introduced into the Wisconsin Assembly in 1889 which would require the yearly attendance of children seven to fourteen years old for twelve weeks in a school in the district of residence, and the teaching of certain subjects in the English language. Recounts the conflict that raged when German Catholics and their Bishops opposed the Bennett Law stating that it violated the rights of parents and church education. Describes how the Bennett Law became a central issue during the Milwaukee mayoral election in 1890 in which Governor Hoard was defeated. Shows how the results of the 1890 elections doomed the Law and declares that Catholics and Lutherans had achieved a measure of independence from state control.

159. Hunt, Thomas C. and Barbara K. Bellefeuille. "The Bible in the Schools: The Edgerton and Schempp Decisions Revisited." *Religion and Public Education* 15 (Summer 1988): 321-30.

Discusses the Edgerton Bible decision of 1890 and the Schempp case of 1963 reviewing the context of each case, the issues involved and the subsequent public outcry. Sees the Edgerton decision in Wisconsin as an indicator of future decisions concerning religious issues in America. Describes the background to the Edgerton Case in which Catholic parents objected to the use of the King James version of the Bible in the schools and explains the major points agreed upon by the five Supreme Court justices who ruled the practice violated the Wisconsin constitution. Presents the history and aftermath of the Schempp Case in which a Unitarian family protested the devotional reading of the Bible in the school contending that it was unconstitutional and infringed upon their rights under the First and Fourteenth Amendments.

160. Jones, William H. "The History of Catholic Education in the State of Colorado." (item 113).

161. Kuhr, Nancy Jane Newton. "Catholic Parochial Schools in the Austin Diocese: Background, Development Since 1849, and Present Status." (item 114).

162. Kunkel, Norlene M. *Bishop Bernard J. McQuaid and Catholic Education.* New York: Garland Publishing, Inc., 1988.

Explains the import of the American Catholic Church in the nineteenth century on the personality of Bernard J. McQuaid who spent his childhood in an orphanage and grew up to become Bishop of Rochester and champion of Catholic education. Discusses McQuaid's campaign to provide a Catholic education for all Catholic children of the diocese and his plan for Christian Free Schools which would serve the rich and poor without distinction. Notes his acceptance of state supervision of secular subjects and examines his efforts to provide teacher training for parochial school teachers. Contends that Bishop McQuaid's school system became a prototype for other American dioceses. Recounts his role in the Wisconsin Bennett Law conflict and his clash with Archbishop Ireland on the School Controversy of the 1890s.

163. Kuznicki, Ellen Marie. "A Historical Perspective on the Polish American Parochial School." *Polish American Studies* 35 (1978): 5-12.

Presents some of the developmental phases of the American Polish parochial school and maintains that anyone evaluating its effect ought first to study the Polish American community in the context of its European roots. Describes the impact of two million Polish arriving in America from 1870 until the 1920s and develops the role of the Polish parochial school which combined the values of Polish heritage with those of the American environment. Reflects that despite its failure to serve the purpose for which it was founded, the Polish Catholic school played an important role in the cultural evolution of the whole Polish American community.

164. Kuzniewski, Anthony. "Boot Straps and Book Learning: Reflections on the Education of Polish Americans." *Polish American Studies* 32 (1975): 5-26.

Examines how Polish education in the United States has been studied and explained by historians focusing on the research of Jozef Miaso whose work, *The History of the Education of Polish Immigrants in the United States*, covers the century following the beginnings of Polish parochial education at the end of the Civil War. Takes issue with Miaso's hidden question of why the Polish immigrant group was less successful than others in using education to advance socially and economically. Contends that the assessment of Polish education in the United States must be made in the light of experience since the relative status of each ethnic group in society often affects how its past is viewed. Describes the rapid growth of the Polish parochial school system between 1880 and 1914 and tells how there was a greater trend after World War I toward quality in the education of the American Polish.

165. Luetmer, Nora. "The History of Catholic Education in the Present Diocese of St. Cloud, Minnesota, 1855-1965." (item 117).

166. McCann, Mary Beatrice. "A Description of Social Studies in the Catholic Secondary Schools of the Archdiocese of Philadelphia, 1890-1976." Ed.D. dissertation. Temple University, 1978.

Investigates the social studies curriculum in the Catholic high schools of the Archdiocese of Philadelphia at certain times -- 1890, 1920, 1950, and 1976, in order to determine the thrust and organizational pattern, the status of history and other social sciences in the list of course offerings, and to discover if any apparent national social studies curriculum movements had any influence on the Archdiocesan course offerings. Finds that history was the dominant social science from 1890 to 1965 but by 1976 the social studies program was concerned with interdisciplinary studies in the world culture and American studies courses which were derived from the State requirements. Explains the correlation of the Catholic curricular offerings with the national trend and recommends further research.

167. McCluskey, Neil G., ed. "Pastoral Letter of the Archbishops and Bishops of the United States (1919)." *Catholic Education in America: A Documentary History* (item 71), pp. 178-92.

Presents the pastoral letter of the American Bishops whose meeting after World War I was the first in a series of annual meetings of the American Catholic hierarchy. Includes the first extract from the introductory section and the entire Section XIII, "Education." Emphasizes the value of higher education under Catholic auspices and determines that the Catholic University will be developed to become an educational center worthy of the Church in America. Expounds on education and the obligation of the Church to maintain a system of education distinct and separate from other systems. States the principles which are the basis of Catholic education and explains the role of the school, the home, and the state in preparing the child to fulfill his obligations to family and society.

168. McKeough, Michael J. "Catholic Secondary Education, 1900-1950." *The Catholic School Journal* 51 (April 1951): 113-15.

Reports that the Catholic high school had developed more slowly than the public high school in America at the turn of the century. Says the private academy and college preparatory schools, economic difficulties, and the general opinion that a Catholic high school education was for the elite were some of the factors involved in the slow growth. Explains the call at the 1903 meeting of the Catholic Educational Association for a free central high school in cities where there were several parishes and discusses the objections to it. Describes the continued development of Catholic secondary schools despite failures and presents the first accurate statistics which were published in 1921. Points out the necessity to have more lay teachers since the religious teachers were overburdened.

169. Maguire, William P. A. "Catholic Secondary Education in the Diocese of Brooklyn." Ph.D. dissertation. The Catholic University of America, 1932.

Depicts the history of Catholic secondary education in the Diocese of Brooklyn, New York, which was created in 1853, to the beginning of the 1930s and records that by 1890 there were twenty-two high schools. Chronicles the continued development of the secondary school system enumerating the arrival of various religious orders of men and women and the opening of each new school and academy. States that in 1923 Bishop Thomas Molloy started a drive for the establishment of free diocesan high schools, opening in 1926 the Bishop Loughlin Memorial High School for boys and the Bishop McDonnell Memorial High School for girls. Provides many tables and a great deal of data concerning the various high schools.

170. Martire, Harriette A. "A History of Catholic Parochial Elementary Education in the Archdiocese of New York." (item 76).

171. Meagher, Timothy J. "The Delayed Development of Parochial Education Among Irish Catholics in Worcester." *Historical Journal of Massachusetts* 12 (1984): 44-59.

Examines the factors involved in the lack of effort by Irish
Catholics to build parochial schools in Worcester, the largest
city in the Springfield Diocese at the close of the nineteenth
century. Describes the Irish parishes and the heavy burden of
debt and financial difficulties they experienced throughout the
late nineteenth and early twentieth centuries resulting in a lack
of money to build schools. Analyzes the indifference of the
Irish laity to parochial education and finds that many of them
were satisfied with the city's public schools. Assesses the import of liberal Catholic ideas among Irish Catholics and their
strong interest in adapting to the American environment. Recounts the gradual change in attitude and the evolving clerical
leadership so that by the 1920s Worcester's Irish Catholics
began to heed the mandate of the Baltimore Council to build
their own schools.

172. Morrissey, Timothy H. "A Controversial Reformer: Archbishop John Ireland and His Educational Belief." *Enlightening
the Next Generation: Catholics and Their Schools 1830-1980.*
Edited by F. Michael Perko. New York: Garland Publishing,
Inc., 1988, pp. 54-66. (The Heritage of American Catholicism).

Analyzes the development of Archbishop Ireland's social
and educational thought which differed from the positions of
his fellow bishops, Bernard J. McQuaid and Michael A. Corrigan. Depicts the debates at the National Educational Association's meetings concerning the role which schools should
play in the moral development of American children and explains the Catholic position stated by Cardinal Gibbons and
Bishop Keane. Cites this as the beginning of the School
Controversy which then centered around Archbishop Ireland
who proposed a single free American school system that
would be state-supported, provide universal and compulsory
education, and include both secular and religious instruction.
Believes that Ireland's approach was based upon his belief in
Americanizing the Catholic population.

173. Murphy, John F. "The Priest's Role in Education in Yester-
day's Church." *The Living Light* 3 (Spring 1976): 145-50.

Deals with the author's reflections on the clergy's role in
American Catholic education during the last decade of the
nineteenth century engendered by his reading of issues of the
American Ecclesiastical Review (AER) from 1889 to 1900.
Discusses the need for a clearly defined role of the clergy in
education during a time of the resurgence of anti-Catholicism,
the prelude to modernism and the Americanism crisis. Remarks that the clergy of the 1890s were sure of their positions
as educators since there was a clearly established role for them
while in the 1970s the clergy seem less certain about that role.
Notes there still remains a strong vestige of the priest as authority, or prime mover. Asks if a rethinking of priorities in
education is needed.

174. Murphy, John F. "Professional Preparation of Catholic
Teachers in the Nineteen Hundreds." *Notre Dame Journal of
Education* 7 (Summer 1976): 123-33.

Recounts how education and schooling were paramount
issues for the American Catholic Church at the turn of the
century, and American Catholics wanted to provide their
children with the learning and schooling of the public schools
but with certain additions. Explains the concern for professionalism and describes the movement led by Thomas Edward
Shields at Catholic University to establish conditions for the
training of Sisters. Explores the establishment of a national
center for the professional education of women religious and
includes a letter of Shields that gives a detailed description of
his own view of the work and its chronology. Observes that
the effort to obtain degrees for religious teachers had taken
root and had been accepted at the highest Catholic levels.

175. Newton, Robert R. "The Evolution of the New York Archdiocesan School System 1800-1967." (item 84).

176. Oates, Mary J. "Organized Voluntarism: The Catholic Sisters in Massachusetts, 1870-1940." *American Quarterly* 30 (Winter 1978): 652-80.

> Demonstrates the implications for religious women with the expansion of parochial schools after the Plenary Council of 1884, especially in the State of Massachusetts which had, up to that time, moved slowly in responding to directives concerning the establishment of parochial schools. Relates that young women entering religious life were encouraged to join teaching communities in order to meet the "critical need" of the Church in Massachusetts to develop a parochial school system. Discusses the concerns of some Catholics with regard to the education of boys, the inadequacy of facilities, large class sizes, and teacher training. Believes parochial schools would have been established when they could be afforded and the Sisters' work would have been enhanced if there had not been a school campaign after the Council of 1884.

177. Oates, Mary J. "The Professional Preparation of Parochial School Teachers 1870-1940." *Historical Journal of Massachusetts* 12 (1984): 60-72.

> Studies the training of the religious teacher in the Catholic schools of Massachusetts during the late nineteenth century and the first half of the twentieth century. Finds that the Sisters learned by doing and by observing experienced teachers. Discusses the results of the inadequate training but records that the Sisters' success in providing a basic education at the elementary level was acknowledged publicly by 1900. Explains that a lack also of professional interchange and exchange with other teachers was counterproductive to change in curriculum, methods of teaching and discipline. Indicates that with state certification requirements during the 1920s and 1930s more Sisters began studying for degrees.

178. Obreza, John Edward. "'Philadelphia's Parochial Schools: An Impressive and Permanent Fact?'" In "Philadelphia Parochial

System From 1830-1920: Growth and Bureaucratization."
(item 85), pp. 151-92.

Discusses the endorsement of curriculum changes and the
adoption of administrative policies formulated during the administration of Superintendent Phillip R. McDevitt. Analyzes
three indicators of his success in making Philadelphia's parochial school system a viable alternative to the public school
system: 1) aggregate growth rates before and after 1895; 2) the
enrollments and services of Roman Catholic High School; 3)
the minutes of the Archdiocesan Parochial School Board.
Contends that these elements considered together indicate that
"resident" historians were less than accurate in their claims.
Finds the problem of Catholic attendance at public schools
was a recurring concern and Catholics were not prepared to
pursue to the same degree the administration's goals.

179. O'Brien, Mary Agnes. "History and Development of Catholic
Secondary Education in the Archdiocese of New York." (item
86).

180. Rector, Theresa A. "Black Nuns As Educators." *Journal of
Negro Education* 51 (Summer 1982): 238-53.

Presents historical sketches of the three Black religious
communities of Roman Catholic Nuns in the United States:
The Oblate Sisters of Providence, The Sisters of the Holy Family, and the Franciscan Handmaids of Mary. Tells how these
Communities were founded by Black women, two dating back
to antebellum times and the third founded in 1916. Addresses
their commitment to provide quality Christian education for
young Black Americans, their ability to survive bigotry, har-
assment, racial prejudice, insufficient funds, rigid rules and regulations, and their continuing contribution to American
Catholic education.

181. Reilly, Daniel F. *The School Controversy 1891-1893.* New
York: Arno Press and the New York Times, 1969. Reprint of
the 1943 dissertation, The Catholic University of America.

(American Education: Its Men, Ideas and Institutions, Teachers College, Columbia University Series).

Researches the full account of the controversy that raged within Catholic ranks from 1891 to 1893 concerning state control over Catholic schools in return for public funds and the right of the state to educate. Examines the background to the conflict and discusses the start of the controversy when Archbishop Ireland gave a speech at the National Educational Association's Convention in 1890 in which he praised the public schools, advocated compulsory attendance and regretted the necessity for parochial schools. Explains his Stillwater and Faribault Plans that would have the state rent parochial school buildings and retain Catholic teachers who would be under the control of the state. Details the intense opposition among Catholic bishops and explores the effects of the controversy. Examines Cardinal Gibbons' report to Pope Leo XIII, Archbishop Ireland's response, and Rome's intervention.

182. Sanders, James W. *The Education of an Urban Minority: Catholics in Chicago, 1833-1965.* (item 131).

183. Scanlon, William G. "The Development of the American Catholic Diocesan Board of Education, 1884-1966." Ed.D. dissertation. New York University, 1967.

Traces the origins and development of the Catholic diocesan board in the United States evidencing that a board of priests and laymen was in existence in Philadelphia in 1852. Depicts the changes in activity and membership that occurred because of chronological and geographical differences. Analyzes why and how the board responded to the educational, cultural, and ecclesial needs of the Church. Shows that this response was accomplished by: 1) administration and supervision; 2) becoming a representative body for those concerned with Catholic schools; and 3) being an institutional adjunct serving the American Church. Recommends that Catholic educators confront the implications of the direction of board development and make provisions to avoid confusion between the role of the board and that of the office of the diocesan superintendent of schools.

184. Shields, Thomas Edward. "Catholic Education: The Basis of True Americanization." *The Catholic Educational Review* 19 (January 1921): 3-19.

> Contrasts the public schools with the Catholic schools in Americanizing foreign-born children and observes that both have endeavored in their own way to form them into American citizens. Believes that Catholic schools maintain certain advantages over the public schools by the inclusion of spiritually oriented objectives and having teachers whose motives are above personal and financial gain. Articulates the virtues that should be developed in all school systems and examines how the public schools and the Catholic schools operate in achieving this desired result. Exhorts the Catholic school to continue to form citizenship in its pupils complying with the legitimate demands of the state without any lessening of its own spirit.

185. Sohn, Frederick H. "The Evolution of Catholic Education in the Diocese of Rochester, New York, 1868 to 1970." (item 132).

186. Sullivan, Mary Xaveria. "The History of Catholic Secondary Education in the Archdiocese of Boston." (item 133).

187. Veverka, Fayette Breaux. *"For God and Country:" Catholic Schooling in the 1920's.* New York: Garland Publishing, Inc., 1988. (The Heritage of American Catholicism).

> Examines the development of Catholic school policy and practices after World War I and the causes of a shift from ethnicity to Americanization. Discusses the defensive spirit of the Church and its educational separatism during the nineteenth century. Describes the growth and improvement of the Catholic school system by the 1920s and identifies the major educational issues at that time. Deals with the nature and

purpose of the Catholic schools in American society; Catholics' defense of their schools from hostile critics; the opposition to federalization and state monopoly of education; and the response and affirmation of Catholic educators toward educational standardization. Observes that educational changes in the Catholic schools both reflected and contributed to social and cultural shifts within the Catholic community in the United States.

188. Voelker, John M. "The Diocesan Superintendent of Schools: A Study of the Historical Development and Functional Status of His Office." Ph.D. dissertation. The Catholic University of America, 1935.

Investigates the office of the diocesan superintendent of schools presenting the background of its origin, its functions and early development. Inquires into the supervision of parochial schools prior to the appointment of the first diocesan superintendent of schools, William Degnan, for the Archdiocese of New York, in 1888, and notes the functions and problems of the pioneer superintendents. Reveals important tendencies such as: 1) the advancement of the diocese, rather than the parish; 2) the making of superintendents, not school boards, solely and directly responsible to the bishop for the administration and supervision of the schools; and 3) the determining of qualifications of teachers and their professional improvement by superintendents. Explains how the superintendent can lead the Catholic school system to higher levels of improvement.

189. Weisz, Howard. "Irish-American Attitudes and the Americanization of the English-Language Parochial School." *Enlightening the Next Generation: Catholics and Their Schools 1830-1980.* (item 172).

Details how the Catholic parochial schools in the latter half of the nineteenth century and into the twentieth century became increasingly like public schools while remaining distinct. Maintains that the American Irish established English-language parochial schools, instilled loyalty to the United States and were responsible for making the Catholic school more like the public schools. Recounts the views and reactions of various bishops and prelates to this assimilation focusing on New York Catholics. Shows how the New York Board of Regents regulations caused Catholic schools to make an effort to qualify for state charters. States that the obvious difference between the parochial schools and the public schools was the concentration of the Catholic schools on providing their students with a knowledge of their religion and inculcating a devotion to it.

CHAPTER 5
A Settled System
1925 - 1945

The two decades which spanned the years 1925-1945 witnessed some organizational, curricular, and professional refinements in the Catholic schools of the nation. Also, it was during this period that Pope Pius XI authored his influential encyclical, *Divini Illius Magistri* ("The Christian Education of Youth"), which provided the ideological basis for Catholic schools for more than three decades.

"The Christian Education of Youth"

Issued on the last day of 1929, amidst a rising sea of totalitarianism, which called for greater civil control over the education of the young, "The Christian Education of Youth" set forth the official Church teaching on that subject. Pius XI began his letter with the statement that education belongs to three societies -- the family, the state, and the Church -- with the last-named having the preeminent mission to educate, a mission with which no agency or person has the right to interfere, since it is God-given. The rights of the family and state are to be in harmony with the Church, which elevates and perfects family and state. Since all of these rights emanate from God, on both the natural and supernatural levels, there can be no contradiction or conflict among or between them, because God cannot contradict Himself nor be in conflict with Himself.[1] In the natural order God communicates fecundity to the family, which is the principle of life. Thus, the family holds the mission and right to educate its offspring directly from the Creator, an inviolable mission and right.[2] A person is a human before he/she is a citizen, so the state may not interfere with this right. However, the familial right is not despotic, ordained as it is to man's last end and subordinated to the natural and divine laws.[3] It is the Church's duty to protect this right, to place herself at the disposal of families as educator, providing schools where her members will not only maintain the faith but also where the faith will grow and prosper in their lives. The importance of the family unit is seen by the lasting effectiveness of the education children receive in a well-ordered and well-disciplined Christian home.[4]

Parents, though, have duties as well as rights. It is their responsibility to enroll their children in schools which by their very nature are subordinate to the family and Church, and to be in perfect accord with these two institutions.[5] Consequently, the so-called "neutral" (or public) school should not be frequented by Catholics, since in practice it is bound to be irreligious, and can at most be tolerated, with the explicit approval of the local Bishop, provided special precautions are taken and under specifically determined circumstances of place and time.[6]

The Jesuit educator, Neil G. McCluskey, arranged some of the key passages of the authoritative papal letter around major educational points, which provide in McCluskey's words, the "theological bases" for Christian education. The headings are McCluskey's; the passages are Pius XI's.

> ITS NATURE. "Since education consists essentially in preparing man for what he must be and for what he must do here below, in order to attain the sublime end for which he was created, it is clear that there can be no true education which is not wholly directed to man's last end...."
>
> IMPACT OF REVELATION. "...In the present order of providence, since God revealed himself to us in the

Person of His Only Begotten Son, who alone is 'the way,
the truth and the life,' there can be no ideally perfect education which is not Christian education...."

THE COMMON GOAL. "...The proper and immediate
end of Christian education, is to co-operate with divine
grace in forming the true and perfect Christian, that is, to
form Christ Himself in those regenerated by baptism...."

THE RESULT. "The true Christian, product of Christian
Education, is the supernatural man who thinks, judges
and acts constantly and consistently in accordance with
right reason illumined by the supernatural light of the example and teaching of Christ."

BROAD SCOPE. "...Christian education takes in the
whole aggregate of human life, physical and spiritual, intellectual and moral, individual, domestic and social...."

SUPERNATURAL PERFECTS THE NATURAL.
"...(Christian education takes in the whole aggregate of
human life) not with a view of reducing it in any way, but
in order to elevate, regulate and perfect it, in accordance
with the example and teaching of Christ."[7]

The Pontiff concluded his letter with an exhortation to Catholic parents that "Catholic education in a Catholic school for all
the Catholic youth" was the ideal to be sought, and with the declaration that anyone who furthered the cause of Catholic education
was performing a work of Catholic action.[8]

Organization of the Schools

As noted in an earlier chapter, the vast majority of students in
Catholic schools were at the elementary school level, connected
with parishes. The secondary schools, far fewer in number and
enrollment, were most likely to be conducted under the auspices
of religious orders. The years between 1925 and 1945 saw a
growth in secondary schools, especially the diocesan or central.
These schools called for new forms of organization, new ways of
financing, and far greater cooperation between parishes, the diocese and religious orders. Agencies, such as the school board, es-

pecially for extra-parochial schools, were established. The issues of overlapping authority resulted, with tension between the professional and the pastoral.

The movement gave rise to curricular questions, such as the place of vocational education in these schools, and the related question of whom Catholic secondary schools should serve, all the youth or mainly college-preparatory.

Involvement in the professional study of education as a field occurred, especially at Catholic University. Here, as well as elsewhere, Catholic educators studied and wrote on issues such as the place of religion in the curriculum, and on the position of Catholic education in regard to the theory of Progressive Education.

Professionalism and Accreditation

The growing concern over professional issues led to the founding of diocesan teachers colleges, such as in Cincinnati, for the preparation of teachers. Plans were formulated for integrating the religious, social, cultural and professional preparation of sisters, who comprised the majority of the teaching force, even at the secondary level.

Concomitant with the trend to professionalism was the growing concern over accreditation. Here, too, secondary education was at the forefront. Elementary schools, under at least the indirect control of the parish pastor, as mandated in Canon Law, faced different challenges.

Enrollment

Catholic schools reported a steady increase in number and enrollment throughout this period. In 1936, for example, in the midst of the depression, Catholic sources reported 1,945 secondary schools with an enrollment of 284,736 and 7,929 elementary schools with a total of 2,102,889 students.[9]

Summary

Catholic schools survived first the Depression, and then World War II. After the War they were to experience unprecedented growth, and with it a host of new challenges. One of them, their relation to the civil state, had its judicial basis change in 1940 when the Supreme Court of the United States made the First Amendment applicable to the state by the Fourteenth.[10] The post-war years, as we shall soon see, were replete with activity for Catholic schools.

Endnotes

1. Pope Pius XI, "Divini Illius Magistri" ("The Christian Education of Youth"), in *Five Great Encyclicals*. New York: The Paulist Press, 1939, p. 44.

2. Ibid., p. 45.

3. Ibid., p. 46.

4. Ibid., p. 57.

5. Ibid., p. 59.

6. Ibid., p. 60.

7. Neil G. McCluskey, *Catholic Viewpoint on Education*. New York: Hanover House, 1959, pp. 77-78.

8. Pope Pius XI, "Divini Illius Magistri," p. 61.

9. Harold A. Buetow, *Of Singular Benefit: The Story of U.S. Catholic Education*. New York: The Macmillan Company, 1970, p. 226.

10. *Cantwell* v. *Connecticut*. 210 U.S. 296, 303 (1940).

Bibliographic Entries

190. Balmain, Alexander F. "The History of Catholic Education in the Diocese of Brooklyn." (item 43).

191. Bollig, Richard Joseph. "History of Catholic Education in Kansas 1836-1932." (item 98).

192. Browne, Henry J. "The American Parish School in the Last Half Century." *National Catholic Educational Association Bulletin* 50 (August 1953): 323-34.

Traces the history of the Catholic parish school during the first half of the twentieth century as reflected in the proceedings of the Elementary Department of the National Catholic Educational Association. Cites Dr. George Johnson as leading the way during the late twenties into the mid-thirties, the revision of the Baltimore Catechism in 1935, and the inauguration in 1938 by American bishops of the Commission on American Citizenship. Describes the parochial schools' relationship with the public schools and the issue of government aid and control of schools. Notes that some of the problems of the immigrant parish schools were not discussed but finds the first fifty years a half-century of progress.

193. Buetow, Harold A. *Of Singular Benefit: The Story of Catholic Education in the United States.* (item 47).

194. Butler, Loretta Myrtle. "A History of Catholic Elementary Education For Negroes in the Diocese of Lafayette, Louisiana." (item 50).

195. Campbell, Paul E. *Parish School Administration.* New York: Joseph F. Wagner, Inc., 1937.

Covers educational theories and their practical applications in the administration of the parish school during the 1930s for pastors, teachers, and administrators, including seminarians whom the author regards as the school administrators of the future. Describes the teamwork that is necessary between the pastor and principal with the pastor exerting an indirect control over school management and discipline. Discusses the responsibilities toward education of both the home and the school and examines the functions of the school principal.

196. Campbell, Paul E. *Parish School Problems*. New York: Joseph F. Wagner, Inc., 1941.

Writes a sequel to *Parish School Administration* with the intention of keeping up with current educational findings. Evaluates the parish school attesting to its expanding functions and discusses teaching beyond the mastery of subject matter. Describes all aspects of parish school administration from practical problems to the teaching of religion, testing and supervision, and the provision for handicapped children. Weaves throughout the roles of the parent and the pastor alongside the principal and teacher. Discusses in the final chapter the direct and indirect methods of control of the parish school by the pastor.

197. Cartagenova, Gonzalo C. "The United States Supreme Court and Religious Liberty in Education, 1930-1980." Ed.D. dissertation. Texas Tech University, 1981.

Examines the opinions of the members of the United States Supreme Court between 1930 and 1980 in cases respecting the free exercise and the establishment of religion in education, identifying the issues decided in cases relating to religious liberty in education, recounting the findings of the court, the bases for the decisions, and the trends resulting from the rulings. Considers the judges' ideological positions, logic, consistency, and approach as reflected in the official Supreme Court records. Discerns the direction of the opinions of the Supreme Court to be moving towards absolute separation between the religious and the secular and the opinions on aid to private schools pointing to compromise.

198. *Christian Education of Youth.* Encyclical Letter of His Holiness Pius XI. (item 5).

199. Connaughton, Edward A. "A History of Educational Legislation and Administration in the Archdiocese of Cincinnati." Ph.D. dissertation. The Catholic University of America, 1946.

Treats educational legislation and administration in the Archdiocese of Cincinnati, limiting the study to the parish elementary school, inter-parochial high schools, schools in diocesan institutions and those schools of the Athenaeum of Ohio which controlled and directed schools of secondary and higher learning. Discusses the early educational efforts of the Archdiocese under Bishop Fenwick and Archbishop Purcell and relates the continued development of the diocesan school system under Archbishops Elder and Moeller who unified diocesan educational activities. Gives an account of the educational leadership of Archbishop McNicholas who, up to the time of the 1940s, had organized an inter-parochial high school system and had established the Athenaeum and the Teachers College.

200. Costello, William J. "The Chronological Development of the Catholic Secondary School in the Archdiocese of Philadelphia." (item 52).

201. Crawford, Sister M. Aloysius. "Preparation of Teachers for Catholic Rural Schools." Ph.D. dissertation. The Catholic University of America, 1941.

Studies the status of teacher training provided for rural teachers in Catholic schools and the course offerings provided by the state teachers colleges and normal schools for public school rural teachers. Describes the socio-economic conditions and the educational opportunities for rural youth explaining the importance of the 4-H Club. Surveys seven studies made of rural teacher training during the years 1917 to 1935 and points out the diversity of opinion regarding teacher preparation. Shows the effort to develop Catholic rural education and gives practical suggestions made by religious teachers to provide differentiated course offerings for rural teaching.

202. Crowley, Francis M. *The Catholic High-School Principal: His Training, Experience, and Responsibilities.* New York: The Bruce Publishing Company, 1935.

Addresses the status of the principals of four-year Catholic high schools in the mid-1930s examining academic and professional training, educational experience, salary, sex, age, duties, and responsibilities. Inventories and analyzes the work day of over two hundred typical Catholic high school principals. Discusses the principal as administrator and supervisor, presents the observations made by principals of their status and gives their suggestions for improvement. Calls for Church leadership to adopt a definite policy for the professional education of highly qualified Catholic school principals and offers some specific training suggestions.

203. Dalton, M. Arthemise. "The History and Development of the Catholic Secondary School System in the Archdiocese of Detroit 1701-1961." (item 53).

204. Deady, Carroll F. "The Place of Vocational Education in Catholic Secondary Schools." *The National Catholic Educational Association Bulletin* 42 (November 1945): 7-15.

Uses the term "vocational education" in a broad sense treating only the education of boys and discusses whether vocational education has a place in Catholic secondary schools, what place it should have, and how much it costs. Believes the vast majority of students have a right to the kind of training they need for their future livelihood and summarizes the objectives of vocational education which are harmonious with the Catholic philosophy of education. Describes the curriculum content stating that vocational education should not exceed forty per cent of the total subjects a student takes. Suggests using the World War II surplus which would be inexpensive and beneficial to Catholic schools.

205. Delaney, John P. "Catholic Social Teaching Through the Regular Curriculum." *The Catholic Educational Review* 39 (November 1941): 513-26.

Advocates practical suggestions for teaching Catholic social principles through every subject in the curriculum of the Catholic schools. Outlines fundamental attitudes to be eradicated and to be inculcated describing how this should be done. Emphasizes that religion is necessarily social and demonstrates the social doctrine evidenced in the Our Father, in the Ten Commandments and in the Sacraments. Expands on the secular subjects listing the post-war problems that could be topics for written assignments, debates, and oratorical contests. Reflects that teachers interested in Catholic social doctrine can find opportunities to teach Catholicism as a way of life.

206. Drouin, Edmond G. "The United States Supreme Court and Religious Freedom in American Education in Its Decisions Affecting Church-Related Elementary and Secondary Schools During the First Three Quarters of the Twentieth Century." (item 148).

207. Faherty, William Barnaby with Elizabeth Kolmer, Dorita Maria Dougherty and Edward J. Sudckum. *From One Generation to the Next -- 160 Years of Catholic Education in Saint Louis.* (item 58).

208. Fitzpatrick, Edward A. "Pope Pius XI and Education." *The Catholic School Journal* 39 (April 1939): 103-8.

Begins with a sampling of the tributes from world leaders paid to the recently deceased Pope Pius XI and discusses the relation of some of Pius XI's major encyclicals to education: the encyclical on "The Christian Education of Youth" which is a succinct but comprehensive basic philosophy of education; "Christian Marriage" in which is found the basis of all education; "Reconstruction of the Social Order" which calls for social reconstruction based on religious and moral education. Sees in the encyclical on "The Christian Education of Youth" education relating the whole man to all of life, an ordered conception of the organization of education, and a study of the social aspects of education though the end is the individual.

209. Friesenhahn, Mary Clarence. "Catholic Secondary Education in the Province of San Antonio: Its Development and Present Status." (item 60).

210. Gallagher, M. Muriel. "Teacher Appraisal of In-Service Education in Catholic Secondary Schools of Pennsylvania." Ph.D. dissertation. University of Pittsburgh, 1942.

   Seeks to identify the agencies and techniques most frequently used in in-service education of teachers and the frequency of their use in the Catholic secondary schools of Pennsylvania. Analyzes appraisals of the agencies and techniques and finds supervising through group methods widely used as a means to promote the growth of teachers. Appraises questionnaire data concerning methods of in-service education used by school systems in cooperation with colleges and universities such as teacher institutes, workshops, and educational conferences. Discusses recommendations for planning an in-service program.

211. Gallagher, Marie Patrice. "The History of Catholic Elementary Education in the Diocese of Buffalo, 1847-1944." (item 109).

212. Hagan, John (Raphael). "Catholic Education and the Elementary School." *Vital Problems of Catholic Education in the United States.* Edited by Roy J. Deferrari. Washington, DC: The Catholic University of America Press, 1939, pp. 59-74.

   Discusses the Catholic elementary school in America sketching the historical background, summarizing the situation of the times and presenting some of the evident problems most of which have a lack of needed financial support as the underlying cause. Reviews the present status and groups the problems of the future under teacher education, diocesan administration, and the relation of the Catholic University to

Catholic elementary education. Considers the school board to be the weak link of the diocesan school system and makes recommendations for strengthening its role in diocesan educational matters. Proposes that the Catholic University develop the field of graduate professional education.

213. Hagan, John Raphael. "The Diocesan Teachers College: A Study of Its Basic Principles." Ed.D. dissertation. The Catholic University of America, 1932.

Covers the internal aspects of the Diocesan Teachers College understood as an independent professional school under the control of the Bishop, having a four-year curriculum leading to a professional degree and attended by religious teaching communities and secular candidates for positions in the Catholic schools. Shows the importance given to the preparation of teachers by the Church, quoting from official Church documents. Discusses how the curricula of the normal school in the United States is determined from its objective and explains the importance of this for Catholic teacher-training institutions. Explores content subjects and discusses the Bishop's responsibility to the Diocesan Teachers College.

214. Harris, Xavier James. "The Development of the Theory of Religious Instruction in American Catholic Secondary Schools After 1920." (item 157).

215. Heffernan, Arthur J. "A History of Catholic Education in Connecticut." (item 64).

216. Johnson, George. "The Catholic Church and Secondary Education." *Vital Problems of Catholic Education in the United States.* (item 212), pp. 75-83.

Reviews the factors involved in the increasing enrollment in secondary schools in the United States and contends that examining the purpose and programs of American secondary education is necessary to meet the needs of three types of youth who will make up the high school population: those with mental ability who will profit from an academic education; those who have mental ability but are not interested in higher learning; and those who will find employment which requires little or no formal education. Discusses the status of Catholic secondary schools which are mainly academic or college preparatory and states the obligation of Catholic leadership towards all Catholic youth.

217. Johnson, George. "The Need of a Constructive Policy For Catholic Education in the United States." *The Catholic Educational Review* 23 (September 1925): 385-94.

Addresses the need for Catholic educators to formulate a program to make their schools better even though they have proved to be as good as any others. Analyzes the present-day crisis in public education and expresses the need for a new philosophy of life and the development of newer social behaviors to meet the changed condition of human affairs brought about by modern industrialism. Asserts that American Catholic schools must not imitate everything being attempted in the public schools and prescribes for the problems to be remedied.

218. Johnson, George. "Our Task in the Present Crisis." *The Catholic Educational Review* 39 (May 1941): 257-64.

Places before Catholic educators at the 1941 meeting of the National Catholic Educational Association the problems facing Catholic education in the face of the threat of war and warns that fundamental changes in the structure of secondary education in the United States will come. Exhorts them to translate the Gospel through the curriculum since children will become true citizens of the United States to the degree they become true Christians. Asks for cooperation with chaplains in the educational and cultural programs in local camps and with the National Catholic Community Service.

219. Johnson, George. "Progressive Education." *The Catholic Educational Review* 38 (May 1940): 257-64.

Confronts the theory of Progressive Education declaring it a philosophical and pedagogical heresy and examines the way to meet its challenge. Declares that Progressive Education has done a service by emphasizing that pupils must not only be hearers but doers also, but states that it has overemphasized the truth or narrowly interpreted it. Discusses the overstressing of teacher activity and the passive receptivity of the child in the conventional school that caused the progressive revolt. Advises Catholic educators to reestablish the "forgotten truth" and to use the term "Christian Education" which is based on a true and valid concept of human nature and human destiny.

220. Jones, William H. "The History of Catholic Education in the State of Colorado." (item 113).

221. Jordan, Edward B. "Apostle of Catholic Education." *The Catholic Educational Review* 42 (September 1944): 393-99.

Summarizes the contributions of Monsignor George Johnson to the cause of Catholic education, especially in the fields of school administration and curriculum construction. Reviews his work as Director of the Department of Education of the National Catholic Educational Association and depicts how the Catholic philosophy of life imbued his spirit and how he realized both the strength and weakness of Catholic education. Describes his membership in the Commission on American Citizenship of which he was chairman at the time of his death on June 5, 1944, and his aim to prove there was no conflict between the truth of Catholic philosophy and American democracy.

222. Jorgenson, Lloyd P. "The Oregon School Law of 1922: Passage and Sequel." *Catholic Historical Review* 54 (October 1968): 455-66.

Gives an account of the Oregon Law requiring all children between the ages of eight and sixteen to attend public school, approved by the voters in 1922 to become effective in 1926. Describes the pressure exerted by organized groups to ensure passage of the bill and the active opposition by Catholics, the secular press, and several Protestant groups. Discusses the challenge to the law by the Sisters of the Holy Names of Jesus and Mary who filed an injunction to restrain the State from putting it into effect. Presents the arguments in the case and relates the Supreme Court's decision in 1925 which said that the Oregon Law went further than mere regulation and that enforcement of it would result in the destruction of parochial and non-public schools.

223. Kohlbrenner, (Bernard) J. "A Plan For Cooperative Super-vision." *The Catholic Educational Review* 31 (June 1933): 334-44.

Assesses the exercise of supervision by the three units of educational organization within the Catholic school system -- the parish, the religious community, and the diocese. Discusses the overlapping of authority and duties in both the Catholic school and the public school systems and explains the differences in the organization of the two systems outlining the principles of supervision employed by the public schools. Describes a suggested division of duties among the Catholic supervisory officials: the diocesan superintendent, the community supervisor, the principal, and the pastor.

224. Kuhr, Nancy Jane Newton. "Catholic Parochial Schools in the Austin Diocese: Background, Development Since 1849 and Present Status." (item 114).

225. Leary, Mary Ancilla. "The History of Catholic Education in the Diocese of Albany." (item 68).

226. Luetmer, Nora. "The History of Catholic Education in the Present Diocese of St. Cloud, Minnesota, 1855-1965." (item 117).

227. McCann, Sister Thomas Maria. "Religion in Catholic High Schools of the United States: A Survey of Content, Method, and Teacher-Training." Ph.D. dissertation. Fordham University, 1939.

Investigates the status of the teaching of religion in the Catholic high schools in the United States during the school year 1937-1938. Attempts to discover the religion courses taught, the methods used, and the training and certification of teachers. Obtains data from questionnaires sent to two hundred and six communities of religious men and women, diocesan superintendents, and various publishers. Reviews the literature in the field, the courses of study and the textbooks used, and examines the special methods and devices used in teaching religion. Indicates the need for diocesan control of courses of study in high school religion, for the adequate training and certification of the high school religion teacher.

228. McClancy, Joseph V.C. "The Office of the Diocesan Superintendent of Schools, Its Possibilities and Limitations." *The National Catholic Educational Association Bulletin* 28 (November 1931): 528-39.

Delineates five fields of service for which the diocesan superintendent of schools is responsible and explains the importance and ramifications of each duty in organizing, directing and developing the schools within the diocese. Views these five fields as religious emphasis, sound secular education, unification of the schools within a diocese, propagation of episcopal educational projects, and leadership. Discusses religion as the primary subject in every Catholic school, and the importance of Catholic schools in the American school system. Points out the efficiency and other positive effects resulting from the superintendent's control of the schools.

229. McGucken, William J. "The Renascence of Religion Teaching in American Catholic Schools." *Essays on Catholic Education in the United States.* (item 15), pp. 329-51.

Discourses on the activity and the development in the field of the teaching of religion that has occurred in American Catholic schools, in Newman clubs, and in study and correspondence courses since the beginning of the century. Considers the development of methods with attention given to how and what is taught, the liturgical movement, and growth in youth movements. Presents the movements from Europe which differ from the catechism method and explains the influence of Fathers Thomas E. Shields and Edward A. Pace in constructing religion textbooks. Discusses the controversy over whether "religion" or "theology" should be taught in the college curriculum.

230. McNeil, Teresa Baksh. "A History of Catholic Education in San Diego County, California, From 1850 to 1936." (item 121).

231. Mang, William. *The Curriculum of the Catholic High School For Boys*. Notre Dame, Indiana: The Ave Maria Press, 1941.

Evaluates the curriculum of the Catholic high schools for boys in twenty states comprising the North Central Association of Colleges and Secondary Schools limited to non-boarding schools and schools for predominantly day students. Appraises the programs of studies finding that the offerings are traditional, preparing a limited group of pupils for college, but not providing for other types of abilities. Reports that the program of studies of the Catholic high school for boys is prescribed by legislative bodies and accrediting agencies to the same extent that it is in public schools.

232. Martire, Harriette A. "A History of Catholic Parochial Elementary Education in the Archdiocese of New York." (item 76).

233. Meyers, Bertrande. *The Education of Sisters: A Plan For Integrating the Religious, Social, Cultural and Professional Training of Sisters*. New York: Sheed and Ward, 1941.

Demonstrates that the professional education of a Sister must be interwoven with a fourfold development comprising religious life, the society or community life, the cultural life as applied to content knowledge, and the active or professional life which requires mastery in teaching. Surveys sixty religious communities to determine the educational programs that would synthesize this development and finds those developed by the Provincial Superior to be the most satisfactory. Makes recommendations for the education of Sisters and provides a detailed plan that would incorporate the four areas of development for religious teachers.

234. Mundie, Catherine Elizabeth. "Diocesan Organization of Parochial Schools: Studies in Catholic Educational History of the United States." Ph.D. dissertation. Marquette University, 1936.

Shows that the legislative basis for the development of the Catholic parochial schools in the United States is through the decrees passed by the Provincial and Plenary Councils and reviews the historical growth of the essential elements that make up the diocesan control of the parochial school system. Discusses the authorization for diocesan control with the bishop as the head of the school system and examines the duty of the pastor, the school board, and board of examination. Details the Philadelphia plan in the organization of parish schools and summarizes the study of a similar organization in ten typical dioceses.

235. Murray, M. Teresa Gertrude. *Vocational Guidance in Catholic Secondary Schools: A Study of Development and Present Status.* New York: Teachers College, Columbia University, 1938.

Investigates vocational and educational guidance as it existed in the Catholic high schools in the United States at the end of the 1930s presenting the strengths and weaknesses and indicating trends and tendencies. Discusses the thinking of Catholic educators on guidance problems as evidenced in the Catholic educational literature, and studies the published research involving statistics and information relative to vocational guidance. Sees Catholic educators as alert to the student's need for vocational guidance and the individual faculty member as the key to progress. Discusses recommendations for the training of teachers and counselors and for college and university course offerings in vocational training.

236. Newton, Robert R. "The Evolution of the New York Archdiocesan School System 1800-1967." (item 84).

237. O'Dowd, James T. *Standardization and Its Influence on Catholic Secondary Education in the United States.* Washington,
DC: The Catholic Education Press, 1936. (The Catholic University of America Educational Research Monographs).

Analyzes the educational standardizing regulations and
procedures of the state and regional accrediting agencies and
their bearing on the Catholic secondary schools. Concludes
that the beneficial influences outweigh any detrimental effects
by helping to raise the standards of the Catholic secondary
school. Cites the criticism that the accrediting agencies tend to
look at the make-up of the school rather than at its educational accomplishments. Recommends more active participation of Catholic educators in the work of accrediting
agencies and a definite formulation of the aims, methods, and
organization of the Catholic high school.

238. Pitt, Felix Newton. "Federal Aid For Catholic Schools?" *The
National Catholic Educational Association Bulletin* 42 (August
1945): 54-74.

Reopens the question of federal aid to education ap-
proaching it from a philosophical viewpoint. Believes that four
factors provide sufficient reason for study, discussion, and re-
consideration of the Catholic stand on opposition to aid that
would involve federal control. Discusses these factors: 1)
General opposition to federal control has been strengthened
by the experience of the totalitarian countries; 2) Equal educational opportunity has been emphasized by war; 3) Catholic
schools have had positive results with federal auxiliary services;
and 4) The Catholic schools cannot expect help from the
states.

239. Pitt, Felix Newton. "The Rural Catholic School." *The Catholic Educational Review* 26 (October 1928): 457-65.

Focuses upon the problems of the rural Catholic school and discusses two reasons for its importance: 1) The rural school serves as a feeder school for the city school and city parish; 2) It must prepare its pupils for both rural and urban life while the city school is homogeneous in its proximate objective. Studies the question of what should be taught in rural parish schools and maintains that rural students must be given the same cultural and social curriculum content as the urban children but with added agricultural training to cope with present-day problems. Proposes how to assist the rural teacher with the problems of curriculum, finances, and school attendance.

240. Ryan, Carl J. "The Central Catholic High School: Its Development and Present Status." Ph.D. dissertation. The Catholic University of America, 1927.

Studies the central Catholic high school, its state of development and as a solution to the increasing number of Catholic pupils who seek a secondary education under Catholic auspices. Describes the methods of financing, the building and equipment, the administration, the curriculum and extra-curricular activities. Concludes that a central high school is preferable to a parish high school and academies and recommends that the diocese adopt a definite policy of financing; that an auditorium, gymnasium and cafeteria be included in the building; that the curriculum be adjusted to the needs of the pupils; and that the school be recognized by an accrediting agency.

241. Ryan, Carl J. "Parents, State, and Education." *Thought* 13 (March 1938): 82-95.

Examines principles that are basic to the American system of education, are in accordance with fundamental American tradition, and are the grounds on which Catholics lay claim to a share in the taxes collected for education. Explains the primary right of the parents to direct the education of the child and points out that with an understanding of the true relationship of the state to elementary and secondary education, the position of private and parochial schools becomes clear. Studies the issues involved in granting funds to sectarian schools and advises that the approach to the problem be through the Federal Government. Explains the benefits that would result from an altered system.

242. Ryan, James H. "The Visiting Teacher." *The Catholic Educational Review* 23 (April 1925): 199-207.

Describes the visiting teacher movement in the public school system and the professional preparation and functions of the visiting teacher who studies the child to understand the factors that might be a handicap to good school work and who provides the needed assistance and guidance to help the child adjust to school situations. Believes this movement has a place in the Catholic educational system and tells what must be considered before outlining a plan for visiting teachers. Advocates the cooperative efforts of the Office of the Superintendent of Schools and the Catholic Bureau of Charities. Refers to the Philadelphia diocesan system of employment of visiting teachers.

243. Ryan, John A. "The Significance of the Supreme Court Decision in the Oregon School Case." *The Catholic Educational Review* 23 (December 1925): 585-88.

Looks at the issue of the Oregon Case which addressed the property and occupational rights of private teaching corporations and not the educational rights of parents. States that the written opinion of the Supreme Court contains an important *obiter dictum*, a statement that reveals the mind of the court. Explains the legal action brought on behalf of the Catholic Sisters who conducted private and parochial schools, maintaining that the Oregon Law caused injuries to property and occupation and was a violation of the "due process" clause of the Fourteenth Amendment. Shows that the rights of parents to send children to private schools have been drawn as a necessary inference.

244. Sanders, James W. *The Education of An Urban Minority: Catholics in Chicago, 1833-1965.* (item 131).

245. Schnepp, Alfred. "Catholic Leadership in Education." *The Catholic World* 146 (October 1937): 22-29.

Confronts the lack of Catholic leadership in the American educational field and the imitative position of Catholic educators following the model of secular public education. Explains the difficulties that Catholics create for themselves, and those that are beyond their control. Discusses what can be done to bring Catholic educators closer to educational leadership in the United States. Challenges them to cultivate scholarship in themselves and in their schools and to keep the Catholic schools in touch with the changing world. Says the great opportunity to show leadership is in the field of moral and religious education.

246. Schumacher, M. A. "Catholic Education: Overdone and Underdone." *The Homiletic and Pastoral Review* 34 (January 1934): 351-61.

Regards as "overdone" the aloofness in the parochial school system's association with non-Catholics and Catholics who do not attend Catholic high schools, and the burden of expenses incurred in maintaining a system of higher education, a burden that is placed on the shoulders of the pastor. Explains as "underdone" the failure to make full use of the parochial schools. Discusses the teaching of religion with regard to the text, the method and the arrangement, and suggests improvement by making the teaching of religion a training of the heart.

247. Seramur, Clarita. "Religion As Integrating Factor in Education." *Journal of Religious Instruction* 15 (June 1945): 869-72.

Explains how religion is the essential element of all education for a universal integration of both the individual and society. Describes how the Catholic educator and the Catholic school prepare the students for life and sees the dualism of religion and education in the United States. States that if moral and religious training is ruled out of the educative process, the student receives the impression that morality is of little consequence.

248. Sohn, Frederick, H. "The Evolution of Catholic Education in the Diocese of Rochester, New York, 1868 to 1970." (item 132).

249. Wilson, Mary Lawrence. "Supervision in Catholic Secondary Schools." Ph.D. dissertation. Fordham University, 1946.

Looks at the supervisory programs in selected Catholic high schools at this juncture of the 1940s and determines the extent of supervisory activities, the supervisory personnel, and the means used to evaluate the programs of supervision. Reports that few schools evaluated their supervisory program, but that teachers wished for more supervision and that principals needed more time to carry out their supervisory duties. Delineates recommendations for an efficient program of supervision in the Catholic secondary schools.

CHAPTER 6
A Period of Unprecedented Growth
1946-1965

In 1959, Neil G. McCluskey wrote that "since the times of Archbishop Hughes of New York and the controversial 1840s, the Catholic position on education has remained substantially the same."[1] McCluskey's assertion was accurate. Catholic schools were crowded; recently-established suburban parishes were often hard-pressed to meet the demands of parishioners for facilities and staff. Nonpublic school population increased 118 percent between 1940 and 1959, compared with a 36 per cent gain in the public sector.[2]

The demand far outstripped the supply, resulting in a number of challenges to Catholic schools. For instance, with facilities and staff for parish elementary schools often limited, what criteria would a pastor employ to choose admittants from the applicants? Which level, elementary or secondary, should receive primary emphasis? How would funding and control operate in inter-parochial secondary schools? How would the growing number of lay teachers be compensated? What professional requirements ought they have? What effect, if any, would there be on the religious mission of the Catholic school by the presence of lay faculty? What should be the role of the lay Catholic community in the operation of these schools? How should lay activity interface with the authority of the pastor and the professional position of the principal and her religious order which ran the schools? How will the schools, with their escalating costs, be supported? Should civil government directly and/or indirectly aid them financially?

The Voice of Authority

Speaking to a group of Italian mothers Pope Pius XII urged them to choose "helpers who are Christians like yourselves" in the education of their children. Then, he pointed out, the mothers were "to cooperate with them" so that their children's character could be formed properly and their piety fostered.[3] Subsequently addressing a group of Italian women engaged in Catholic education, the Pope maintained that the home needed the school, not any school, but one with "teachers who side by side with Christian mothers...develop the training of their (the children's) minds, characters and hearts, bringing them up in a spiritual and moral atmosphere."[4]

Catholic Church authorities in the United States viewed attendance at Catholic school as an important religious matter. A majority (55 of 104) of Catholic dioceses who responded (104 of 131) to a survey in 1958 replied that there was a statute which required Catholic parents to send their children to a Catholic school. Nine of the 49 that did not have a statute had some restrictions on attendance at public schools. Twelve of the 55 dioceses that had a statutory regulation imposed a reserved sin (one "reserved" to the Bishop for forgiveness) on parents who defied the regulation; 38 of the 55 required parents to apply formally for permission to send their children to a public school.[5]

The Question of Financial Aid--The Role of the Courts

The burgeoning Catholic school population, accompanied by increasing costs for new facilities and by personnel, led to a renaissance of the question of governmental financial aid to Catholic schools. Arguing from the premises that education is based on morality which in turn is founded on religion, and that parents, not civil authorities, are the primary educators of their children,

Catholic leaders in the mid-19th century had called on civil government to provide fiscal support for their schools, usually in the form of aid to the parents who would then select Catholic schools (in accordance with Church teaching) for their offspring. Under pressure from nativists, sometimes quite virulent, Catholic authorities in the United States in the late 19th century had retreated from this position and settled for a "hands off" policy from government.

The "separation of Church and State" doctrine in the United States, with its many religions, made the issue of aid more complex. The Supreme Court, under the Fourteenth Amendment, had dealt with the thorny issue of church-state relationship in education twice in the 1920's. In *Meyer*, it had limited the authority of civil government over non-public schools and their curricula,[6] and in *Pierce*, the Court had ruled that nonpublic schools had the right to exist and parents had the prerogative to send their children to them.[7] The First Amendment became involved in church-state disputes in matters of schooling through the Fourteenth in 1940.[8]

Catholic authorities and educators were not of one mind on the question of governmental aid to their schools. The different kinds of aid further complicated the issue. Some did not want any aid at all, relishing their independence, and fearing civil aid would ultimately bring governmental control. Others favored *indirect* aid, such as bus transportation, loan of secular textbooks, or vouchers or tax credits to parents. Still other wanted *direct* governmental financial assistance to the schools. There were vexing constitutional, as well as political, questions to be answered. Division within the legal community existed on these questions.

The United States Supreme Court rendered a ruling in 1947 which bore on the issue. It adjudged, by a 5-4 vote, that providing bus transportation to pupils who attended church-affiliated schools was constitutional because: 1) it was the children, not the church, who were assisted (child benefit principle); and 2) that a public purpose (safety) was served by the practice.[9] The kind of aid, not who received it, was viewed as critical by the Court. Recognizing that the Church did receive some benefit from its decision, the Court averred that the state could not exempt itself from the obligation of protection of its citizens who attended schools operated by churches. Cognizant of the emotion engendered by the tenet of "separation of church and state" as witnessed in the arguments of dissenters who contended that tax funds were being used for a religious purpose and by the narrow (5-4) margin, the Court set down prohibitions which have become known as the "Everson Dicta," intended to guide civil government officials in dealing with the establishment and free exercise clauses of the First Amendment.

The court would not rule again on any case that directly affected Catholic schools *per se* during this period. It did, however, address the question of released-time religious instructions in 1948[10] and 1952,[11] ruled on school-sponsored prayer in 1962,[12] and, in a far-reaching decision in 1963, passed on devotional Bible-reading.[13] The implications of this last decision will be treated in the next chapter.

The "Traditional" Catholic Approach to Education

Reginald Neuwien, in his study on Catholic schooling published in 1966, commented that there had been a marked continuity of thought by the teaching authority of the Church on education.[14] Derived in large part from the encyclical on education by Pius XI, and reaffirmed often by Pius XII, this "God-centered" educational theology-philosophy remained the touchstone of Catholic orthodoxy throughout this period. The reasoning ran something like this. Education involves three agencies--church, state and family. The family's rights are primary, but that unit is dependent on the other two to carry out its mission. The state is obligated by God to protect and foster the primary rights of the family. This is so because God has charged parents by the natural and divine law with the spiritual and temporal well-being of their children. Thus the state's function is to encourage and support the family, substituting for the family in case of default.[15] The Church, meanwhile, has been commissioned in its teaching mission by God, since education is intrinsically connected with man's last end, the supernatural goal of eternal happiness. Catholic parents, then, are bound to follow the teachings and regulations of the Church regarding the education of their children, because they have these children as stewards, delegated by God to see to their proper upbringing, in a sense to stand for God here on earth. The parents are to heed the Church's teaching regarding all matters connected with education.[16]

Following this line of reasoning led McCluskey to conclude as follows:

1. Secular education should be integrated with religious education;
2. Weekly catechism lessons are inadequate substitutes for Catholic schools;
3. Attendance at public schools, because of Protestant and secular influence, can prove harmful for a Catholic child;
4. Ideally, Catholic children should be educated in a Catholic school;
5. Catholic parents have the paramount right to direct the education of their children;
6. The free exercise of this right is contingent upon access to the practical means;
7. The state taxes all citizens alike to form a common pool for the support of education, which, for reasons of conscience, Catholic parents are unwilling to patronize;
8. These parents, because of their religious convictions, are forced to pay twice for the education of their children.[17]

The Citizens for Educational Freedom

Pay twice for "God-centered" education? "No" thundered the Citizens for Educational Freedom (CEF). Organized in the late 1950's to get what they termed their "fair share" of their tax dollars for "independent" (from government) schools, and to seek freedom and excellence in education, this non-sectarian (but heavily Catholic), mainly lay group, entered the political arena in support of their positions.[18] A Jesuit political scientist, Virgil Blum, was the leading theoretician and articulate spokesman for CEF. He argued that the state should recognize its youth as its chief asset, and maintain an active interest in their development. Government's purpose in education was to seek the good of the individual child, which will benefit not only the child but also the common good. The Fourteenth Amendment not only prohibits discrimination but also demands equal treatment under the law. This right of a child is a personal, constitutional right. The state, in turn, may not demand that the child surrender his/her freedom of mind and religion as a condition for sharing benefits due him/her as a citizen. When government subsidizes one particular kind of school (public) and not others (non-public) its action is arbitrary, unreasonable and discriminatory. According to the Constitution, Blum argued, a student may not be classified when exercising the basic right of choice of schools to attend. If that happens, then the state is not fulfilling his/her right of equal protection. The state, which is required to be neutral to religion, may not shirk its equal protection responsibility to its citizens because of religion. Such an action would make the state hostile to religion, causing religion to become a liability to a citizen. Consequently, students who choose religiously-affiliated schools should not be prevented from sharing in common benefits. If this occurs, then the state is guilty of violating those students' freedom of mind and religion.[19]

Blum maintained that Christian and Jewish schools were "God-centered" because they try to give their students an understanding of:

1. The central truths of religious faith.
2. The moral values that are rooted in religious commitments.
3. Man's relation to God and to his fellow man.
4. The meaning and purpose of life, and the ideas that inspire the religious man.[20]

Public schools are constitutionally prohibited from the attempt to inculcate this value framework in their students, are therefore secular, which means that God is officially dead in the school and thus in the education of the students.[21] Consequently, the "why" of "God-centered" education.

As noted above, CEF was composed of a number of religious groups. These agreed on the following tenets:

1. The individual, not the school, is primary in education. This means students and parents, not particular educational systems, deserve tax aid.

2. Personal constitutional rights are not received through a person's church, but through his/her citizenship. All, regardless of their religious belief, are equal before the law and should receive a proportionate share of all government services they need -- including education.
3. In questions of Federal aid for schools, the primary consideration is justice for everyone. If Federal aid is forthcoming, it must be nondiscriminatory and given equally to all children, not simply to those who attend public schools.[22]

The rationale for the CEF position, is, understandably, most similar to the official Catholic stance. Were CEF's policies to be adopted, then Catholics would receive financial assistance in choosing Catholic schools for their children. What benefits would accrue to the child? McCluskey answers the question this way:

1. The child learns systematically and thoroughly about his religion. He obtains a formal knowledge of the truths of the Christian Revelation, including the existence and nature of God, Christ's Incarnation and Christ's Church and the workings of the Holy Spirit within it, the history of the chosen people and of the Church.
2. He enjoys regular opportunities, direct and indirect, for the deepening of his sense of religious dedication. He has ready access to the Mass and the Sacraments; he learns to live a fuller life of prayer; he acquires a practical knowledge and love of the church's liturgical life.
3. The child learns an ordering of knowledge in an atmosphere in which the spiritual and the supernatural hold the primacy in the hierarchy of temporal and eternal values. He learns that his faith is not something apart but is related to the whole texture of life.
4. He acquires a "Catholic" attitude or outlook on life based upon the firm knowledge of his duties and privileges as a follower of Christ; he gains pride and love -- and loyalty to -- his Catholic heritage.[23]

The Beginnings of Change

In 1957 Archbishop (of Milwaukee) Albert G. Meyer, who was then President of the National Catholic Education Association (NCEA) praised both the quantity and quality of Catholic elementary and secondary education.[24] Catholic enrollment, in 1958-59, stood at 4,101,792 in elementary and 810,768 in secondary schools.[25] The Catholic historian, John Tracy Ellis, was among a distinct minority who faulted the schools. Ellis felt that there was an overemphasis on the school "as an agency for moral development" which led to a deficient concern for the intellectual life.[26]

It was a book authored by a lay Catholic, Mary Perkins Ryan, entitled *Are Parochial Schools the Answer?*, which was to be a portent of things to come for Catholic schools. Briefly, Mrs. Ryan (who answered her own question in the negative), held that: immigrant Catholic parents were in no position to correct or supplement what their children were taught in the Protestant-oriented and dominated public schools in the 19th century, so Catholic schools were established. These schools served a dual purpose: to protect the faith and culture of the immigrants. The structure of Catholic life in the United States was "clericalized," which resulted in two distinct spheres in the Church, clergy and laity. The Church had taken up a defensive posture, had been in a "state of siege." The only way to learn religion, to preserve the faith, was through Catholic schools; else, as one clergyman put it, "...we might as well let the devil take over right away.[27] The parochial school had become, following this rationale, the center of parish life, involving parents through instruments such as choirs, altar boys, and the celebration of religious events (such as the 40 hours devotion) in addition to academics. As a result, parents never developed confidence in their ability to instruct their children in religion. While in theory the Church had affirmed the primary rights of parents in the education of their children, in practice parents fulfilled this right (and concomitant responsibility) by sending their children to parochial schools. With the changing theology of the 1960s, which emphasized involvement in the world (incarnational) rather than withdrawal from the world (separational), and with the growing emphasis on the formative role played by the liturgy, Mrs. Ryan opted for placing emphasis on adult education, the liturgy, and instructing parents that the task of educating children is theirs, not the parochial school's.[28]

The reaction of Catholic educators demonstrated that Mrs. Ryan had struck a tender nerve. Responses included an article entitled "Yes, Parochial Schools *Are* the Answer" and personal attacks on her Catholicism, the latter leading to a defense of her orthodoxy by her husband.

Other events, most notably the convening of the Second Vatican Council by Pope John XXIII in October 6, 1962, contributed to the stirrings which led to a drastic change in the saga of Catholic schools in the United States. That story will be told in the next chapter.

Endnotes

1. Neil G. McCluskey, *Catholic Viewpoint on Education.* Garden City, NY: Hanover House, 1959, p. 167.

2. Ibid, p. 107.

3. Vincent A. Yzermans, ed., *Pius XII and Catholic Education.* St. Meinrad, IN: Grail Publications, 1957, p. Xi.

4. Ibid., pp. 6-9.

5. McCluskey, *Catholic Viewpoint on Education*, pp. 117-18.

6. *Meyer* v. *Nebraska.* 262 U.S. 390 (1923).

7. *Pierce* v. *Society of Sisters.* 268 U.S. 510 (1925).

8. *Cantwell* v. *Connecticut.* 210 U.S. 296 (1940).

9. *Everson* v. *Board of Education.* 330 U.S. 1 (1947).

10. *McCollum* v. *Board of Education.* 333 U.S. 203 (1948).

11. *Zorach* v. *Clauson.* 343 U.S. 306 (1952).

12. *Engel* v. *Vitale.* 370 U.S. 421 (1962).

13. *School District of Abington Township* v. *Schempp.* 374 U.S. 203 (1963).

14. Reginald A. Neuwien, ed., *Catholic Schools in Action.* Notre Dame, IN: The University of Notre Dame Press, 1966, p. 19.

15. McCluskey, *Catholic Viewpoint on Education,* pp. 80-87; James A. Burns and Bernard J. Kohlbrenner, *A History of Catholic Education in the United States.* New York: Benziger Brothers, 1937, p. 152.

16. McCluskey, Ibid., pp. 88-89; Burns and Kohlbrenner, Ibid, p. 153; Russell Shaw, *50 Questions and Answers on Federal Aid to Education and Related Matters.* Washington, D.C.: The National Council of Catholic Men and the Education Department of the National Catholic Welfare Conference, pp. 7-8.

17. McCluskey, Ibid., p. 167.

18. CEF Brochure, *Citizens for Educational Freedom.*

19. Virgil C. Blum, *Freedom of Choice in Education.* New York: The Paulist Press, 1963, pp. 98-105.

20. Blum, *Education: Freedom and Competition.* Chicago: Argus Communications Co., 1967, p. 35.

21. Ibid., p. 17.

22. James R. Brown, "Citizens for Educational Freedom," *America*, 8 February 1964, p. 195.

23. McCluskey, *Catholic Viewpoint on Education,* pp. 89-90.

24. Harold A. Buetow, *Of Singular Benefit: The Story of U.S. Catholic Education.* New York: The Macmillan Company, 1970, p. 276.

25. McCluskey, *Catholic Viewpoint on Education,* p. 100.

26. John Tracy Ellis, *American Catholics and the Intellectual Life.* Chicago: The Heritage Foundation, 1956, p. 46.

27. Mary Perkins Ryan, *Are Parochial Schools the Answer?* New York: The Guild Press, 1963, pp. 34, 36, 46-47.

28. Ibid., pp. 65-67, 116-117.

Bibliographic Entries

250. The American Hierarchy. "The Place of the Private and Church-Related Schools in American Education." *The Catholic Mind* 54 (February 1956): 111-16.

> Presents the joint statement issued by the American Bishops at the close of their annual meeting in Washington, DC, November 20, 1955, which was submitted "...in quiet confidence that the national sense of justice will stand firm...." Declares private and church-related schools in America exist by right which the Supreme Court made implicit in the Oregon School Case and explains why parents have the vested right to educate their children. Discusses the private and church-related school as part of the American system and reminds critics that America is a pluralistic society and these schools reflect the American spirit which demands unity in the essentials of citizenship.

251. Ann Virginia, Sister. "The Cruel Choice Facing Catholic Education." *The Catholic World* 195 (September 1962): 343-49.

> Explains and defends the choice of Catholic secondary education over elementary if only one level can be maintained because of financial and personnel problems. Proposes that all students who ask for admission be taken at the terminal level which in most dioceses is the secondary level. Gives five short-range objectives which can be reached only at this maturer level: 1) working out a fair admissions policy; 2) offering a high level of religious education; 3) keeping intellectual re-

spect for Catholic education; 4) studying the sources of vocations, all girl and boy high schools; and 5) providing education
for all of life. Calls for accepting all Catholic children in grade
14 if terminal education moves up to include the junior college.

252. Bless, William. "Role of the School in the Religious Formation of Youth." *Lumen Vitae* 12 (March 1957): 99-112.

Treats the issues of responsibility in education and shows
how the school completes the task for the Church, the family
and the state in the formation of youth. Discusses the school's
competence in helping students to become adult and independent and its place in their religious formation. Distinguishes between direct and indirect religious formation and
believes that Catholic education is only possible in the Catholic school where there is a commitment to both. States
that secular teaching and education have their own autonomous value and should be brought out as completely as
possible in Catholic schools. Maintains that secular subjects
should be treated as such, but they should stand against a
background of a Christian concept of life.

253. Buetow, Harold A. *A History of United States Catholic
Schooling.* (item 46).

254. Buetow, Harold A. *Of Singular Benefit: The Story of Catholic
Education in the United States.* (item 47).

255. Butler, Loretta Myrtle. "A History of Catholic Elementary
Education For Negroes in the Diocese of Lafayette, Louisiana." (item 50).

256. Carmody, Charles J. "American Catholic Religious Education: From 1776 to the Eve of Vatican II." (item 145).

257. Cartagenova, Gonzalo C. "The United States Supreme Court
and Religious Liberty in Education, 1930-1980." (item 197).

258. Clark, Mary Catherine. "A National Survey to Investigate the Status of Supervision in Catholic Secondary Schools." Ph.D. dissertation. St. John's University, 1962.

Explores supervision of instruction in the Catholic secondary schools of the United States determining and evaluating the current supervisory practices, the pattern of supervision, the extent to which the lay supervisor is used in the system, and the principal's evaluation of supervisory influences as they affect his school. Finds a variety of supervisory practices are used and the principal of each school implements the recommendations and directions from the parish, the diocese, and the state departments. Points out the strengths and weaknesses of supervision in the Catholic high school and finds that supervision is above average. Makes recommendations for strengthening the secondary school department of the diocesan office of education.

259. Corcoran, Sister M. Jerome. *The Catholic Elementary School Principal.* Milwaukee: The Bruce Publishing Company, 1961.

Discusses the profession of the Catholic elementary school principal in all areas of administration and supervision. Reviews educational principles that are basic to all Catholic elementary education, the relationship of the principal to other personnel, and provides an analysis of the principal's main functions. Deals with defining good teaching, the in-service growth of teachers, community relations in education, principles of evaluation, and special services for children. Has special chapters by John P. Treacy, "Introduction: The Role and Status of the Catholic Elementary Principal;" Leo R. Ward, "Principles for Principals;" and W. W. Thiesen, "The School Plant." Devotes the last chapter to the principal's evaluation of herself.

260. Costello, William J. "The Chronological Development of the Catholic Secondary School in the Archdiocese of Philadelphia." (item 52).

261. Curran, Paul F. "The Coinstitutional High School -- A Study of the Problems and the Rewards." *National Catholic Educational Association Bulletin* 62 (November 1965): 1-66.

Uncovers the factors which influence effective administration of the coinstitutional high school which is considered a desirable alternative to coeducation and involves separate classes for boys and girls at the secondary level. Studies the administrative roles discussing the three ways in which final authority develops and explains both the good and adverse aspects of each alternative: 1) in one person who is either a diocesan priest or a member of a religious order; 2) in two principals, one for boys and one for girls; and in a division of authority vested in a business manager and either one or two principals responsible for educational matters. Defines the role of the principal and concludes that if there is a multi-community situation, written policies and rules are essential for continuity.

262. Daele, Mary Caroline. "The Participation of Nonpublic Schools and Nonpublic Teachers in the Programs of the National Defense Act of 1958." Ph.D. dissertation. The Catholic University of America, 1963.

Investigates the extent of participation of nonpublic schools in the National Defense Education Act Programs, the reasons for any lack of participation and changes that should be made in the Act to bring about more participation. Examines four of the ten NDEA titles: Title I, Financial Assistance for Strengthening Science, Mathematics, and Modern Foreign Language Instruction; Title V, Guidance Counseling, and Testing; Title VI-B, Language Development; and Title IX, Science Information Service. Finds much less participation by nonpublic schools because of inequitability, apparent discrimination and the failure of nonpublic school administrators to take advantage of opportunities afforded by NDEA Institutes to bring about better communication between public and Catholic school personnel. Makes recommendations for better participation and for affecting change in the NDEA.

263. Dalton, M. Arthemise. "The History and Development of the Catholic Secondary School System in the Archdiocese of Detroit, 1701-1961." (item 53).

264. Dever, Daniel J. "Catholic Schools of Hawaii." *Educational Perspectives.* (item 103).

265. Drayer, Adam M. "A History of Catholic Secondary Education in the Diocese of Scranton, Pennsylvania." (item 147).

266. Drinan, Robert F. "Can Public Funds Be Constitutionally Granted to Private Schools?" *Social Order* 13 (March 1963): 18-32, 48.

Reviews pertinent Supreme Court decisions showing that funds can be alloted to private schools within the framework of the Constitution. Discusses the public dimensions of private schools and public-welfare legislation where benefits may not be granted or denied to citizens because of their religion or lack of it. Refers to the incidental aid to religion in state programs upheld by Supreme Court opinions in Sunday-law cases. Declares there is persuasive argument for violation of the establishment clause in the Court rulings precluding sectarian teaching and religious practices in public schools and concludes that neither Congress nor the United States Supreme Court have confronted the claim of parents who dissent from the orthodoxy which the public school represents.

267. Drouin, Edmond G. "The United States Supreme Court and Religious Freedom in American Education In Its Decisions Affecting Church-Related Elementary and Secondary Schools During the First Three Quarters of the Twentieth Century." (item 148).

268. Engles, Leo James. "A Study of Catholic Education in Oklahoma With Special Emphasis on the Diocese of Oklahoma City and Tulsa (1875-1970)." (item 152).

269. Faerber, Louis J. "Provisions For Low-Ability Pupils in Catholic High Schools." Ph.D. dissertation. The Catholic University of America, 1948.

    Investigates to what extent low-ability pupils are admitted to or excluded from Catholic high schools and to what extent schools that admit low-ability pupils provide for them. Finds the majority of Catholic high schools do not extend the same admission privileges to low-ability pupils as they do to those of higher mentality. Studies the schools which admit slow learners and finds the philosophy in providing for them is in keeping with the ideals of Catholic education. Notes a lack of organized guidance programs for these students. Details the provisions made for low-ability pupils in selected schools. Presents a general summary of recommendations for the diocesan superintendent and the administrators of both large and small Catholic high schools.

270. Faherty, William Barnaby with Elizabeth Kolmer, Dolorita Maria Dougherty and Edward J. Sudckum. *From One Generation To the Next -- 160 Years of Catholic Education in Saint Louis.* (item 58).

271. Fichter, Joseph H. "Are Parochial Schools Worthwhile?" *The Catholic World* 188 (February 1959): 362-67.

    Looks at some of the disadvantages and advantages of the parochial school in comparison to the typical suburban public school. Finds that in the parochial schools the classrooms are crowded, lay teachers are paid less and do not have the number of degrees held by public school teachers. Notes superior physical facilities in the public schools and more departmentalization in the upper grades. Assesses the advantages of the parochial school and finds that children receive more and better explicitly stated rationales for good behavior and constructive attitudes and have a better attendance record. Discovers that tests administered to public and parochial school children reveal almost no difference in the mean score. Concludes that the parochial school is worthwhile and serves the total community.

272. Fichter, Joseph H. *Parochial School: A Sociological Study*. Notre Dame: University of Notre Dame Press, 1958.

Researches St. Luke's parochial school, a mid-western American Catholic parish elementary school, in a day-by-day sociological study over the course of a normal school year. Studies the parish school along with parish organization, family life and the patterns of religious behavior. Compares the children in the upper grades of both the parochial school and the near-by public school through a series of tests and questionnaires and finds a similarity between the two groups in all cultural areas that do not deal directly with religious questions or personalities, but discovers a difference in the parochial school children's rationales for their decisions about social problems.

273. Fleege, Urban H. "Catholic School Curriculum, 1939-1965." *The Catholic Educator* 35 (April 1965): 149-53.

Compares the Catholic school curriculum of the mid 60's with that of the 30's addressing whether or not there is a coherent curriculum, its impact, the more important changes that have taken place, and any evidence of significant differences. Notes that the curriculum is different and the schools have become more "Catholic" in their instruction. Gives the background to the major effort in developing a curriculum guide, *Guiding Growth in Christian Social Living* and the reasons for its negligible educational impact. Discusses the ways in which the curriculum has changed and concludes with a reflection on the effect of the Catholic school curriculum on Catholic behavior, singling out the findings of Father Andrew M. Greeley. (item 275).

274. Freeman, Roger A. "Tax Credits and the School Aid Deadlock." *The Catholic World* 194 (January 1962): 201-08.

Examines the question of public benefits to private schools that was broadly debated in 1961 and discusses the arguments and rejoinders on distributive justice, double taxation and interference with freedom of choice. Points out the distinction made between levels of education in authorizing loans and financial aid and the aims expressed to justify it. Contends that public institutions did not fear competition in higher education but on the elementary and secondary level. Considers tax credits as the only form of public aid to students at denominational schools that is free from constitutional challenge, and the more attainable objective in the movement to obtain equity for all children.

275. Galvin, William A. "Ecclesiastical Legislation On Christian Education With Special Application to Current Problems." *The Jurist* 14 (October 1954): 463-80.

Discusses possible solutions for the problems involved in the fulfillment of Church law regarding the Christian education of Catholic youth of elementary and high school age. States the Ecclesiastical legislation and presents historical aspects of Catholic education in the United States. Notes that only half of Catholic school children are enrolled in Catholic elementary schools and attributes this to lack of facilities, lack of financial support, and the dearth of religious vocations in proportion to the Catholic birthrate. Offers possible solutions such as consolidating schools, eliminating the elementary school and devoting talents and resources to educating the adolescent.

276. Grant, Philip A., Jr. "Catholic Congressmen, Cardinal Spellman, Eleanor Roosevelt, and the 1949-1950 Federal Aid to Education Controversy." *Records of the American Catholic Historical Society* 90 (1979): 3-13.

Tells the story of the federal-aid-to-education bipartisan bill introduced in the United States Senate in 1949 and its revision which stirred up a debate involving Graham A. Barden, who authored the revised measure that provided funds solely for public schools and had no requirement for a distribution of funds to segregated schools. Discusses Cardinal Spellman's address accusing Barden of writing an anti-Catholic and anti-Negro bill and Eleanor Roosevelt's articles in her column "My Day" insinuating that Spellman had precipitated the controversy and declaring that no federal aid, including bus service, should go to parochial schools. Recounts the outcome of the bill which was not approved, ending consideration of educational legislation in the eighty-first Congress.

277. Greeley, Andrew M., Peter H. Rossi, and Leonard J. Pinto. *The Social Effects of Catholic Education.* Chicago: National Opinion Research Center, University of Chicago, 1964.

Compares Catholics who went to Catholic schools with Catholics who did not, evaluating the differences between public school and parochial school Catholics and a control group of non-Catholics. Attempts to determine whether a common educational experience is required to maintain a consensus of common American values in a pluralistic society. Suggests that the parochial school system is a result of the vitality of Catholicism in the United States and not vice versa. Finds that those educated in Catholic schools were more likely to engage in behavior encouraged by Catholic norms, but finds no differences among Catholics or Protestant groups in social attitudes, respect for civil liberties, or interest in public affairs. Determines that Catholic schools have made a unique contribution to acculturation of the immigrant groups.

278. Gross, M. Mynette. *Teaching Success of Catholic Elementary School Teachers: A Study of Factors Which Condition Success in Teaching in the Catholic Elementary School.* Washington, DC: The Catholic University of America Press, 1953.

Identifies the factors that Catholic elementary school teachers, mainly religious sisters, consider important for success in teaching and determines the differences between superior and below average teachers in personal qualities, in teaching skills, and in their personal, educational, and teaching backgrounds. Discusses factors for success such as spiritual motivation, instructional strategies, preparation time, and ability to understand pupils. Notes that emotional stability and good judgment had the most bearing on success or failure and indicates that good teachers also possessed more education than the poorer teachers. Recommends cooperative evaluation of the teacher-learning situation by supervisors and teachers.

279. Hamilton, Clinton D. "Theory of the Roman Catholic Church in the Support and Control of Education, With Special Reference to the United States." Ph.D. dissertation. Florida State University, 1965.

Ascertains from statements or decrees issued by Church Councils or from encyclicals or decrees of a pope what the theoretical position of the Roman Catholic Church is with regard to the support and control of education, especially in the United States. Examines the Church's position within the milieu of the debate on separation of Church and State. Shows that the original aim of the Church in America to support her own school system has broadened to include the goal of receiving federal aid to support Catholic schools.

280. Hicks, Harold Edward. "The Growth of the Educational System of the Archdiocese of New York From 1940 to 1964." Ph.D. dissertation. Fordham University, 1964.

Surveys the growth and development of the elementary and secondary educational system of the Archdiocese of New York comparing its status in 1940 and in 1960 in order to measure the progress made during the twenty years. Focuses mainly on changes that occurred in the administration and organization in regard to students, personnel, and the school plant. Discusses the educational decrees of the Archdiocesan Synod of 1950 which clarified the authority of the Superintendent of Schools and the Secretary of Education, and entitled a seat, when possible, in a Catholic school to each child. Explains the inauguration of the *Cooperative Entrance Exam-*

ination Programs and the *Administrative Manual for the Elementary Schools.*

281. Hochwalt, Frederick G. "Presents Trends In Secondary Education." *National Catholic Educational Association Bulletin* 43 (August 1946): 367-72.

   Focuses upon the trends and tasks that confront secondary education in the post World War II era and considers the articulation of the secondary school program with the elementary school and the college as a primary area of investigation. Believes the question of acceleration to be a major problem involving the curriculum. Sees evaluative criteria used more frequently as a measure of secondary proficiency and expects greater interest in the analysis of the high school curriculum. Notes better organized programs in guidance with the improved professional training of teachers and discusses the results of a strong development in the field of secondary school supervision. Indicates more of a demand for student activities and the expansion of facilities.

282. Holland, Howard K. "What Public and Parochial Teachers Can Learn From Each Other." *The Catholic Educational Review* 57 (April 1959): 227-35.

   Describes how public school and Catholic school educators can help each other in their mutual task of teaching America's children through cooperation, exchange of ideas and reciprocal understanding. Suggests lessons for Catholic schools: Public schools play an important role by enrolling all types of children. Guidance programs using precepts of developmental psychology should be added to assist learning. Points out how public school teachers can profit from Catholic schools by centering the curriculum around virtuous human behavior and emphasizing personal qualifications in the hiring of new teachers. Urges the joining of hands in educating the country's children.

283. Horrigan, Donald Charles. "Frederick G. Hochwalt: Builder of the National Catholic Educational Association, 1944-1966." Ed.D. dissertation. Columbia University, 1976.

Examines the work of Frederick Hochwalt as a leader in the development of the National Catholic Education Association (NCEA) while he served as its Executive Secretary during the two decades following World War II. Explores the history of NCEA, founded in 1904, and presents a detailed account of what Hochwalt did to build the Association and bring about the professionalization of American Catholic educators. Raises questions for further research as Catholic institutions become more thoroughly Americanized.

284. Hunt, Thomas C. and Barbara K. Bellefeuille. "The Bible in the Schools: The Edgerton and Schempp Decisions Revisited." (item 159).

285. Hunt, Thomas C. and Norlene M. Kunkel. "Catholic Schools: The Nation's Largest Alternative School System." (item 65).

286. Kuhr, Nancy Jane Newton. "Catholic Parochial Schools in the Austin Diocese: Background, Development Since 1849 and Present Status." (item 114).

287. Long, Mary Brideen. "An Evaluation of Catholic Elementary School Teachers' Pre-Service Education." Ph.D. dissertation. The Catholic University of America, 1952.

Studies the pre-service professional education programs of Catholic elementary school teachers whose classroom experience ranges from one to ten years by surveying the teachers themselves rather than the institutions engaged in the preparation of teachers. Determines to what extent the pre-service programs prepared Catholic elementary school teachers for their teaching tasks and concludes that there should be a four-year program. Recommends differentiating pre-service programs for elementary and secondary school teachers. Proposes a general course in methods which applies the principles of psychology and a provision of opportunities for directed observation.

288. Luetmer, Nora. "The History of Catholic Education in the Present Diocese of St. Cloud, Minnesota, 1855-1965." (item 117).

289. M. Eleanor, Mother. "Two Blueprints For Education." *The Catholic Educational Review* 55 (March 1957): 173-85.

Places the theories and practices incorporated in the three-volume Catholic school curriculum, *Guiding Growth in Christian Social Living* against the position of Progressive Education presented by Carleton Washburne in his book, *What is Progressive Education?*, highlighting the areas of agreement and disagreement. States that the disparity lies in the realm of God in the curriculum, the spiritual nature of the child, and the role of grace in the educative process. Sees concurrence in the importance of learning activity and experiences outside the classroom. Examines both works with regard to education for democracy, the place of the supernatural and methods and techniques.

290. McCann, Mary Beatrice. "A Description of Social Studies in the Catholic Secondary Schools of the Archdiocese of Philadelphia, 1890-1976." (item 166).

291. McCarren, Edgar P. "What the Informed Public Should Know About ESEA 1965." *The Catholic Educational Review* 63 (November 1965): 505-23.

Analyzes the Elementary and Secondary Education Act of 1965 which provides educational services and equipment for both public and nonpublic schools, adapting to their special needs and treating them on an equitable basis. Explains that the future development of the legislation will depend on the way it works. Discusses three of the six titles in ESEA: Title I for the educationally deprived; Title II for books and instructional materials for all pupils; and Title III for supplementary educational centers and services. Provides ten practical suggestions for the implementation of the three Titles.

292. McCluskey, Neil G. "The Dinosaur and the Catholic School." *Catholic Mind* 58 (July-August 1960): 323-31.

Discusses four challenges to American Catholic education which necessitate major adaptations lest the fate of the dinosaur that could not adapt to new conditions overtake it. Identifies and explains the challenges: 1) the growth in population; 2) the beginning of extensive federal aid to education; 3) the demand for excellence; and 4) the changing attitude of the American community towards things Catholic. Suggests major modifications concerning administration, finance, and emphasis. Believes all Catholic schools should become diocesan schools, centralizing educational matters and recommends that formal Catholic schooling start with the seventh grade or junior high school.

293. McKenna, Mary Olga. "Dilemma For American Catholic Parents: Elementary or Secondary Schools?" *The Catholic Educational Review* 60 (1962): 289-302.

Expounds on the trend in thinking by some American Catholic educators that Catholic elementary schools should be abolished in favor of more Catholic secondary schools because of the financial crisis, population explosion, and clear message that Catholic schools are not going to get financial aid from the federal government. Expects the solution will flow from Catholic principles of education that consider the earliest years in a child's life the most formative. Says the answer is not to drop grades but to aim for the ideal Catholic education on all levels and demand economic justice along with religious freedom.

294. McManus, William E. "Ten Points For Catholic Education." *Catholic Mind* 52 (December 1954): 710-17.

Considers the future of Catholic elementary and secondary schools bright citing their tradition and presenting statistical evidence of growth. Outlines a ten-point program for the future that includes prayer for vocations, recruitment of lay teachers, high professional standards, admission procedures, religious instruction and activities for Catholic pupils in public school, expanded high school facilities, the economical management of operating costs, the equalization of the financial burden, and the development of a home school association in every parish.

295. McNamara, Mary Patrice. "Supervision and Supervisors in the Catholic Elementary School Systems of the United States." Ph.D. dissertation. Fordham University, 1949.

Explores the organization of supervision, the preparation and scope of supervisors' work, and their supervisory practices in the Catholic elementary schools of the United States. Describes the two supervisory patterns: the Diocesan pattern in which the religious supervisor works directly under the jurisdiction of the diocesan superintendent, and the Community pattern in which the supervisor operates only in the schools conducted by her own religious congregation. Explains the plans of supervision and their relative merits and finds supervisors well-prepared and familiar with the best supervisory techniques but aware of their own supervisory shortcomings. Recommends provision for a diocesan reading room of professional materials and opportunities for educational research.

296. McNicholas, John T. "Five Educational Considerations For the Postwar World." *The Catholic School Journal* 46 (June 1946): 185-88.

Asks the Catholic educators attending the convention of the National Catholic Educational Association to weigh five considerations when evaluating their work in education after World War II: first, the false principle of totalitarianism that places no value on human life; second, the illiteracy in America which was revealed by the draft and which showed some of the defects of the educational system; third, the widespread juvenile delinquency; fourth, the educational inequality among American children; and fifth, the value of Catholic education in the United States which should be appreciated. Examines each consideration and emphasizes the need for moral training, for recognizing the rights of children and parents in education and for arousing public opinion against illiteracy and poor instruction.

297. Martire, Harriette A. "A History of Catholic Parochial Elementary Education in the Archdiocese of New York." (item 76).

298. Mary Dorothy, Sister. "Are Catholic Schools Progressive?" *The Catholic Educator* 21 (October 1950): 116-19.

Appraises Catholic education as "progressive education" insofar as the term connotes change in educational methods, not in aims or principles. Explains the development of progressive education from its beginnings in ancient Greece to modern secular systems describing the compounding of "isms" whose theories and aims are the basis for the modern progressive system. Compares the basis of Catholic education which is the individual's relationship to God with the basis of progressive education which is the individual. Shows how Catholic schools appreciate aspects of the activity method and make an effort to keep abreast of the changing world about them.

299. Mary Joan, Sister and Sister Mary Nona. *Guiding Growth in Christian Social Living.* Washington, DC: Catholic University of America Press, 1944.

Details a curriculum for the Catholic elementary schools throughout the United States specifying objectives that would carry out its main purpose of guiding the growth of children in Christian social living. Organizes a school program that would show the contribution of school learning activities to the child's practice of Christ-like living. Divides the work into three volumes with each adapted to a division of the elementary school -- Primary, Intermediate, and Upper Grades. Complies with the request of the United States bishops to launch an education program based on Christian principles and designed to carry out the instruction of Pope Pius XI to clarify and re-emphasize the teaching of Christ in their application to the problems of contemporary American life.

300. Miller, Mary Janet. *Catholic Secondary Education: A National Survey.* Washington, DC: National Catholic Welfare Conference, 1949.

Reports on the comprehensive 1946 Biennial Survey of Catholic secondary education in the United States by the Department of Education of the National Catholic Welfare Conference. Finds a great system of Catholic high schools in every state and an increase in enrollment of over 500% since 1915 but calls for new ways of expansion and significant changes in curriculum to assure Catholic high school education for all Catholic youth. Discusses the goals of Christian general education, addresses the need for experimentation and calls for programs of studies suited to the diversified abilities, interests, and aptitudes of the increased student body.

301. Miller, Mary Janet. "General Education in the American Catholic Secondary School." Ph.D. dissertation. The Catholic University of America, 1952.

Analyzes the development of general education and its characteristics in American democracy revealing a universal acceptance of the ideal of secondary education for all American youth which means programs correctly related to carefully determined outcomes. Outlines the implications of the general education movement for program planning in Catholic secondary schools and shows that general education must be related to the life needs of individuals and society. Suggests the possibilities that exist for integration through Christian social principles.

302. Motz, Herman A. "The Catholic Priest As a High School Counselor." Ed.D dissertation. University of Denver, 1965.

Determines the advantages and disadvantages of being both a priest and counselor in a Catholic high school from the point of view of the priest counselor and examines the factors which would weaken or strengthen his position. Includes in this study priest counselors whose major responsibility is counseling students in Catholic high schools that have formal counseling programs. Finds that training and the right type of personality were considered more important to counseling than being a priest but, as a priest, a spiritual rapport can develop with the student. Recommends the introduction of counseling courses into the seminary curriculum and suggests further studies of questions raised.

303. Newton, Robert R. "The Evolution of the New York Archdiocesan School System, 1800-1967." (item 84).

304. Nossell, Eleanor Jane. "The Utilization of Community Services by Catholic Secondary Schools." Ph.D. dissertation. St. John's University, 1964.

Investigates how Catholic secondary schools in the United States incorporate the use of community resources in their educational program. Determines the extent of availability of community services to Catholic schools and the degree to which the schools are utilizing these services. Analyzes the factors that either contribute to or impede availability and utilization and assesses the attitude of Catholic school administrators toward community services and their schools' use of them. Finds availability affected by geographic location and that utilization of community services never equals the amount of their availability. Proposes that diocesan superintendents prepare broad and flexible policies in the area of school-community cooperation.

305. O'Brien, John J. "Catholic Schools and American Society." *Social Order* 12 (February 1962): 77-89.

Maintains that certain Catholic school practices and means used to achieve laudable ends inhibit effective action for social reconstruction in a pluralistic society. Discusses the qualities that inhibit social action and claims they result from the historic-cultural situation in which the Catholic schools emerged and from the primary concern of religious survival. Singles out negativism as the quality from which others spring and which is a result of the negative moral approach to religious aspects of the Catholic educational system. States that students of schools that have eliminated negativism and any misconception of the proper order of virtue, placing charity first, will identify with the American social system as fully participating members.

306. Power, M. Theophane. "Home and School Relationships in the Catholic Elementary Schools of a Number of Selected Dioceses." Ph.D. dissertation. The Catholic University of America, 1950.

Presents a study of the parent teacher association as it functions in Catholic elementary school as an agency for coordinating the work of the home and school in the development of Christian character. Includes nine archdioceses and nine dioceses in the study and finds that organized parent teacher associations are the exception rather than the rule in Catholic elementary school, although some form of home and school relations exist in every school. Describes the general aims of the Catholic parent teacher associations affiliated with the National Committee of the National Council of Catholic Women and considers home and school relationships most satisfactory where a diocesan federation of parent teacher groups has been established.

307. Reilly, Mary Louise. "An Evaluation of Business Education Practices in Catholic Diocesan High Schools in the United States." Ph.D. dissertation. Fordham University, 1957.

Surveys the practices in business education in two hundred ten diocesan high schools for the school year 1954-1955 evaluating them in accordance with criteria derived from professional literature including opinions of Catholic educators concerning the improvement of business education practices. Indicates that Catholic diocesan high schools conform to accepted standards in regard to curriculum, community business relations, general and vocational business education, personnel, instructional materials and guidance. Recommends making the business department facilities available for adult education, offering a work-experience program, and utilizing school and community relationships in curriculum planning and revision.

308. Reinert, Paul C. "American Catholic Educators Face New Responsibilities." *The National Catholic Educational Association Bulletin* 49 (August 1952): 56-61.

Reviews the obligation Catholic educators have inherited from their predecessors who built the American Catholic educational system and analyzes the new responsibilities they must assume. Exhorts them to look upon teaching in a Catholic school as a vocation and a profession maintaining a vital interrelationship between teaching activities and a personal spiritual life. Discusses three duties resulting from modern social and economic conditions: to move toward closer working relationships between the schools and the home; to repudiate the pedagogy of John Dewey; and to develop better mutual understanding and appreciation between Catholic educators and non-Catholics.

309. Ryan, Francis A. "The Significance of 'The Harvard Report' For Secondary Schools." *The National Catholic Educational Association Bulletin* 42 (November 1945): 16-28.

Addresses the "Harvard Report" published at Cambridge in 1943 after a committee inquiry into the problem of the objectives of a general education in a free society. Evaluates the report's interpretation of the necessity for pupils to understand our common heritage and the dignity of man. Looks at the areas of general education in secondary schools and discusses the suggestions of the report for implementing general education. Notes that Catholic secondary schools already have certain necessary aspects of general education but could adopt suggestions in the organization and administration of course materials and aspects of method. Points out that the "Harvard Report" embraces the "whole man" while ignoring religion.

310. Sanders, James W. *The Education of An Urban Minority: Catholics in Chicago, 1833-1965.* (item 131).

311. Scanlon, William G. "The Development of the American Catholic Diocesan Board of Education, 1884-1966." (item 183).

312. Sharkey, Don. *These Young Lives: A Review.* New York: W. H. Sadlier, Inc., 1950.

Reviews Catholic education in the United States in a comprehensive essay of 84 folio pages with pictures and picture credits and covers every aspect of the American Catholic educational system from kindergarten to the university. Tells the story of the Catholic elementary schools and Catholic high schools describing every area of school life and presents a picture of a strong and vital educational system.

313. Sloyan, Gerard S. "The Catholic High School: Idea and Reality." *The Catholic Educational Review* 51 (1953): 217-33.

Discourses on the needs of the American student whom the author considers the most sinned against individual in contemporary American life because of neglect and misunderstanding. Shows how the Catholic high school's potential weakness lies not in its goal or message, but in secondary school teachers who stand for ideas rather than ideals, disregarding the spiritual and religious needs of adolescents and who are concerned largely with knowledge both abstract and concrete. Exhorts Catholic educators to take care of the deepest needs of students without fear or favor and reminds them that students pressured from many sides are free and that good schools allow them to choose to be good.

314. Sohn, Frederick H. "The Evolution of Catholic Education in the Diocese of Rochester, New York, 1868 to 1970." (item 132).

315. Synon, Mary. "The Three Rs and a Fourth." *Lumen Vitae* 7 (January-March 1952): 99-106.

Expounds on the necessity of inculcating the social philosophy of the Church through the curriculum of the elementary and secondary Catholic schools. Explains the history and accomplishment of the Commission on American Citizenship of the University of America whose curriculum, *Guiding Growth in Christian Social Living*, built courses of study in dioceses and archdioceses of the United States. Describes how the curriculum is based on the five goals of Catholic education: physical fitness, economic literacy, social virtue, cultural development, and moral perfection. Discusses social teaching, Catholic citizenship, and expresses the hope of the Commission that the work already accomplished is only a beginning of the movement in social education.

316. Tinnelly, Joseph T. "The Right to Educate -- The Role of the Parent, the Church and the State." *Catholic Lawyer* 4 (Summer 1958): 198-209, 251.

Deals with the respective rights of parents, the Church and the State in educating children, articulating the basis of these rights. Believes there is a need for clear delineation of the principles and policies in the American educational system which is being challenged on the soundness of many current philosophies of education. Gives a brief account of the Catholic parochial schools and their contribution to the educational progress of America and relates their difficulties to obtaining state aid. Discusses the various Supreme Court decisions restricting state aid to religious schools and to children in New York. Explains that the Zorach vs Clauson case of 1952 concerning the New York "released time" program, and upheld by the Supreme Court, provides a hopeful note for parents in the supervision of the education of their children.

317. Titzer, John Baptist. "Theory and Practice of Discipline: A Study of Boys' Catholic High Schools." Ph.D. dissertation. Fordham University, 1948.

Evaluates the state of discipline in 103 Catholic high schools for boys in the United States according to the concept of discipline as expressed by Catholic authorities and considered from the administrator's viewpoint. Defines discipline as a means of training the immature to assume more and more control of their own conduct and discusses the theory of discipline set forth in general and specific criteria. Applies the criteria to the current administrative disciplinary practices and recommends that all Catholic schools conform to the criteria. Provides recommendations such as greater emphasis on self competition and rewards for success.

318. Tracy, Henry Marshall. "Status of the Lay Teachers in Catholic High Schools in the United States." Ph.D. dissertation. Fordham University, 1958.

Investigates the lay teacher problem in the Catholic high schools of the United States with the purpose of ascertaining what is being done about it and what should be done. Recognizes the need to recruit lay teachers in order to maintain the present status of Catholic high schools. Describes recruitment practices and selection and all the issues affecting lay teachers. Declares that a diocesan-wide program should be planned for the hiring of lay teachers. Their financial status should be made comparable to that of public school teachers and tenure should be granted. Observes the variety of opinions of Catholic administrators as to the importance of the lay teacher's contribution to Catholic education.

319. Velardi, Angelica. "Aspects of the Preparation of Sister Teachers For Teaching in Secondary Schools." Ph.D. dissertation. Fordham University, 1959.

Surveys the academic, professional, and specialized curricula of pre-service programs for preparing Sisters for teaching in secondary schools; investigates their professional laboratory experiences through directed observation and student teaching and studies the supervisory activities used. Reports that the majority of responding institutions were liberal arts colleges and Religious Communities engaged in Sister Teacher education programs which required a bachelor's degree and almost all encouraged higher studies. Indicates a significant trend in Sister teacher formation with a direction toward a strong liberal arts background. Recommends a five-year preparatory program with the fifth year devoted to internship with opportunities to work with all types of children.

320. Ward, Leo R. *Federal Aid to Private Schools*. Westminster, MD: The New Press, 1964.

Analyzes the issues of federal aid to private schools presenting the basic argument that the private and church-related school has been and is state-aided, that there has been and continues to be collaboration between Church and State, that a single monolithic educational system would not only be unfortunate but un-American, that to pressure private and church-related schools into mediocrity would be a denial of religious liberty and of freedom of choice in education. Cites the obstacles to frank and open discussion of aid to students in church-related schools and concludes with a list of popular assumptions about church, state, and school issues with over eighty relevant quotations.

321. Welch, Constance. "The National Catholic Educational Association: Its Contribution to American Education A Synthesis." Ph.D. dissertation. Stanford University, 1947.

Traces the organization and development of the National Catholic Educational Association from its foundation in 1904 and evaluates it according to its stated objectives. Examines the Association's influence in the formulating of educational doctrine and how it puts its philosophies into practice. Appraises the effect of the Association in the development of Catholic institutions and studies its effectiveness in promoting the major thesis of Catholic education that religion is the principle and foundation on which true education rests. Points out that the Association is an advisory body providing an opportunity for Catholic educators to focus on common problems, to exchange ideas and to propose views for adjustment and development of curriculum.

322. Yzermans, Vincent A. "Our Holy Father Pope Pius XII on Catholic Education." *The Catholic Educational Review* 54 (November 1956): 516-25.

Demonstrates the contributions of Pope Pius XII in the field of educational thought, having delivered over sixty addresses on the subject of education. Discusses his explanation and delineation of the principles of education expressed in the encyclical of Pope Pius XI on the *Christian Education of Youth*. Tells of Pius XII's warning against three dangers in education: statism whereby the state aims to remove the influence of the family and the Church in education; superficial knowledge which is "...no more than a smattering of widely different subjects;" and ignorance of religious truth. Reflects on Pope Piux XII as the builder of Catholic education who applies the principles enumerated by the Holy See for centuries.

CHAPTER 7
The Second Vatican Council and the Beginning of the Decline
1966-1971

Numerically, Catholic school enrollment reached an all-time high of 5.6 million pupils (elementary and secondary) in 1965-66,[1] when they constituted 87 percent of the nonpublic school population.[2] In the years following 1966, however, Catholic school enrollment plummeted. What is most interesting, though, is that the schools' major assailants now hailed from an internal, rather than external, source.

There were other challenging issues which confronted Catholic schools and their advocates in this period. Among them were questions related to segregation (were some schools "racial escape valves" as charged in some quarters?); what was the proper functioning of the growing school board movement, and related issues stemming from the professional-pastoral dilemma; and finally, how to deal with the burgeoning percentage of lay teachers in the schools with attendant questions, both financial and spiritual.

The Attack from Within

The role in the assault on the *raison d'être* of Catholic schools played by Mary Perkins Ryan has been described in the previous chapter. The most surprising contribution to the questioning of the fundamental purpose of Catholic schools came from the Catholic hierarchy.

No major controversy about the existence and need for Catholic schools in the United States had arisen since the letter of Pope Leo XIII to the American Bishops in 1893. In the 1960s though, the roots of the criticisms of Catholic schools can be traced to the Second Vatican Council (Vatican II), which generally speaking, "opened up" the Church to the world. In Vatican II, the Church fathers' most direct response to Catholic schools, schooling being one of the proposed areas of rapprochement with the world, was in "Gravissimum Educationis" ("Declaration on Christian Education"). The Bishops declared in this document that "the Church's involvement in the field of education is demonstrated by the Catholic school." They stated further that the Catholic school was to be "evidenced by the gospel spirit of freedom and charity"; that it was to prepare the young for their world and for "the advancement of the reign of God"; and reminded parents of their "duty to entrust their children to Catholic schools when and where this is possible, ..."[3]

Individual bishops questioned the efficacy of the schools. Bishop Joseph Dammert of Peru pointed out the disparity between the Church's educational efforts within and without the schools. He listed the large number of priests, brothers, and sisters engaged in Catholic schools and showed the sharp contrast of this figure with the relatively minute number of religious personnel working in religion programs with a much larger body of Catholic youth in state or public schools. He reminded his fellow bishops that by virtue of their Baptism all Catholics had a right to a Christian education. Dammert doubted that justice was being served under the present arrangement.[4]

The American bishops who served on the education committee of the Council also had concerns. Among these were: 1) freedom of choice by parents to select the school of their choice for their children, assisted financially by government, and 2) the Church must promote both Catholic schools and the other forms of education for those not in Catholic schools, such as the Confraternity of Christian Doctrine.[5] Here the bishops gave voice to a long-standing concern that the view which equated Catholic education with Catholic schooling had resulted in the neglect of the religious education for Catholic youth outside Catholic schools.[6] For example, in Milwaukee $1.21 was expended per child for the religious education of Catholic children who attended public schools in 1967-68. Per pupil costs for Catholic secondary school pupils, meanwhile, ranged into the hundreds of dollars.[7]

Questions about the effectiveness of Catholic schools, especially when viewed in the context of the investment of personnel and money they required, were raised in other quarters at this time. Shortly before his death Cardinal Ritter of St. Louis, a strong advocate of Catholic schools, stated that if the Church in the United States had the choice to do it all over again, that it would not have invested so heavily in Catholic schools.[8] Religious orders, such as the Marist Brothers, announced that they would not accept any more assignments in Catholic schools, but would concentrate on experimentation in religious education.[9] Liberal groups of lay people, such as the Association for Church Renewal in St. Paul, protested the Archdiocese's allocation of 60 percent of a $3.5 million campaign to parish schools, and only 25 percent to the poor.[10]

The authors of *The Perplexed Catholic*, one a non-Catholic layman, the second a Catholic priest, described the Church's record as "shameful" for neglecting its youth in public schools at a price of supporting parochial schools. Not only have Catholic schools been unnecessary for the Church's survival as the Greeley-Rossi study on Catholic schools brought out,[11] they contended, but the schools have a dismal record in social justice.[12]

Shared Authority -- Catholic School Boards

In the wake of Vatican II, which called for more lay participation in Church affairs, Monsignor O'Neil C. D'Amour spearheaded the movement which called for changed governance patterns for Catholic schools. D'Amour advocated altering the administrative structure of the schools to reflect the social and political realities of American life. In the process D'Amour recommended that parish school boards be established with real, not advisory, powers. Pointing out the difference between the realms of the "pastoral" and "professional," D'Amour found pastoral concern an inadequate substitute for professional competence.[13] He termed "clerical-controlled" schools anachronistic. In the years that followed, D'Amour developed his model further, calling for diocesan and area boards of education, and outlining their powers and duties, which he believed could be operated in accord with Church law.[14]

D'Amour's leadership had its effects. In 1967 the National Catholic Educational Association (NCEA) issued a report on the board movement in Catholic educational circles. While it did not embrace all of D'Amour's recommendations, it did conclude that lay boards extended the schools' "base of support" and fostered the "cooperation of the community" on behalf of Catholic schools. Written by Catholic school superintendents, this document contained a rationale for the boards' existence as well as guidelines for their functioning.[15]

As seen in the previous chapter, the Citizens for Educational Freedom (CEF) were primarily lay, and ardently activist. As might be expected, CEF officials supported the board movement. For example, in 1967 Stuart Hubbell, CEF President, called for the establishment of school boards which would move Catholic schools to excellence as well as provide parents the opportunity to examine their rights and duties in the education of their children.[16]

The literature records the breadth of the interest in Catholic school boards which D'Amour had generated in Catholic educational circles at the time. Articles, ranging from the consideration of the relative rights of pastoral and professional, to laymen of the parish painting a parochial school, were published under the aegis of the school board topic.[17]

Minorities in the Schools

In the second half of the 19th century Catholic parish elementary schools were founded, in the main, to protect the faith of a poor, immigrant population. Supported by contributions to the Sunday collection for the most part, they were, in a sense, Catholic "common schools." In the post-World War II years, Catholics moved in considerable numbers from the central cities to the surrounding suburbs. They were replaced in the inner cities by minority groups, especially blacks, most of whom were not Catholic.

The 1960s witnessed the "War on Poverty," the Elementary and Secondary Education Act (ESEA), and attempts at desegregating public schools. The concern was raised in some quarters that Catholic urban parish elementary schools, perhaps under financial pressure, were serving as racial "escape valves," as well as abandoning the urban poor in favor of the affluent suburbs.[18]

Msgr. James C. Donohue, at the time director of education at the United States Catholic Conference (USCC), the civil arm of the American bishops, called for pairing Catholic inner city and suburban schools, and for cooperation with public schools in urban areas, even to sharing facilities. Donohue viewed with alarm the fact that many of the 452 Catholic schools which had closed in 1966-67 were in the inner city. He thought the Church would be deficient in meeting Christ's Second Great Commandment ("Love thy neighbor as thyself") if it failed to provide educational opportunities for the urban poor.[19] The following year, in 1968, he addressed the issue again. This time he called on Catholic schools to focus on two goals in the urban ghettos: 1) academic excellence, and 2) the development of a Christian elite, based not on financial standing but on the potential of developing Christian values.[20]

Similar sentiments to those put forth by Donohue were expressed by Martin Ahmann, the executive director of the National Catholic Conference for Interracial Justice, when in 1968 he charged the Church with an inadequate record in the schooling of black Americans.[21] To a degree, he echoed the concern conveyed five years earlier that Catholic schools in innercity settings were examples of *de facto* segregation.[22]

Rising costs made the Church's educational efforts among the urban poor, many non-Catholic, more difficult. The Superintendent of Schools in the Archdiocese of Philadelphia, feared that the escalating costs would result in the "virtual withdrawal from our primary apostolate in the poor and Negro area."[23] A different interpretation was voiced by a Pittsburgh priest, Father Donald McIlvain, who worked with inner city youth. He charged that "the Catholic school system is making only feeble efforts at integration of its schools."[24] For instance, several dioceses, among them Baltimore and Milwaukee, provided financial assistance to inner city students and/or schools. Minority students who were not Catholic were among the aid recipients.[25]

It is evident that attempts, albeit uneven, were made by Catholic educators and authorities to provide schooling for minority children.[26] It is also clear from the data presented by the Berkeley sociologists, Charles Glock and Rodney Stark, that the lay Christian did not follow the lead of the clergy, Protestant or Catholic, in excess of 75 percent of whom were working actively against racial discrimination, in matters of racial justice. The lay people were not only prejudiced, they also denied "the right of the churches to challenge their prejudice." The laymen, Glock and Stark's report revealed, want the Church to "tend to the private religious needs of its members and to stay out of such questions as peace, social justice and human rights."[27]

Data on Catholic school closings and openings, as contained in the following table, indicate that the church was attempting, at least in some cities, to serve the urban poor. The data also revealed that Catholic schools had tended to follow the Catholic population to the suburbs.

Table 1
Catholic School Closing and Openings, 1966-1968

	Innercity	Suburban	Rural	Total
Secondary school openings:	21	31	8	60
Secondary school closings:	85	37	95	217
Elementary school openings:	48	72	27	147
Elementary school closings:	182	44	194	420

Source: Cited in *The National Catholic Reporter*, 4 September 1968, p. 3.

The call from the well-known Washington priest, Monsignor Geno C. Baroni, who labored in the inner city, for Catholic authorities to take concrete steps to guarantee that Catholic schools in those areas be integrated came from his concern over the rising black-white crisis in the cities. Fearful that Catholic secondary schools in particular were not educating their white students to an understanding of this crisis, Baroni maintained that taking such steps, which he spelled out in several publications, would put the Church in the position of working towards a solution of a major contemporary social issue, racial justice.[28] Baroni's ideas are yet another illustration of the disagreement extant within the Church over the role Catholic schools should play in the education of minority children, usually non-Catholic. This difference of opinion in turn reflects divergent views on the very mission of the Church itself.

The Question of Aid

In 1963 the Supreme Court had ruled that government was to be neutral to religion. Neither the purpose, nor the primary effect of a statute, could either advance or inhibit religion, if a law was to be constitutional.[29] Under growing financial pressure, brought about at least in part by the increasing numbers of lay teachers, some Catholic leaders intensified their efforts for governmental fiscal aid to their schools. Their efforts met with some success, most notably in the loan of secular textbooks. The Supreme Court ruled in 1968 that a New York practice of loaning such books which were on the state-approved list for public schools to pupils in church-related schools was permissible, invoking the child benefit and religious neutrality principles.[30]

The Court went further. It stated that church-affiliated schools had two purposes: 1) sectarian or religious training, and 2) secular instruction. These schools, under this latter purpose, served a secular end.

Following the concept that church-related schools serve a secular function, Pennsylvania passed a law in 1971 which provided financial support of these schools for "those purely secular educational objectives achieved through non-public education...."[31] The state compensated the schools for these services, which included teachers' salaries, textbooks, and instructional materials. No state funds were permitted for any materials which dealt with worship or religious training.

The Court ruled that the Pennsylvania legislation, and the Salary Supplement Act of Rhode Island, were unconstitutional.

(The Rhode Island statute called for a 15 percent supplement to be paid to teachers in nonpublic schools, provided they did not teach religion and used only materials employed in the public schools.) Basically, the Court found that the statute fostered "excessive entanglement" between church and state, and hence violated the establishment clause of the First Amendment.[32]

The Court established far-reaching guidelines in its decision which were to be applied in subsequent church-state rulings in education. The tripartite test for the constitutionality of legislation affecting church-state issues henceforth would be: 1) the legislation must have a secular purpose, 2) the legislation neither inhibits nor promotes religion, and 3) the legislation must not create excessive entanglement between government and religion. This test would be used to the dismay of the proponents of government financial aid to church-related schools, as we shall see in the next chapter.

Summary

The Catholic bishops of the country issued an official pronouncement in 1967 entitled "Catholic Schools Are Indispensable." In it, the hierarchy, cognizant both of the current spiritual crisis which Catholic schools were undergoing and of the initial stages of declining enrollment with attendant financial difficulties, predicted that "not in the too distant future ... the trials and troubles of the present moment will be seen for what they really are, steps toward a new era for Catholic education."[33]

In 1971, but four years after the bishops' pronouncement, that future appeared bleak, indeed. A scant five years before, in 1965-66, Catholic schools had reached the peak of their enrollment. Despite some doubters, most notably Mary Perkins Ryan, optimism about their future abounded. The latter 1960s had witnessed the growing distinction between Catholic education and Catholic schooling. The period saw Catholic schooling as the conventional arrangement of a combination of religion and secular subjects taught in a "God-centered" environment challenged from within -- by cleric, religious and lay Catholic alike. Many of the educators themselves, priests, brother, nuns, had an "identity crisis."[34] Questions about the necessity of Catholic schools had been raised at an Ecumenical Council. Indeed, in less than a decade's time Catholic schools, especially their *raison d'etre*, in the United States had fallen from their zenith to a state of disarray.

Endnotes

1. *U.S. News and World Report*, 18 August 1975, p. 55.

2. *Education Week*, 30 March 1983, p. 14.

3. "Declaration on Christian Education," in *The Documents of Vatican II*, ed. Walter M. Abbott. New York: America Press, 1966, p. 77.

4. Mark J. Hurley, *Commentary on the Declaration of Christian Education*, Study Club Edition. Glen Rock, NJ: Paulist Press, 1966, p. 77.

5. Ibid., p. 23.

6. See for example, Vincent P. Lannie, "Church and School Triumphant: The Sources of American Catholic Educational Historiography," *History of Education Quarterly* 16 (Summer 1976): 142.

7. *The National Catholic Reporter*, 24 April 1968, p. 1.

8. Ibid., 27 September 1967, p. 5.

9. Ibid, 25 October 1967, p. 3.

10. Ibid, 5 March 1969, p. 5.

11. Andrew M. Greeley and Peter H. Rossi, *The Education of Catholic Americans*. Chicago: Aldine Publishing Co., 1966.

12. John L. Reedy and James E. Andrews, *The Perplexed Catholic*. Notre Dame, IN: Ave Maria Press, pp. 64-65, 155-158.

13. O'Neil C. D'Amour, "Parochial Schools without Parochialism," *Ave Maria*, 24 April 1964, pp. 12-14.

14. A sampling of D'Amour's writing in this field includes: "Restructuring Patterns of Education," in C. Albert Koob, *What Is Happening to Catholic Education?* Washington, DC: National Catholic Educational Assocation, 1966, pp. 25-37; "School Boards of the Future," *America*, 25 September 1965, pp. 316-17; "The Parish School Board," *National Catholic Educational Association Bulletin* 62 (August 1965): 248-49; "Catholic Schools Must Survive," Ibid., 65 (November 1968): 3-7; "The 'Control' Structure of Catholic Education," Ibid., 63 (August 1966): 267-74; and "Structural Changes in Catholic Schools," *Catholic School Journal* 66 (June 1966): 27-29.

15. National Catholic Educational Association, *Voice of the Community: The Board Movement in Catholic Education.* Washington, D.C.: National Catholic Educational Association, 1967, Preface.

16. Stuart Hubbell, "Citizens for Educational Freedom in New York: Outlook for the Future," *National Catholic Educational Association Bulletin* 64 (August 1967): 89-91.

17. A sample of the literature published in Catholic sources on various aspects of the school board movement at this time includes: Olin J. Murdick, "Parish School Board," *America*, 22 January 1966, pp. 132-36; Aloysius F. Lacki, "Pastor's Viewpoint on School Boards," *National Catholic Educational Association Bulletin* 64 (August 1967): 161-63; M. Simeon Wozniak, "School Boards in American Catholic Education," Ibid.: 163-65; Ellen Casey, "The Diocesan Board and the Parish Board," Ibid.: 97-103; William C. Bruce, "A Few Thoughts on Parish School Boards," *Catholic School Journal* 67 (December 1967): 65; "Some Don'ts for a Parish School Board," Ibid., 68 (April 1968): 90; "Advice for New School Board Members," Ibid., 65 (October 1965): 27; and Interview with Msgr. J. William Lester, "How a Diocesan Board Upgrades Lay Teachers," Ibid., 65 (September 1965): 76-78.

18. See, for example, Peter Schrag, *Village School Downtown.* Boston: Beacon Press, 1967; Martin Ahmann, "The Church and the Urban Negro," *America*, 10 February 1968, pp.

181-85; "Are Parochial Schools Racial Escape Valves?" *Christian Century*, 26 October 1968, p. 1298; and John P. Sheerin, "Our Segregated Catholic Schools," *Catholic World,* March 1963, pp. 333-34.

19. James C. Donohue, "Catholic Education in Contemporary Society," *National Catholic Educational Association Bulletin* 64 (August 1967): 13-17.

20. Donohue, "New Priorities for Catholic Education," *America*, 13 April 1968, pp. 476-79.

21. Martin Ahmann, "The Church and the Urban Negro," p. 81.

22. Sheerin, "Our Segregated Catholic Schools," pp. 333-34.

23. "Service for Sale: Tapping Pennsylvania's Till," *Commonweal* 7 June 1968, pp. 350-51.

24. Ibid., p. 351.

25. *Crux of the News*, 7 November 1969, p. 3; 17 October 1969, p. 3.

26. See, for instance, Robert J. Starratt, "The Parochial Schools in The Inner City," *The National Elementary Principal* 46 (January 1967): 27-33; M. Melathon, "Response to the Challenges of Schools in Disadvantaged Areas," *National Catholic Educational Association Bulletin* 64 (August 1967): 173-79; and Ann M. Wallace, A New York City Program for Disadvantaged Students," *National Catholic Educational Association Bulletin* 64 (February 1968): 19-26.

27. *The Wisconsin State Journal*, 31 May 1969, p. 10.

28. Geno C. Baroni, "The Inner City: A New Challenge to the Catholic High School," in *Trends and Issues in Catholic Education*, eds. Russell Show and Richard J. Hurley. New York: Citizens Press, 1969, pp. 232-46.

29. *School District of Abington Township* v. *Schempp.* 374 U.S. 203 (1963).

30. *Central School District* v. *Allen.* 392 U.S. 296 (1968).

31. *Lemon* v. *Kurtzman.* 403 U.S. 602, 609 (1971).

32. *Lemon* v. *Kurtzman, Earley* v. *DiCenso, Robinson* v. *DiCenso.* 403 U.S. 602 (1971).

33. *Catholic School Journal* 67 (January 1968): 25-27.

34. See Michael O'Neill, "Personal Dimensions of the Future of Catholic Schools," *Notre Dame Journal of Education* 2 (Spring 1971): 36-43.

Bibliographic Entries

323. Abbott, Walter M., ed. *The Documents of Vatican II.* New York: Herder and Herder, 1966.

Presents the sixteen promulgated texts of the Second Vatican Council in a new and definitive translation with commentaries and notes by Catholic, Protestant and Orthodox authorities signifying dialogue and ecumenical support. Makes note in the commentary by Most Rev. G. Emmett Carter on the "Declaration on Christian Education," of the Declaration's insistence on integration of Christian education into the whole pattern of life in all its aspects. Gives the response by Dr. John C. Bennett who states that the goals outlined for Christian education are sound and believes concessions from both sides are necessary in the use of taxes in the support of nonpublic schools.

324. Anibas, Marcella. "Toward Renewal: The Future of Catholic Elementary Education in the Light of Vatican II." pp. 99-107. (item 11).

Analyzes similar educational implications of the Vatican II documents *Declaration on Christian Education*, the *Constitution on the Church in the Modern World*, the *Decree on the Apostolate of the Laity*, and *Decree on Ecumenism*, and the *Declaration on Religious Freedom*. Summarizes and discusses the implications stating that change must be accepted as a necessary component of meaningful and effective educational renewal. Emphasizes that Catholic education must provide for complete Christian formation and requires flexible, univeral, and ecumenical structures with provision for direction and freedom. Notes that the form these structures takes depends upon the needs of a particular situation and the perceptive reading of the times.

325. Ball, William B. "Justice in Federal Aid After Vatican II." *Catholic Mind* 64 (November 1966): 25-34.

Demonstrates how five of the Council documents are relevant to the school aid question providing a climate of change that reduces tensions between Catholic schools and the community. Points out that the *Declaration on Christian Education* says schools are to provide education for the world; the *Decree on the Apostolate of the Laity* calls for an emerging Catholic laity who will bring particular insights into Catholic education; the *Decree on Ecumenism* and the *Declaration on the Relationship of the Church to Non-Christian Religions* are most important in breaking down the image of Catholic exclusiveness; and the *Declaration on Religious Freedom* indicates freedom in education as a significant aspect of religious freedom.

326. Blum, Virgil C. *Catholic Education: Survival or Demise?* Chicago: Argus Communications Co., 1969.

Confronts the question of the survival of Catholic schools and urges the Catholic community and its leaders to become active and involved in saving freedom and diversity in education. Discusses the Council Fathers' commitment to religious freedom and parents' rights in the education of their children. Contends that the rapid decline in Catholic school enrollment is largely the result of a growing financial crisis and must be solved if Catholic schools are to survive. Clarifies the tuition-grant program explaining its provisions and contends that the enaction of legislation for such programs would stimulate competition, economy and efficiency, equality of opportunity for the poor, and freedom of choice in education.

327. Bowling, Ann Virginia. "Two Emerging and Evolving Administrative Structures in Catholic Education in the United States: Diocesan and Parish Boards of Education." Ed.D. dissertation. Wayne State University, 1968.

Studies the historical development and organizational structure of diocesan boards of education and parish boards of education as they emerge on the American Catholic educational scene. Supplies, in Part I, background information necessary to understand the material presented in the study: a summary of the present situation in Catholic schools in the United States, factors that may have been responsible for the evolution of new administrative structures, and the relationship of the diocese and parish to the schools. Describes the study in Part II and discusses its findings concerning the diocesan and parish boards for the year 1967. Concludes that Catholics intend to keep their school system, strengthening it at the diocesan level with greater stress on quality education.

328. Brockman, Norbert. "The Inner City and Catholic Secondary Education." *The Catholic Educational Review* 67 (November 1969): 155-61.

Deals with the relationship of the Catholic secondary school and the emerging urban culture of the contemporary United States. Believes that Catholic education is basically healthy and can survive any crisis except the crisis of confidence. Argues that to meet this crisis, the complexity of urbanism must be addressed. Delineates the issues of the new urbanism, its life-style with the characteristics of community and participation, and the resulting new patterns for Catholic high schools. Explains how Vatican II has confronted major social issues concerning the relation of person and institution which means that the Catholic educational system must devote its energies to integrating the community in contemporary American society, not just the inner city.

329. Brown, William E. and Andrew M. Greeley. *Can Catholic Schools Survive?* New York: Sheed and Ward, 1970.

Exhorts the Catholic community to do the good that can and should be done about the crisis in Catholic education affirming the need for Catholic schools. Organizes the work into two parts with five appendices which deal with the financing and maintaining of Catholic schools. Explores in Part 1 the crisis in Catholic education stating that Catholic educators have lost confidence because the old rationale is no longer adequate. Outlines the beginnings of a specific theology of Catholic education in a post-Vatican, post-immigrant era. Develops in Part 2 Christian approaches to Catholic education presenting a program of action and believes that the Catholic community has the required capabilities and resources to solve any problems.

330. Buetow, Harold A. *A History of United States Catholic Schooling.* (item 46).

331. Buetow, Harold A. *Of Singular Benefit: The Story of Catholic Education in the United States.* (item 47).

332. Cartagenova, Gonzalo C. "The United States Supreme Court and Religious Liberty in Education, 1930-1980." (item 197).

333. Cordasco, Francesco. "The Catholic Urban Schools: Patterns of Survival." *Notre Dame Journal of Education* 2 (Spring 1971): 61-67.

Confronts the decline in enrollments in Catholic schools, their financial straits, and the fiscal burdens imposed on the public schools when children leave a Catholic school which has closed or has reduced operations for financial reasons. Believes Catholic educators have erred in attributing the imperiled condition of Catholic schools to the need for money and in arguing for public support in the rhetoric and language of the 50's and 60's. Declares that the Catholic schools are related to the contemporary urban environment and Catholic educators must define their urban poor as their major constituency. Says the Catholic schools must provide the animus which gives meaning and dimension to educational programs, governance and participation.

334. Davies, Daniel R. and James R. Deneen in association with Russell Shaw. *New Patterns For Catholic Education: The Board Movement in Theory and Practice.* New London, CT: Croft Educational Services, 1968.

Writes for members of Catholic boards of education conveying to them a sense of the traditions, goals, needs and problems of the Catholic educational system and a sense of the importance of the board's role in guaranteeing the continuing and effective presence of the Church in education. Describes the emergence of the boards of education for Catholic schools discussing the basic functions of a board and its relationship with the administrator, superintendent or principal. Discusses practical ways by which the board can serve most effectively and states that boards of education cannot ignore possible controversy and must be alert to contemporary challenges.

335. De Ferrari, Teresa Mary. "American Catholic Education and Vatican Council II." *The Catholic Educational Review* 63 (November 1965): 532-41.

Elucidates two important distinctions in Catholic education: the distinction between Catholic education as such with the type of theology at the core of its curriculum, and Catholic education as a loose combination of religion and secular subjects taught in a so-called religious atmosphere. Points out the confusion added to the problem of Catholic education when writers and speakers do not make these distinctions and reminds critics of Catholic education in the United States of the kind of theology that Catholic educators had to work with up to the Vatican II Council. Recognizes the need to educate young Catholics not attending Catholic schools and to provide for Catholic adult education.

336. Deferrari, Roy J. *A Complete System of Catholic Education Is Necessary*. Boston: St. Paul Editions, 1964.

Divides the work, which is a reply to *Are Parochial Schools the Answer?*, into two parts: Part I, "The Nature of Catholic Education" and Part II, "Mrs. John Julian Ryan and Catholic Education." Answers Mrs. Ryan's question asserting that only by the application of the Catholic philosophy of education systematically and completely from the beginning to the end of a person's growth can the true end of Catholic education be achieved. Refutes many of the statements in each chapter of the Ryan book and discusses two general errors: 1) the failure to understand fully the nature and importance of academic integration; and 2) the lack of understanding of the nature and methods of true scientific scholarship.

337. Deno, Lawrence M. "A Study to Describe, Classify, and Evaluate Diocesan-Sponsored Catholic School Research." Ph.D. dissertation. University of Notre Dame, 1970.

Describes, classifies, and evaluates diocesan-sponsored Catholic elementary and secondary school research and establishes criteria by which this school research could be classified and evaluated. Notes that slightly less than half of the American dioceses had or were sponsoring Catholic school research projects conducted by university educational researchers, private researchers or self-research. Finds school research conducted by individual superintendents to be less comprehensive and consistent. Recommends that university researchers be hired for diocesan-sponsored school research and that an administrative researcher be a member of the diocesan education staff. Makes suggestions for advancing school research as a more scientific endeavor.

338. Dever, Daniel J. "Catholic Schools of Hawaii." (item 103).

339. Dolan, Jay P. "Schools." (item 55).

340. Donovan, John D., Donald A. Erickson, and George F. Madaus. *Issues of Aid to Nonpublic Schools.* Volume II: *The Social and Religious Sources of the Crisis in Catholic Schools.* Prepared for the President's Commission on School Finance by Center for Field Research and School Services, Boston College, 1971.

Identifies the factors responsible for the contemporary crisis in Catholic schools throughout the United States and provides the perspectives and data essential to an understanding of the complexities of the forces involved. Gives an historical perspective of the Catholic schools from the colonial era to the twentieth century and describes the existing Catholic school system in terms of its basic units, policy and administrative structures, financing and staffing. Analyzes the roots of the crisis in terms of the interaction of contemporary social and religious forces and explores the significant changes in the American religious mentality and in the goals and structures of Catholicism since Vatican Council II.

341. Drouin, Edmond G. "The United States Supreme Court and Religious Freedom in American Education In Its Decisions Affecting Church-Related Elementary and Secondary Schools During the First Three Quarters of the Twentieth Century." (item 148).

342. Elford, George. "School Crisis -- Or Parish Crisis?" *Commonweal* 93 (January 29, 1971): 418-20.

Asks if the Catholic school crisis is merely a symptom of the parish crisis and if so, suggests that the remedies must go far beyond the school. Formulates several hypotheses for further discussion: 1) In the typical Catholic parish, the parish school is the only major program in operation; 2) The typical parish, when measured against the theological model of a parish would fare badly; 3) There are serious differences between contemporary theology and the concepts which support the day-to-day operation of the typical parish; and 4) parishes which function more in agreement with the theological ideal show evidence of less tension and greater flexibility when faced with educational problems. Asserts that a school-centered parish infused with the spirit of Vatican II needs leadership of a high caliber.

343. Ellis, John Tracy. "The Catholic School: Commitment or Compromise?" *Notre Dame Journal of Education* 2 (Spring 1971): 13-29.

Expresses the belief that the Catholic school should continue as part of the American Catholic community's commitment to the United States. Discusses the history of the "commitment" rather than "compromise" of Catholics for almost two centuries. Explains the reasons why Catholic schools should be maintained wherever possible, but holds the reservation that they must be in a position to provide a high quality of education. Understands the burden of fiscal pressures and the reduced numbers of teaching religious but offers motives from the American Catholic past to move forward into an uncertain future. Reiterates that the Catholic schools contribute a moral element to American society that it desperately needs.

344. Engles, Leo James. "A Study of Catholic Education in Oklahoma With Special Emphasis on the Diocese of Oklahoma City and Tulsa (1875-1970). (item 152).

345. "ESEA and Catholic School Children -- An Appraisal." *The Catholic Educator* 38 (September 1967): 53-56.

Reviews the progress of the Elementary and Secondary Education Act (PL 89-10) and the extent that Catholic schools have been aided by the ESEA programs by surveying diocesan superintendents. Discusses Title I projects which varied with children's needs noting that the program mentioned the most was remedial reading. Cites Title II as the most successful ESEA program explaining its impact for libraries in Catholic schools and describes the projects and programs under Title III declaring them interesting educational experiments. Points out some serious problems for Catholic school children caused by provisions in state constitutions against nonpublic school participation in particular programs.

346. Faerber, Louis J., ed. *The Emerging Objectives of Catholic Education.* (item 11).

347. Faherty, William Barnaby with Elizabeth Kolmer, Dolorita Maria Dougherty and Edward J. Sudckum. *From One Generation to the Next -- 160 Years of Catholic Education in Saint Louis.* (item 58).

348. Ganss, Karl Peter. "American Catholic Education in the 1960's: A Study of the Parochial School Debate." Ph.D. dissertation. Loyola University of Chicago, 1979.

Studies the history and development of the educational debate of the 60's from the publication of Mary Perkins Ryan's book, *Are Parochial Schools the Answer?*, to the promulgation of the statement on Catholic education by the Washington Symposium in 1969. Examines the thought of Mrs. Ryan who was the catalyst for much of the discussion generated during this time and analyzes the basic issues underlying her argument to abandon Catholic schools. States that the book helped to clarify the distinction between Catholic education and Catholic schooling and helped the American Catholic Church face the changes initiated by Vatican II. Deals with wider issues of the debate and presents scientific evidence supporting the effectiveness of parochial schools.

349. Greeley, Andrew M. and Peter H. Rossi. *The Education of Catholic Americans.* Chicago: Aldine Publishing Company, 1966.

Reports on a comprehensive study of the education of Catholic Americans in the Catholic school system by the National Opinion Research Center at the University of Chicago and conducted by Greeley and Rossi. Centers on issues concerned mainly with the effects of a Catholic education that are still manifested in adulthood. Finds that those who have a religiously oriented education were more likely to exhibit the desired behavior, were slightly more successful in their study and work and, after college, more tolerant. Shows that the Catholic schools have not been the reason for the health and survival of the American Catholic Church, but they have accomplished something and "are neither as bad as their most severe critics portray them nor as good as they might be."

350. Green, John J. "New Concept of Catholic Education." *The Priest* 27 (July-August 1971): 9-17.

Believes that the Catholic school is a practical necessity but that it must change its concept of itself and its function in order to answer the needs of modern young Catholics, helping them to understand their faith and providing them with concrete experiences of living in a genuinely Christian community. States that the Catholic school must acknowledge the genuine values of the world and prepare its students to live a sacral life in a secular society. Discusses the approaches to be taken which involve teaching students how to think and implementing programs of liturgical services and Christian Social Action. Contends that Catholics continue to want their schools to do something that the public schools cannot do.

351. Harper, Mary-Angela. "Identity Crisis of Catholic Education." *Catholic School Journal* 70 (April 1970): 30-34.

Explores what it means to be a post-Vatican II Catholic and what contemporary Catholic education is. Says that the identity crisis of Catholic education is that it has forgotten its right and duty to have an identity. Explores the contemporary stress on the personal dimension of faith and shows how Catholic children within the atmosphere of the Catholic school may deepen, enrich, and make explicit their Catholic-Christian witness. Enjoins Catholics to remember that their national and post-Council religious heritages share a common vision of community -- unity in diversity and perfection in mutual interaction with others.

352. Hesburgh, Theodore M. "Catholic Education and the Challenge of the Seventies." *Notre Dame Journal of Education* 2 (Spring 1971): 5-12.

Proposes that by trying to understand the situation of the young, Catholic education can understand its own current critical situation. Explains the state of revolution that young people are in, discussing the reasons, the meaning, direction and future of it, and what Catholic educators can learn from it. Cites as the basic cause the rapidity of monumental change in America and the world since 1950 with the problems and challenges related to the moral issue of the dignity of man. Describes two theories about the significance of the present revolution: 1) a counter revolutionary force reacting to the new technotronic society and 2) a counterculture threatening the establishment by attempting to transform modern society.

353. Hoffer, Paul J. "The Catholic School in an Era of Technology," pp. 82-98. (item 11).

Describes technical humanism and how it conditions all people including the young. Discusses its fundamental characteristics: the need for rationality and for efficacy, the requirement of working in teams and of projection or foresight. Explains that there are direct positive aspects of the technical mentality that could prove beneficial to Christianity. Addresses the negative attitude to the technical world and states what the Christian school must give to the young people of a technological age in order to strengthen them in their faith, to help them understand how to situate and judge technical power and how to be efficient for a purpose that gives meaning to their lives.

354. Hoffer, Paul J. "Insights Into the Elaboration of the Declaration On Christian Education," pp. 33-51. (item 11).

Gives an historic account of the origin and initial development of the Second Vatican Council's document on Christian education calling upon Catholic educators to accept it as it is, to study it thoroughly, and to apply it intelligently in practice. Recounts the continued revisions, dissatisfactions, even the call to abandon the schema. Discusses the will of the Council Fathers regarding the Christian education of all the youth of the world and the conciliar spirit of the text. Gives the interventions of the various Cardinals and Bishops when a discussion of the text was begun. Concludes with an account of the correction and approbation of the Declaration and its promulgation by the Pope on October 28, 1965.

355. Hunt, Thomas C. and Norlene M. Kunkel. "Catholic Schools: The Nation's Largest Alternative School System." (item 65).

356. Koob, C. Albert. "Catholic Education: Today and Tomorrow." *Notre Dame Journal of Education* 2 (Spring 1971): 30-35.

Relates that Catholic educators are aware of the dissatisfaction expressed concerning Catholic schools and that there is a great deal of activity to meet the crisis. Interprets some of the activity as reactionary and other activity as genuine efforts to create better educational systems out of existing ones. Finds that changing management patterns and reorganization are most important and explains the basic elements that have to enter into any redesigning for Catholic education. Discusses alternatives to the present school system and emphasizes the importance of understanding the program of religious education and how it relates to the total program.

357. Koob, C. Albert, ed. *What Is Happening to Catholic Education?* Washington, DC: National Catholic Educational Association, 1966.

Contains essays that are adaptations of speeches given in conjunction with two NCEA workshops on Catholic secondary school administration. Presents new ideas and recommendations for improvement of the Catholic schools in an age of transition. Covers restructuring patterns, religious administrators, changed roles for teachers and principals, the nongraded high school, principles of administration, supervisory activities, use of tests, financial management of the Catholic high school, and public relations. Includes an observation of Catholic schools after Vatican II and takes a look at their future.

358. Koob, C. Albert and Russell Shaw. *S.O.S. For Catholic Schools: A Strategy For Future Service to Church and Nation.* New York: Holt, Rinehart and Winston, 1970.

Believes that the present crisis in Catholic schools can become an avenue of growth and progress and calls for a commitment to service to the Church and society. Discusses the need for a radical change of attitude and method explaining that the old structures for policy-making and for action are no longer adequate. Notes that foresighted educators already have begun the work of reorganization and reorientation. Finds merger and consolidation essential for restructuring and says "Catholic school" must no longer be synonymous with "parochial school." Demonstrates that Catholic schools will survive with the support of the Catholic community and that crisis is essentially a sign of movement and of transition.

359. Kuhr, Nancy Jane Newton. "Catholic Parochial Schools in the Austin Diocese: Background, Development Since 1849 and Present Status." (item 114).

360. McCann, Mary Beatrice. "A Description of Social Studies in the Catholic Secondary Schools of the Archdiocese of Philadelphia, 1890-1976." (item 166).

361. McCarty, Shaun. "Catholic Education in the 70's: Burial or Resurrection?" *The Homiletic and Pastoral Review* 70 (September 1970): 902-08.

Addresses the need for an honest assessment of issues involved in order to save Catholic education. Advocates the renewal and adaptation of educational structures to articulate the constant Catholic values for a new time, place, and people. Describes what the trends will be in Catholic schools during the 70's and sees the irony in re-evaluating goals and structures from necessity rather than a genuine commitment to progress. Believes the constants must include academic excellence and Christian formation, and the variables mean discovering new ways of operating the schools and alternatives to schools such as CCD and adult education.

362. McCluskey, Neil G. *Catholic Education Faces Its Future.* Garden City, New York: Doubleday and Company, Inc., 1969.

Discusses the major problems confronting Catholic education analyzing and suggesting approaches to them and emphasizes Catholic education rather than the formal Catholic schooling. Speaks of atmosphere and values as key words in the continued support of Catholic schools and looks at the revolutionary changes taking place noting the extent of lay involvement. Sees this as a healthy sign of the coming of age of Catholic education in America.

363. McCluskey, Neil G. "Values, Anyone?" *Notre Dame Journal of Education* 1 (Fall 1970): 208-16.

Considers how a person acquires a sense of values and the pivotal place of the school in any discussion of values. Explains how the learning process cannot be completely separated from the acquisition of values and that a value-free school is a myth. Observes the trend developing in American educational policy that recognizes that public goals may be achieved through private and religious sponsored agencies. Shows how there are values associated with every human action and asserts that the social approach to the problem of religion and education must be stressed. Says that America must take a stand on basic social values or risk engulfment by alien value systems.

364. McLellan, Joseph. "The Statistics of Crisis." *Commonweal* 93 (January 29, 1971): 421-23.

Offers the first comprehensive statistical report on Catholic elementary and secondary schools for the years 1967-68 to 1969-70 and examines the significance of the data derived from the NCEA survey. Sees the parochial school as the institution in trouble while other parts of the Catholic educational system are holding firm or expanding. Claims that the school controlled by a pastor is not the model for the Catholic school of the future and reports the trend in setting up a cluster plan which eliminates parish schools and develops interparochial schools that serve two or more parishes. Explains how Vatican II and the polarization that followed have made a major impact on Catholic schools.

365. McManus, William (E). "The Future of Catholic Education." *Notre Dame Journal of Education* 2 (Spring 1971): 44-53.

Describes Catholic education's future within the context of the Vatican Council Fathers' description of the Church as a Mystery, a Sacrament, a Symbol of Unity, and as servant and pilgrim. Believes it is a prophetic call for Catholic educators to develop creative plans for continuing the good and successful in Catholic education and for initiating innovative and experimental ventures. Lists significant movements which, though in their initial stages, give promise of full development.

366. Maher, Joseph A. "Close a School?" *Catholic School Journal* 70 (January 1970): 30-32.

Explains the school-closing program of a small academy in a suburban borough of New York City describing each step of the phasing-out period as agreed to by the administration and parents. Emphasizes the determination to provide a good education for the remaining students and cites the extension of accreditation by the Middle States Association based on the maintenance of the school's high standards. Tells of the social activity and the sports program and describes the final functions of the school. Regards attitude as the most important issue claiming that the phasing-out program should be approached as an opportunity to give a superior education to the remaining students.

367. Neuwien, Reginald A. *Catholic Schools in Action: A Report.* The Notre Dame Study of Catholic Elementary and Secondary Schools in the United States. Notre Dame, IN: University of Notre Dame Press, 1966.

Presents the report of the study of Catholic elementary and secondary schools in the United States which evaluated religious and secular outcomes and gained insight into the strengths, weaknesses, and major problems of Catholic schools. Describes the procedures used and analyzes the resulting data on enrollment, staff, religious understanding, student attitudes, and opinions -- as well as the expectations of the Catholic parents. Finds that parents consider the most important goals to be self-discipline and hard work, knowledge of God, and citizenship. Shows evidence of academic success as measured by standardized tests whose scores were well above the national average.

368. Newton, Robert A. "The Evolution of the New York Archdiocesan School System 1800-1967." (item 84).

369. Nordberg, Robert B. "Catholic Education, 1966: An Overview." *The Catholic Educational Review*, 64 (1966): 505-16.

Cites three studies about Catholic education and comments on indicated trends: The Notre Dame Study; the preliminary report of the National Opinion Research Center directed by Father Greeley and Peter Rossi; and an issue of the *Catholic High School Quarterly Bulletin* devoted to "Guidance: Integral and Professional" which incorporates findings from a study by James M. Lee. Discusses the finding of the studies and examines the danger points of interpretation. Maintains that critics of Catholic education fault it not for partial failures to reach its goals but for the goals themselves. Indicates that better teachers, more meaningful teaching of religion, more attention to guidance problems, and more respect for the humanistic tradition of Christian education would help to solve the problem.

370. O'Donnell, Harold J. "The Lay Teacher in Catholic Education." *Notre Dame Journal of Education* 2 (Spring 1971): 84-86.

Deals with the historical examination of the attitudes toward lay teachers in Catholic education noting that prior to the nineteenth century and well into it, teaching in the parish schools was done mainly by the laity. Tells how Catholic education grew and developed with the formation of religious communities of women in the United States, and how Sisters and Brothers who served as teachers began to play a larger role than lay teachers. States that school boards must become an active, effective force if lay teachers are expected to commit themselves to Catholic school teaching, and attitudes toward lay teachers must change or the efforts to save Catholic education will come to naught.

371. O'Laughlin, Jeanne Marie. "The Change Process of Catholic Elementary Schools; Implications For Administrators." Ph.D. dissertation. University of Arizona, 1970.

Intends to determine if changes have occurred in eleven Catholic schools in the diocese of Tucson, Arizona, since the Notre Dame Study published in 1966, a study in which the same eleven schools participated. Divides the data obtained into two categories: data for comparison to the Notre Dame Study, and data concerning the change process. Finds change occurring in the social-civic attitudes of the students and in the attitudes of parents towards the goals of the Catholic schools and the schools' success in accomplishing them. Perceives that administrators are the major agents of change, but teachers do initiate and support change.

372. O'Neill, Michael. "Four Myths About Parochial Schools." *America* 116 (January 21, 1967): 82-86.

Discusses four common assumptions concerning American Catholic schools, pointing out the lack of factual support for each: 1) every Catholic child should be in a Catholic school; 2) parochial schools represent different social and economic classes; 3) Catholic schools are inferior; and 4) parochial schools will soon be discontinued or radically curtailed as a result of general disillusionment and criticism. Notes that the Greeley-Rossi study found support for parochial education among American Catholics and explains the function that elementary schools serve within the parish structure providing a center of communication and action.

373. O'Neill, Michael. "Personal Dimensions of the Future of Catholic Schools." *Notre Dame Journal of Education* 2 (Spring 1971): 36-43.

Assesses the personal and emotional realities of the Catholic school question and believes that the real crisis lies in "middle management" -- Priests, Nuns, and Brothers who have been undergoing a severe identity crisis. Relates the causal factors and the added impetus of Vatican II, pointing out the confusion when ideas and ideals were being shaken and American Catholics began attacking each other. Explains that the vitality and effect of Catholic education have always been in direct proportion to the strength and quality of professional religious life. Advocates a strong relationship with religious communities, parishes, and dioceses eliminating overdependency and depicts a restructured relationship.

374. Ryan, Mary Perkins. *Are Parochial Schools the Answer? Catholic Education in the Light of the Council.* New York: Holt, Rinehart and Winston, 1964.

Purports to initiate discussion as to whether or not a Catholic school system is ultimately either essential or desirable in attaining the objectives of the Vatican II Council. Asks if the Catholic school is the only possible solution to the problem of religious formation and shows how the Church has used other methods in the past to ensure that Catholics obtain their Christian formation. Examines the mentality behind the school system and indicates that the new mentality must realize that the educational effort of the Church should be extended to the whole adult community. Describes what should be done, and what might be done both with or without a Catholic school system.

375. Ryan, Mary Perkins. "One Year Later: Further Thoughts on Are Parochial Schools the Answer?" *Commonweal* 82 (April 23, 1965): 139-41.

Analyzes the reasons for the controversial reception of the book *Are Parochial Schools the Answer?* Finds that the book's appearing to attack an established institution with which people strongly identify arouses controversy and that the timing of the book, which appeared after an attack on parochial schools in the secular press, helped to fuel the controversy. Explains that religious communities had not yet re-examined their life and role in the light of the Council, Catholic educators were feeling that things were beginning to improve, and Vatican II's *Constitution on the Liturgy* had not yet been promulgated. States that the question is how change can be made with the least pain and confusion from the attitude of triumphalism to the pilgrim and servant mentality authenticated by the *Constitution of the Church.*

376. Seidl, Anthony A. *Focus on Change -- Management of Resources in Catholic Schools.* New York: Joseph F. Wagner, Inc., 1968.

Provides the guidelines for the management of resources in the Catholic schools. Identifies basic areas of school business administration, relating them to the total organizational structure, and developing the principles essential to successful financial and business management within the educational process. Includes appendices on school business administration criteria and worksheets for development of a ten-year financial plan for Catholic schools.

377. Shaw, Russell and Richard J. Hurley, eds. *Trends and Issues in Catholic Education.* New York: Citation Press, 1969.

Contains writings by various experts in their field on questions of policy ideas in Catholic elementary and secondary education. Includes material from books and periodicals as well as articles commissioned for the work. Devotes a section to the rationale for Catholic education and examines the new look in religious education. Confronts financing of Catholic education, discussing federal aid and shared time. Evaluates Catholic education's responsibilities for the disadvantaged, exploring the inner city and parochial education. Includes trends in curriculum and instruction pertinent to Catholic education and concludes with a section that looks into the future.

378. Sheridan, Michael P. and Russell Shaw, eds. *Catholic Education Today and Tomorrow.* Proceedings of the Washington Symposium on Catholic Education, November 5-10, 1967. Washington, DC: National Catholic Educational Association, 1968.

Reports the proceedings of the national meeting of Catholic school people, representatives of other Catholic educational programs, public and private school educators and many others, held to discuss Catholic education in an era of educational, sociological, and theological change and as a response to a morale problem in Catholic education. Incorporates four position papers: *Social Functions of Catholic Education* by Robert J. Havighurst; *Efficiency, Equity and the Economics of Catholic Schools* by Ernest Bartell, C.S.C.; *The Role of the Layman in Catholic Education* by John J. Meng; and *The Structure of Catholic Schooling* by John I. Goodlad.

Recognizes that education is, in one sense, the central mission of the Church and that the most significant educational goals are achieved in an atmosphere of freedom.

379. Shuster, George N. *Catholic Education in a Changing World.* New York: Holt, Rinehart and Winston, 1967.

Reflects on the impact of Vatican II on Catholic education, discussing the challenges presented by the new dimension of freedom and modernity. Uses the empirical evidence revealed by the studies at Notre Dame and the National Opinion Research Center to examine and evaluate the elementary and secondary Catholic schools concluding that American Catholic schools have been considerably better than their reputations, and are here to stay. Discusses the finances of Catholic schools. Reflects that the financial future is not encouraging, but observes that the sources of Catholic support for education have not been thoroughly explored. Anticipates a cutback in Catholic elementary schools and advancement in Catholic high schools.

380. Sohn, Frederick H. "The Evolution of Catholic Education in the Diocese of Rochester, New York, 1968 to 1970." (item 132).

381. Toale, Thomas E. "An Evaluation of Catholic Secondary Schools Within the Archdiocese of Dubuque, Iowa and Throughout the United States on Selected Quality and Quantity Indicators From 1966 to 1986." Ph.D. dissertation. University of Iowa, 1988.

Compares and analyzes the changes in quantity and quality indicators that occurred in secondary schools in the Archdiocese of Dubuque, Iowa, in the twenty-year period between 1966 and 1986 with the same or similar quantity and quality indicators from a national sample of Catholic secondary schools. Finds that despite fewer pupils and higher per-pupil costs in the secondary schools of the Archdiocese, they provide an education that is increasing in quality. Notes that during the twenty-year period, the impact of the Second Vatican Council began to be felt, and the changing role of the laity and declining number of Religious Sisters and Brothers had a direct effect upon the changing governance structure of the Catholic schools.

CHAPTER 8
Reevaluation and Regrouping
1972 - 1982

In 1971-72 there were 10,841 Catholic schools (8,982 elementary, 1,859 secondary), with an enrollment of 4,034,785 (3,075,785 elementary and 959,000 secondary).[1] A decade later, their number had declined to 9,494 (7,996 elementary, 1,498 secondary), with an enrollment of 3,094,000.[2] The schools had thus endured a population decline of almost one million in this decade. The dwindling numbers reflected a mounting loss of sense of purpose and dedication.

Official Church Support

In 1972 the nation's Catholic bishops issued a pastoral letter to the country's Catholics, *To Teach as Jesus Did*. In this document the bishops proclaimed the Church's educational ministry as: 1) to teach doctrine, the message of hope contained in the gospel; 2) to build community, "not simply as a concept to be taught but as a reality to be lived"; and 3) service to all humans, which arose from the sense of Christian community.[3] Catholic schools were identified as offering the "fullest and best opportunity to realize the threefold purpose of Christian education among children and young people." Only in the "unique setting" of a

Catholic school could the young "experience learning and living fully integrated in the light of faith." The teachers who, aided by the curriculum, model an "integrated approach to learning in their private and professional lives," are empowered to bring about the "integration of religious truth and values." It was this integration with life which set Catholic schools apart from other schools, and entitled them to the support of the Catholic community.[4] Recognizing the loss of spirit which had adversely affected Catholic schools, the bishops urged their flock to confront the enormous challenges which faced Catholic schools, and above all, to "avoid a defeatist attitude."[5]

Then, in 1977, the bishops addressed the purpose of Catholic schools when they wrote that "Catholic schools are unique expressions of the Church's efforts to achieve the purpose of Catholic education among the young.... Growth of faith is central to their purpose."[6] The bishops' words were supported by Pope John Paul II in 1979 when he described the primary mission of Catholic schools, which at once both sets them apart from public schools and justifies their existence and support by the Catholic community:

> The special character of the Catholic school, the underlying reason for it, the reason why Catholic parents should prefer it, is precisely the quality of the religious instruction integrated into the education of the pupils.[7]

The Catholic school, the Pope declared, should be the place where the gospel would "impregnate the mentality of the pupils" with the resulting "harmonization of their culture" in the "light of faith." According to the Pope, the task of developing a "community of believers" was embodied in the very mission of the schools.[8]

Together with the writing of the Pope, the bishops' statements identify the rationale for the professed uniqueness and distinctive quality of Catholic schools. As such, they simultaneously serve as a fitting preface to this chapter.

The Catholic School as "Faith Community"

In 1976, then-President of the National Catholic Educational Association (NCEA), John F. Meyers, suggested that Catholic education consider the question "how are we different?" from public schools, rather than wondering whether Catholic schools were as good as their public counterparts.[9] The NCEA sponsored workshops for Catholic school superintendents that were organized around the theme of the school as a Christian educational community. The superintendents then conducted similar meetings for their principals and teachers. The NCEA-published document, *Giving Form to the Vision*, was designed to give Catholic school people tangible assistance to implement the bishops' message in *To Teach As Jesus Did*.[10]

The development of the concept "faith community" was to occupy a prominent place in Catholic school circles in the 1970s. Picking up on the notion that Catholic schools should become more of an alternative, concentrating on their uniqueness, Michael O'Neill emphasized intentionality as the most critical factor in the schools becoming faith communities.[11] For O'Neill, intentionality was the sharing of basic values that conditioned everything that goes on in the school.[12] It is "collective intentionality" which enables the school to do all that it does extremely well, and distinguishes it from all other kinds of schools in the process.[13]

Challenges to the "Faith Community"

The Professional Staff

Building principals play a crucial role in developing the "faith community." The *National Catechetical Directory*, for example, holds principals accountable for recruiting teachers who are in harmony with the school's "goals and character." Then, the principals are responsible for making opportunities available for spiritual growth for the teachers, including promoting "community among faculty and students."[14]

Teachers, who have regular direct contact with the students, must also be active agents in instilling in the pupils the religious principles necessary for a school to be a "faith community." The charge of imbuing teachers with the capacity to build faith has become more complex. A generation ago most of the teachers were members of religious orders. As such, they had been steeped in the traditions of the order, and lived a community life in accord with those traditions. Table 1 reveals that the number of religious teachers dropped sharply from 1968-69 to 1981-82 (from 56.7 percent of the staff to 24.8 percent). New means were required in order to foster spirituality in the largely lay staff, indispensable for the schools to be distinctively Catholic, to constitute "faith communities."

Table 1

Number and Percentage of Religious and Lay Teachers in Catholic Schools

	1968-69		1978-79		1981-82	
Elementary						
Sisters	63,204	54.7%	28,453	28.9%	23,289	24.0%
Male Religious	1,278	1.1%	502	.5%	577	.6%
Lay Teachers	51,079	44.2%	69,584	70.6%	72,981	75.4%
Total	115,561	100.0%	98,539	100.0%	96,847	100.0%
Secondary						
Sisters	20,428	39.4%	10,616	21.5%	8,738	17.7%
Male Religious	10,073	19.4%	5,880	11.9%	5,139	10.4%
Lay Teachers	21,416	41.2%	32,913	66.6%	35,448	71.9%
Total	51,917	100.0%	49,409	100.0%	49,325	100.0%
All Schools						
Sisters	83,632	49.9%	42,396	28.1%	32,027	21.9%
Male Religious	11,351	6.8%	6,951	4.6%	5,716	3.9%
Lay Teachers	72,495	43.3%	101,301	67.3%	108,429	74.2%
Total	167,428	100.0%	150,648	100.0%	146,172	100.0%

Source: Cited in *Catholic Schools in America: Elementary/Secondary*, 1982 ed. (Englewood, Colo.: Fisher Publishing Co., 1982), p. xviii.

Collective Bargaining in Catholic Schools -- A New Phenomenon

The growing number of lay teachers led to a new phenomenon in the annals of Catholic schools -- teachers forming associations of their choice which will in turn represent them in bargaining with their employer, in this instance the Catholic Church (diocese, parish, religious order, or lay school board). The Catholic Church had a long-standing tradition of supporting this right of workers, dating back to the encyclical of Pope Leo XIII, *Rerum Novarum* ("On the Condition of Labor"), published in 1891. In this document Leo declared that employers had the responsibility to respect the rights of workers to organize, a right which he insisted was founded on social justice.[15] Four decades later Pope Pius XI reaffirmed Leo's teaching, referring to "Rerum Novarum" as the "Magna Carta" of the social order[16]

In the 1960s the Church again addressed the role of the worker. In *Gaudium et Spes*, approved at Vatican II, the Church Fathers stated that "Among the basic rights of the human person must be counted the right of freely founding labor unions," said unions "truly able to represent the workers and to contribute to the proper arrangement of economic life." Workers should be able to so participate "without risk of reprisal," and with the realization that in the process they are "associates in the whole task of economic and social development and in the attainment of the universal common goal." In the event of disputes, the bishops recognized the necessity of strikes, as the "ultimate means for the defense of the workers' own rights and the fulfillment of their just demands."[17]

Given this official teaching of the Church on workers' rights, the stance taken by some Catholic leaders, lay and clerical, toward the collective bargaining efforts by lay teachers in Catholic schools raised some questions. In the strife which occurred in Chicago, which judicially ended with the United States Supreme Court denying jurisdiction to the National Labor Relations Board (NLRB) over teachers in church-operated schools,[18] it is interesting to note that the lay teachers bitterly criticized the archbishop and pastors on religious grounds, including the failure to recognize their rights guaranteed them in Church teaching.[19] The Church's position on social justice in Chicago was chastised as "wanting in its own vineyard," inconsistent with the Bishops' own words in *To Teach As Jesus Did*, which called for lay teachers to function as "full partners in the Catholic educational enterprise."[20] The President of the Federation of Catholic Teachers in New York joined in the criticism, calling on the bishops to "practice what you preach." He charged that the bishops were using the "faith community" label as a "shroud" in which to "bury Catholic teacher unionization efforts."[21]

Putting aside the legal ruling of the Supreme Court, and considering only the religious policy issues, the position and tactics taken by some Catholic educational leaders -- lay as well as clerical and religious -- seem at odds with the Church's historic posture on the rights of workers. A new approach to labor-management disputes in the Church was called for and developed. Recognizing the rights of *all* parties involved, and the "uniqueness" of the Catholic school, this collaborative approach bears promise for "labor peace."[22] It is similar, indeed, to the ideas advocated by the long time Catholic labor leader, Monsignor George Higgins, in his 1979 Labor Day Address. In that talk Higgins called for a "voluntary substitute for the National Labor Relations Board," which would, on the one hand, guarantee that Catholic social teaching would be followed and, on the other, take into account the difference between "church-related" and public schools.[23]

Minorities in Catholic Schools

This issue was treated at some length in the previous chapter. It remained a question for Catholic social policy, however. Some writers, inside and outside of the Church, criticized Church leaders for what they felt was an unsatisfactory commitment to schooling the urban poor.[24] On the other side, a number of instances could be cited in this decade to document extraordinary effort (especially with the limited financial resources available) on the part of Catholic dioceses, clergy, and/or religious orders to serve inner city youth in Catholic schools, regardless of their religious affiliation.

As the 1980s progressed, spurred in part by the publication of James S. Coleman's *Public and Private Schools*, debate reopened with renewed vigor over the relative effectiveness of public and private high schools on the educational achievement of their students. Using data garnered from the longitudinal study, *High School and Beyond*, in a section entitled "Minority Students in Catholic Secondary Schools," the priest-sociologist Andrew Greeley wrote that attendance at Catholic high schools benefitted minority students more than attendance at public high schools.[25]

In 1982 the Catholic League for Religious and Civil Rights denied, in *Inner-City Private Elementary Schools*, the myth that Catholic schools are elitist. Using a randomly selected sample of sixty-four schools in eight cities, fifty-four of which were Title I recipients, and with a minority population of at least 70 percent, the study found strong support for the schools by their patrons. Located in rundown buildings, beset with financial problems, mostly Catholic-affiliated but with a third of the students Protestant, these schools provided a safe environment, fostered moral values and emphasized basic learning skills in their pupils. Fifty-six percent of the school population in these schools was black, 31 percent was Hispanic, statistics which demonstrate the Church's commitment to racial minorities, according to the schools' supporters.[26]

These data notwithstanding, the differences of the opinion as to the role of Catholic schools as "faith communities," in the sense that they served as witnesses of faith to the poor in the central cities, persisted throughout the 1970s and into the 1980s.

The Question of Government Aid to Catholic Schools

Michael O'Neill described the Catholic school as "faith community" in the following way:

When people in a school share a certain intentionality, a certain pattern or complex of values, understandings, sentiments, hopes, and dreams that deeply conditions everything else that goes on, including the math class, the

athletic activities, the dances, coffee breaks in the teachers'
lounge, everything.[27]

The American bishops had emphasized the religious nature of
Catholic schools, which as a result made these schools unique.[28]
Indeed, the very name "faith community" itself depicts an entity
that is fundamentally (and some would say totally) religious, not
secular. Yet, Catholic educational authorities had sought governmental financial support to "purchase the secular services" from
these schools. The question is, then, how could these schools,
"faith communities," have anything secular in them? Nonetheless,
attempts to gain state fiscal support continued throughout the period, concurrent with the emphasis on the schools as "faith communities."

The three-pronged test Chief Justice Warren Burger put forth
in *Lemon*[29] would be used to the chagrin of both supporters and
opponents of government aid to church-related schools. The
Court later reaffirmed the test in 1973 when it said,

> ...when it [aid] flows to an institution in which religion is
> so pervasive that a substantial portion of its functions are
> subsumed in the religious mission or when it funds a spe-
> cifically religious activity in an otherwise substantially se-
> cular setting...

then a constitutional violation may be present.[30]

Backers of aid to church-related schools felt this test would
be harmful to their cause. A few days before the *Lemon* decision
in 1971, the NCEA reported that 35 states were providing some
form of financial aid to Catholic schools.[31] Some worried about
the future of their programs. Others, like the Jesuit Father Virgil
Blum, claimed the decision demoted Catholics to second class citizens. Blum, a leader in the formation of the Citizens for Educational Freedom in the 1950s and 60s, compared the decision to
that of *Plessy* v. *Ferguson* in 1896 which authorized the segregation
of the races, provided facilities were "equal." He contended that
Catholics should learn from the Blacks and Jews, and from political action groups to seek their basic civil rights.[32]

Church-state cases involving aid to Catholic schools and/or their patrons continued to be pressed in the courts. In *Brusca*, Catholic parents in Missouri were unsuccessful in their attempt to gain aid on the grounds that the denial of same constituted a violation of their Fourteenth Amendment right of equal protection.[33] A year later, in a case which emanated from New York, the Court denied that state the right to provide for maintenance of church-operated schools, tuition reimbursements to parents whose children attended them, and tax relief to those parents who were not included in the reimbursement program.[34] Also in 1973, again from New York, the Court ruled, on the grounds of excessive entanglement, that reimbursing church-operated schools for the expenses they incurred in fulfilling state-required activities, such as the testing program, was unconstitutional.[35] Catholic leaders expressed their dissatisfaction with this decision, but noted that aid in the form of textbooks, transportation and health services remained.[36]

The violation of the tripartite test established in *Lemon* provided the basis for the Court's ruling in *Meek* vs. *Pittenger* (1975). Aid in the form of "auxiliary services," such as instructional materials and services for exceptional, remedial or educationally disadvantaged students, was forbidden; only the loan of secular textbooks received the Court's approval.[37]

The decision was resoundingly denounced by leaders in the Church. Protests, ranging from a parade in Philadelphia to a letter-writing campaign, were organized.[38] A priest-principal of a Catholic high school commented that "it's tough to be a fetus or Catholic"[39]; a priest-editor penned that the decision was due to the bias of the court's members:

We have said it repeatedly; any Supreme Court decision that denies auxiliary services to parochial and private school children comparable to those in public schools is based not on any constitutional difficulty but purely and simply on the personal prejudices of the parties who deny such aid.[40]

Archbishop Joseph L. Bernardin, at the time President of the National Council of Catholic Bishops, also censured the decision, alleging that the Court "had distorted the restrictions of the establishment clause of the First Amendment to the point where it now requires hostility rather than neutrality toward religion."[41]

There were other Court decisions and many more comments on their effect on Catholic schools in this period. The above have been presented to provide a flavor of the temper of the times as far as the topic of governmental aid to Catholic schools is concerned.

Legal challenges continued. In 1976, according to the Commission of Law, Social Action and Urban Affairs of the American Jewish Congress, there were 13 cases on the docket of the Supreme Court regarding governmental aid to church-affiliated schools. People wondered whether the Court would follow the principle of separation of church and state, as in *Lemon, Nyquist* and *Meek*, or whether it would choose accommodation as it had in *Everson* and *Allen*. Doubt also existed as to the stance of popular opinion on the issue. For instance, the Gallup Poll of 1969 reported 59 percent in opposition to government aid to church-related schools, 38 percent in favor. In 1974, though, 52 percent supported such aid and 35 percent were opposed.[42]

One fact is certain: the issue will not fade away. The attainment of aid, whether direct (to the schools) or indirect (to the schools' patrons) would assist parents of limited means to opt for Catholic schools for their children and would increase the capability of the schools to deliver educational services and pay their professional lay personnel a salary that would be more competitive and commensurate with their responsibilities. Yet that aid could bring with it government control of at least part of the schools' programs and have the potential to render the "faith community" concept nonexistent.

Student Population and Community Support

Andrew Greeley *et al.* reported in 1976 that enrollment in Catholic elementary schools had continued to decline but that the Catholic high school population had approached one million that year, near its high point of 1965.[43] In this study Greeley *et al.* noted that Catholic schools still enjoyed the strong support of the laity. While only 35 percent of Catholic parents of school-age children surveyed reported having children in parochial schools, 38 percent of the remainder said no parochial school was available. Moreover, 89 percent of those surveyed rejected the idea that "the Catholic school system is no longer needed in modern day life," and 80 percent responded that they would contribute more money to save a financially beleaguered parish school. Seventy-six percent said the schools should receive financial aid from the federal government. Finally, the authors averred that this data indicated that Catholic schools were successful in influencing students in the area of values.[44]

An article by James L. Morrison and Benjamin H. Hodgkins, written in 1978, suggested that the steady high school enrollment reported by Greeley *et al.* reflected a rationale that is inconsistent with the nature and goals of "faith communities." They argued that:

> ...although the original purpose of Catholic education was to serve religious ends, the contemporary Catholic educational system is primarily secular and specifically oriented to facilitating the social mobility of selected Catholic youth.[45]

They viewed the shift in emphasis from elementary to secondary schools as one factor that suggests that "religious training, important as it still might be -- is rapidly becoming of secondary importance to an institutional concern in preparing at least a segment of Catholic youth" for contemporary society.[46] Greater institutional autonomy within the Catholic Church can be expected to strengthen that tendency. While admitting that their data were not taken from representative public and Catholic senior high schools, they concluded that Catholic high schools may be becoming like many Protestant colleges -- religious in name only.[47] They call for more "systematic research" to "verify or correct" their interpretation. If Morrison and Hodgkins are correct, the notion of "faith community" could not exist in such a high school.

Summary

In the "Afterword" to *Catholic Schools in a Declining Church*, Andrew Greeley suggested that the Catholic hierarchy get out of the school business and turn control over to the laity, who were able and willing to run the schools. Then, and only then, he maintained, would the Catholic schools be healthy.[48] Regardless of whether his recommendation was accurate, the bishops have not followed it.

The Church did, however, create new means for developing the kind of spiritual qualities in teachers and administrators called for by Catholic leaders with the purpose of becoming "faith communities." Examples of these steps are evident in the 1981 document, *The Christian Formation of Catholic Educators* and in *The Pre-Service Formation of Teachers for Catholic Schools*, published in 1982.[49]

The issue of the rights of lay teachers to organize and bargain collectively remains. The treatment of the lay teachers in New York City, for instance, at the hands of a lay school board headed by Seraphim Maltese, the head of the New York State Conservative Party, did little to reflect social justice.[50] It is erroneous, in the view of this writer, to assume that Catholic laity will be of one mind as to policy and practice regarding Catholic schools. In fact, the laity may well be less observant of the tenets of Catholic social teaching than their clerical or religious forerunners. It may take the efforts of the hierarchy, contrary to Greeley's suggestion, to ensure that lay teachers in Catholic schools are dealt with in accord with the canons of the social teaching of the Church.

In his keynote address at the NCEA convention in 1982, Alfred McBride, a former NCEA official, identified three major challenges which faced Catholic schools in the 1980s. The "most basic one," according to McBride, was to "keep Catholic schools Catholic, institutionally, morally, and spiritually." The second was to "increase academic excellence competitively, professionally, and creatively." The third, and last challenge, was to "secure a financial basis for...schools through endowments, development programs, and government aid."[51] The next, and final chapter of this book, will deal with those challenges.

Endnotes

1. Kenneth A. Simon and W. Vance Grant, eds., *Digest of Educational Statistics*. Washington, D.C.: U.S. Department of Health, Education, and Welfare, 1987, p. 56.

2. Ibid.

3. National Conference of Catholic Bishops, *To Teach As Jesus Did*. Washington, D.C.: United States Catholic Conference, 1973, pp. 1-9.

4. Ibid, pp. 28-29, 31-33.

5. Ibid, p. 34.

6. National Conference of Catholic Bishops, *Sharing the Light of Faith, National Catechetical Directory for Catholics in the United States*. Washington, D.C.: United States Catholic Conference, 1979, pp. 143-44.

7. Pope John Paul II, *Catechesi Tradendae*, 1979, paragraph 69. (For the complete English text of *Catechesi Tradendae*, see *The Living Light* 17 (Spring 1980): 44-89.

8. Ibid.

9. *The National Catholic Reporter*, 22 October 1976, p. 8.

10. National Catholic Educational Association, *Giving Form to the Vision: The Pastoral in Practice*. Washington, D.C.: National Catholic Educational Association, 1974.

11. Michael O'Neill, "Catholic Education: The Largest Alternative System," *Thrust*, 7 May 1978, p. 26; O'Neill, "Toward a Modern Concept of Permeation," *Momentum* 10 (May 1979): 48-49 .

12. Ibid, p. 49.

13. Ibid, pp. 49-50.

14. *Sharing the Light of Faith*, p. 131.

15. Pope Leo XIII, "Rerum Novarum" ("On the Condition of Labor"), in *Five Great Encyclicals*. New York: Paulist Press, 1939, pp. 1-30.

16. Pope Pius XI, "Quadragesimo Anno" ("Reconstructing the Social Order"), in Ibid, pp. 125-67, p. 137.

17. "Gaudium et Spes" ("Pastoral Constitution on the Church in the Modern World"), in Walter M. Abbott, ed., *The Documents of Vatican II*. New York: Guild Press, 1969, pp. 277-78.

18. *National Labor Relations Board* v. *The Catholic Bishop of Chicago*, et al. 99 S. CT. 1313 (1979).

19. J.J. Reilly, "Teachers' Unions, Catholic," *The New Catholic Encyclopedia*, 17. New York: McGraw Hill, 1979, p. 648.

20. Rita C. Schwartz, "Social Justice for Catholic School Teachers: Trouble in the Vineyard." Paper prepared for the 1980 Convention of the National Association of Women Religious, published by the National Association of Catholic School Teachers, Philadelphia, pp. 1-3.

21. Harold J. T. Isenberg, "If You Want to Teach: Catholic Teacher Unionization Without the NLRB," *America*, 3 November 1979, pp. 260-62.

22. John J. Augenstein, *A Collaborative Approach to Personnel Relations*. Washington, D.C.: National Catholic Educational Association, 1980, pp. 3-7.

23. *The National Catholic Reporter*, 17 September 1982, p. 6.

24. The Chicago Archdiocese, under the leadership of John Cardinal Cody, constitutes one local church which was under heavy indictment for failure in this matter. *The National Catholic Reporter* is one source for these criticisms.

25. *The Catholic Herald Citizen*, 9 July 1981, p. 1.

26. James G. Cibulka, Timothy J. O'Brien, and Donald Zewe, *Inner-City Private Elementary Schools: A Study*. Milwaukee: Marquette University Press, 1982.

27. O'Neill, "Toward a Modern Concept of Permeation," *Momentum*, p. 49.

28. *To Teach as Jesus Did.*

29. *Lemon* v. *Kurtzman*. 403 U.S. 602 (1971).

30. *Hunt* v. *McNair*. 413 U.S. at 743 (1973).

31. *The National Catholic Reporter*, 18 June 1971, p. 3.

32. *The Catholic Herald Citizen*, 14 August 1971, p. 1.

33. *Brusca* v. *State of Missouri*. 92 S. Ct. 1493 (1972).

34. *Committee for Public Education and Religious Liberty* v. *Nyquist*. 413 U.S. 756 (1973).

35. *Levitt* v. *Committee for Public Education and Religious Liberty*. 413 U.S. 472 (1973).

36. See, for instance, *The Catholic Herald Citizen*, 30 June 1973, p. 2; and *Ibid*, 7 July 1973, p. 2 for comments from a range of Catholic officials.

37. *Meek* v. *Pittenger*. 421 U.S. 349 (1975).

38. *The National Catholic Reporter*, 4 July 1975, p. 1; *Ibid*, 1 August 1975, p. 4.

39. *Ibid*, 1 August 1975, p. 4.

40. Andrew R. Breines "Parochiaid: A Myth of Equality," *The Catholic Herald Citizen*, 7 June 1975, p. 8.

41. *The National Catholic Reporter*, 6 June 1975, p. 1.

42. *The New York Times,* 29 June 1969, p. 25; George H. Gallup, "Sixth Annual Poll of Attitudes Toward Public Education," *Phi Delta Kappan:* 56, 1 (September 1974): 20-32.

43. Andrew M. Greeley, William C. McCready, and Kathleen McCourt, *Catholic Schools in a Declining Church.* Kansas City, KS: Sheed and Ward, 1976, p. 301. (The study, published in 1976, was based on two samples of American Catholics taken at the National Opinion Research Center: the first in 1963, the second in 1974.)

44. *Ibid.*

45. James L. Morrison and Benjamin J. Hodgkins, "Social Change and Catholic Education," *Education* 98 (March-April 1978): 264.

46. Ibid, p. 276.

47. Ibid, pp. 276-77.

48. Greeley, et al., *Catholic Schools in a Declining Church,* pp. 324-25.

49. Alfred A. McBride, *The Christian Formation of Catholic Educators.* Washington, D. C.: Chief Administrators of Catholic Education, National Catholic Educational Association, 1981; and Russell M. Bleich et al., *The Pre-Service Formation of Teachers for Catholic Schools: In Search of Patterns for the Future.* Washington, D. C.: The Chief Administrators of Catholic Education, The Association of Catholic Colleges and Universities, National Catholic Educational Association, 1982.

50. *The National Catholic Reporter,* 17 September 1982, p. 6; *Ibid,* 1 October 1982, p. 6.

51. McBride, "Major Challenges Facing Catholic Education in the 1980s," *Momentum* 13 (December 1982): 10-11.

Bibliographic Entries

382. Amato, Nicholas Paul. "The Impact of Parish Subsidy Reductions On the Goals and Attitudes of Members of Catholic School Communities and Its Consequent Implications For School Planning Within New Ecclesial Structures." Ed.D. dissertation. Boston University, 1977.

Considers the issues of parish subsidies, goals satisfaction, and powerlessness in the Catholic schools of Baltimore in order to help the schools better understand their aims and plan for their future at a time of reorganizational change. Finds that parish subsidies of any kind do not impact on the goals for Catholic schools, which indicates that goals and priorities can be set despite a school's financial difficulties. Shows that satisfaction toward financial management is related to occupational level, role, and age group, and emphasizes that a successful school comes from community involvement and community ownership.

383. Augenstein, John J. "Teacher Unions, the Courts, and Catholic Schools." Paper Presented at the Annual Meeting of the National Catholic Educational Association (New Orleans, LA, April 7-10, 1980).

Addresses the status of teacher organizations in Catholic schools in the United States, discussing the history, rationale, and conclusion of the Supreme Court decision of 1979 which ruled that church-operated schools do not fall under the jurisdiction of the National Labor Relations Board. Gives the results of a national survey of Catholic school superintendents and the heads of teacher organizations showing a steady growth of teacher unions and a consensus for a third party to settle disputes. States that there must be agreement of both administrators and teachers on the overall mission of the Church, its educational mission, and the place of the school within that mission.

384. Austin, Gilbert R. and Stephen P. Holowenzak. "Catholic
    Schools and Public Aid: The Elementary and Secondary Ed-
    ucation Act and the Principle of Accommodation." *Notre
    Dame Journal of Education* 3 (Winter 1973): 373-82.

    Shows the evolving of the principle of accommodation or
    acceptability in the case of public monies for nonpublic school
    education first established by the Federal Government in the
    Elementary and Secondary Education Act (ESEA 1965). Re-
    ports research findings that strengthen the importance of the
    ESEA principle and alleges that it will be the basis for argu-
    ment by nonpublic schools for state and local aid. Outlines the
    factors which determine the participation of the nonpublic
    schools in Title I, ESEA, and advises the Catholic educational
    leadership to be watchful that the progress made since 1965
    be maintained.

385. Brady, Charles and Mary Sarah Fasenmyer, eds. *Giving Form
    to The Vision: The Pastoral in Practice*. Washington, DC: The
    National Catholic Educational Association, 1974.

    Provides a process of implementation of five principles of
    Catholic education as presented in the American Bishops'
    Pastoral on Catholic education, *To Teach As Jesus Did*: Edu-
    cational Policy-Making, Adult Education, Religious Educa-
    tion Outside the School, Catholic Elementary School, and
    Catholic Secondary School. Gives direction and structure to
    the implementation of activities within each of the leadership
    groups cited providing the instruments needed to assess the
    quality of the Catholic education program and to determine
    the actions to be taken in order to be more completely in ac-
    cord with the Pastoral's vision of Catholic education.

386. Buetow, Harold A. *A History of United States Catholic
    Schooling*. (item 46).

387. "Catholic Secondary Schools and the Educational Reform
    Movement in American Secondary Education." Washington,

DC: National Catholic Educational Association Special Bulletin, 1976.

Critiques the report of the National Association of Secondary School Principals (NASSP), *This We Believe: Secondary School in a Changing Society*. Concurs with many of the document's proposals but points out omissions in philosophy and in proposals and sets forth a "Statement Regarding Catholic Secondary Education." Presents Victor Hickey's analysis of the NASSP document in two parts: 1) a review and critique of the reform proposals including compulsory education and graduation requirements; and 2) a review and critique of the five reform reports. Declares that the NASSP fails to define the need of religious, moral, spiritual and humanistic values.

388. Cartagenova, Gonzalo C. "The United States Supreme Court and Religious Liberty in Education, 1930-1980." (item 197).

389. Charron, Rose Mary. "Parental Perceptions of the Unique Qualities of Catholic Schools: An Exploratory Study, With Implications For Teacher Formation." Ph.D. dissertation. Michigan State University, 1980.

Identifies the unique and desirable qualities of Catholic schools as perceived by parents of children enrolled in Catholic schools and discusses some implications these qualities have for the formation of Catholic school teachers. Reviews the historical background of the Catholic school and outlines the role of the teachers as stated in Church documents. Finds parents perceive that it is the Catholic school teachers and the goals of Catholic education that give the Catholic school its unique character. Shows that comprehensive religious instruction is the specific aspect of education that parents want for their children. Believes the study is significant in its contribution to an understanding of the survival of the Catholic schools into the 1980's.

390. Coleman, James S. "Quality and Equality In American Education: Public and Catholic Schools." *Phi Delta Kappan* 63 (November 1981): 159-64.

Examines four basic assumptions and ideals underlying American education (the common school, local control, local financing, and *in loco parentis*) and indicates that failure to establish a new set of attainable goals necessitated by change in society has hurt both the quality and equality of American education. Arrives at conclusions resulting from Coleman's study, "Public and Private Schools" noting there is higher academic achievement in basic cognitive skills in Catholic schools than in public schools. Explains study results that show greater quality in the Catholic schools and suggests that the ideal of the common school is more nearly met in the Catholic schools than in the public schools.

391. Dempsey, Michael J. "An In-depth Study of Five Key Changes of Direction Indicated For Catholic Schools by Vatican II and Technology." Ph.D. dissertation. Fordham University, 1973.

Analyzes changes in directions in five areas of religious education in American elementary and secondary schools as a result of Vatican II and developments in technology. Contrasts them with past objectives establishing guidelines to evaluate progress made in new directions. Finds that changes have occurred with substantial implications for instructional systems of Catholic schools but little research has been concentrated on translating the new directions into feasible instructional design and programs. Notes that the implications of technology are little understood and states that technological development is at the root of the culture change.

392. Dolan, Jay P. "Schools." (item 55).

393. Donohue, John W. "A Vatican Statement on Education." *America* 137, 20 August 1977, pp. 67-70.

Appraises a statement on education by the Vatican's Congregation for Catholic Education released July 5, 1977. Says the task of any Catholic school "...is fundamentally a synthesis of faith and life." Calls for the coexistence and cooperation of diverse educational systems and reminds Catholic schools that they should serve the cause of social justice and be open to all. Explains that the tone and perspective reflect Vatican II and Pope Pius XII.

394. Drouin, Edmond G. "The United States Supreme Court and Religious Freedom in American Education In Its Decisions Affecting Church-Related Elementary and Secondary Schools During the First Three Quarters of the Twentieth Century." (item 148).

395. Dulles, Avery. "Catholic Theology and the Secondary School." *Catholic Mind* 71 (September 1973): 15-24.

Discourses on five principles found in the statement of guidelines issued by the Jesuit Secondary Education Association's Commission on Research and Development (CORD). Identifies the principles as normative for the educational process: 1) future-oriented learning; 2) participatory learning; 3) climate of trust; 4) pluralism of values; and 5) orientation to service. Discusses the relationship of the five principles to the fundamental principle of a strong emphasis on religious studies and maintains that the new vision of the Church after the Council requires theological updating in the curriculum, student counseling and in the moral and spiritual attitudes of the teachers.

396. Duminuco, Vincent J. "Catholic High Schools: 2001." *Religious Education* 73 (January-February 1978): 22-35.

Depicts the Catholic high schools of the future influenced by Christian optimism and providing a positive environment for personal and religious affirmation. Highlights the need for an integrated synthesis in school programs and environment, and examines the new kind of young person growing up in a new kind of world. Comments upon the historian Thomas Berry's view of what makes it different from the old: universalism, developmental change, and humanism. Discusses distinguishing characteristics of the Catholic high school of the future and believes the synthesis of the Christian vision with method and technology is necessary if the Catholic high schools are to be effectively called Catholic.

397. Elford, George. "The Year That Was: A New Era For Catholic Education?" *Today's Catholic Teacher*, 7, September 1973, pp. 38-40.

Views the events of the school year 1972-73 -- Watergate, the Supreme Court's abortion decision, the Court's veto of the tax credit, the United States Bishops' Pastoral *To Teach As Jesus Did*, the faith community movement in education, the funding by the Ford and Danforth Foundations of the Council for American Private Education -- as impacting on Catholic education in the 70's and 80's. Explains the impact as threefold: 1) Events highlight the need for an effective system of Catholic education; 2) The Pastoral establishes the Church's commitment to total education; and 3) Catholic schools, freed from the expectation of receiving state aid, can bolster their sense of identity and develop a distinctively Catholic school.

398. Faherty, William Barnaby with Elizabeth Kolmer, Dolorita Maria Dougherty and Edward J. Sudckum. *From One Generation to the Next -- 160 Years of Catholic Education in Saint Louis.* (item 58).

399. Faricy, Robert L. "Toward an Understanding of the Catholic School." *Homiletic and Pastoral Review* 72 (March 1972): 26-32.

Communicates an understanding of what makes a school Catholic, why it is important to keep the Catholic schools and where their future lies. Philosophizes why schools exist, explaining their function in the process of human progress. Describes the Catholic school as true to its nature and summarizes its uniqueness: 1) Religion is taught; 2) Christian witness is given by the teachers and there is explicit educational experience of the Christian community. Elucidates how each curriculum subject including religion must have an identity of its own and affirms the need for Catholic teachers personally committed to Christ and teaching in Catholic schools.

400. Fasenmyer, Mary Sarah. "The Pastoral Message: Present and Future." *Notre Dame Journal of Education* 6 (Winter 1975): 293-98.

Considers the response to the pastoral statement of the American Hierarchy, *To Teach As Jesus Did*, and evidences that serious study of the text is an ongoing process among the Catholic educational and pastoral ministries. Contends it is known and being heeded within the teaching ministry and new models of educational ministry are emerging. Summarizes five principles of the pastoral message that speak to Catholic educators and asserts that the internalization of these principles creates the climate for educational renewal.

401. Flynn, Anthony. "Effective Leadership Styles for Catholic High Schools Under the Threat of Closing." Ph.D. dissertation. University of Notre Dame, 1975.

Explores types of leadership effectiveness that would be most helpful in the kind of situational stress challenging the Catholic high school facing the threat of closing. Uses a model based on Fiedler's Theory of Leadership Effectiveness and finds that the teachers who perceived the threat of the school closing more than their principal, rated the principal's leadership effectiveness lower than those teachers who perceived the same threat less than their principals. Indicates that the negative teachers harbor a feeling of hopelessness while positive teachers show reliance on their leaders in a time of stress. Suggests further research to discover if positive teachers are motivation-oriented, and if negative teachers are hygienic-oriented, avoiding pain and discomfort and regarding security as a maximum value.

402. Ford, Elinor R. "The Saga of America's Catholic Inner-City Schools." *Catholic Mind* 78 (December 1980): 5-16.

 Looks at the beginnings of Catholic inner-city schools noting certain universals associated with them and examines the present-day Catholic inner city schools in the light of these universals: 1) They are established and maintained as the greatest need of urban youth; 2) They are the concern of the whole church and must be financed by the sacrifices of all church members; 3) They are administered and staffed by professional educators; 4) A particular school will survive only with the committed support of everyone; and 5) The struggle for government and business support must never be abandoned. Discusses who is served and the performance of present Catholic inner-city schools as well as why they are so popular among Catholics and non-Catholics alike.

403. Gaffney, Edward McGlynn, Jr. "Postscript: Meek, Wolman and the 'Fear of Imaginable But Totally Implausible Evils' in the Funding of Non-Public Education." *Freedom and Education: Pierce v. Society of Sisters Reconsidered.* Edited by Donald P. Kommers and Michael J. Wahoske. Notre Dame, IN: University of Notre Dame Law School, 1978, pp. 79-93.

 Analyzes the decisions handed down by the United States Supreme Court on the public funding of nonpublic schools in *Meek* v. *Pittinger* (1975) and *Wolman* v. *Walter* (1977). Tells how the Supreme Court reversed the Pennsylvania district court judgement in the *Meek* Case and the Ohio district court's decision in *Wolman* ruling that the loan of instructional materials and equipment to nonpublic school students violated the no-establishment clause of the first amendment. Contends that in *Meek* and *Wolman* the Court is divided and the distinctions made by the Justices make little sense as coherent constitutional doctrine and as clear guidelines for educators.

404. Gilbert, John (R). "Teaching Values in the Catholic School." (Item 12).

405. Greeley, Andrew M. *Catholic High Schools and Minority Students*. New Brunswick, NJ: Transaction Books, Rutgers University, 1982.

Examines data collected in the High School and Beyond (HS & B), a national study carried out the National Opinion Research Center (NORC) under contract with the National Center for Education Statistics. Ascertains the plans and activities of young people as they pass through school and into adulthood. Focuses on minority students attending Catholic secondary schools and seeks to discover from the data why black and Hispanic students attending Catholic high schools display higher levels of academic effort and achievement than black and Hispanic students attending public schools. States that the Catholic school outcomes are due partially to the kinds of young people attending the schools, quality of discipline, and quality of teaching.

406. Greeley, Andrew M., William C. McCready, and Kathleen McCourt. *Catholic Schools in a Declining Church*. Kansas City, KS: Sheed and Ward, Inc., 1976.

Researches the value-oriented education of the Catholic schools in the United States under the stress of social change. Replicates the 1963 National Opinion Research Center (NORC) study analyzing the impact of Catholic schools on adult religious behavior and attempts to see whether the impact has changed in the turbulent decade in the Church that followed the first study. Finds a positive and a negative force at work in the American Catholic Church since 1963 -- a positive reaction to the Vatican Council and a negative response to the encyclical *Humanae Vitae*. Discovers that support for Catholic schools among American Catholics is strong and the importance of Catholic education has increased.

407. Harper, Mary-Angela. *Ascent to Excellence in Catholic Education: A Guide to Effective Decision-Making*. Waterford, CT: CROFT-NEI, Prentice-Hall, Inc., 1980.

Provides policymaking guidelines for Catholic boards of education encompassing the theory and practice of boardsmanship and the concept of Catholic policymaking as a ministry. Explains the roles, responsibilities and relationships of the Catholic education board and delineates the criteria for judging the effectiveness of models for participatory decision-making. Describes the steps to be taken for a successful meeting and elucidates the role of committees. Demonstrates the necessity for recruiting quality board members and for training for excellence in educational policymaking. Appends a model constitution and bylaws, checklists and various forms.

408. Heath, Mark. "To Teach As Jesus Did: A Critique." *The Living Light* 10 (Summer 1973): 284-95.

Analyzes the pastoral message *To Teach As Jesus Did* from the viewpoint of religious educational theory and describes its vision of the educational mission of the Church as an integrated ministry embracing teaching, community and service. Explains the apparent structural division of catechetics and education and observes that the overall thrust of the pastoral message is in a unity of educational ministry bringing together many institutions, programs and activities that extend to the entire Catholic community. Calls for unified models of Christian education that can be expressed from administrative structures.

409. Holtz, Gregory M. "Research Needs in Catholic Elementary and Secondary Education." *Notre Dame Journal of Education* 6 (Spring 1975): 92-96.

Covers two research areas and methodologies concerned with Catholic schools: diocesan studies and selected secondary analyses, and follow-ups to past research. Demonstrates why the typical diocesan study has overrelied on the methodology of sociology and economics. Makes suggestions for team research efforts of dioceses and universities with the university supplying the new knowledge and the diocese testing, refining and disseminating findings. Sets forth the kind of research that should be done and states that there must be scholarly team-work in the formulation of a methodologically sound research design coupled with leadership, organization and funding.

410. Hunt, Thomas C. "Catholic Schools Today: Redirection and Redefinition?" *The Living Light* 17 (Fall 1980): 203-10.

Looks at the time of the 60s when Catholic parochial schools came under attack from within the Catholic commu-nity. Tells of the American Bishops' statements of support for Catholic schools in the 70s. Reviews the position of the Ca-tholic schools entering the 1980s, addressing the question of how changes will affect their uniqueness and rationale for ex-istence. Expresses the emphasis in Catholic education on de-veloping a faith community and discusses the principal's role in this development of a mostly lay faith community. Men-tions concerns about financial aid to Catholic schools and the characteristics of the contemporary Catholic education system and its students, but notes the confidence to meet the chal-lenges.

411. Hunt, Thomas C. and Norlene M. Kunkel. "Catholic Schools: The Nation's Largest Alternative School System." (item 65).

412. Koppes, Albert P. "Measuring Change in Catholic Schools." *NASSP Bulletin* 59 (September 1975): 94-96.

Compares educational practices evidenced in a selected group of innovative Catholic schools with those advocated by the NASSP Model Schools Project established by J. Lloyd Trump and William Georgiades. Finds three concepts within the twelve areas of change easiest to implement: small group discussion as a teaching methodology, independent study, and making more flexible use of present facilities. Gives a lack of the proposal and the citing by faculty of a lack of time as the specific reasons why certain changes were not made. Suggests inservice training for faculties and setting up residences in high schools where change has occurred. Notes the importance of the principal's continued support and of publicizing the educational changes.

413. Kuhr, Nancy Jane Newton. "Catholic Parochial Schools in the Austin diocese: Background, Development Since 1849 and Present Status." (item 114).

414. Laria, Joseph A. "Role Expectations for Catholic Secondary School Lay Principals." Ph.D. dissertation. Fordham University, 1974.

Attempts to determine and compare the expectations for the ideal role of the lay principal as perceived by parents, lay teachers, lay administrators, and religious teachers and communities in Catholic secondary schools in the Diocese of Brooklyn. Studies the effects of greater lay involvement in decision making on the administrative level and ascertains if the lay principal is expected to provide for the development of both religious and secular values of Catholic secondary schools. Finds that lay principals are expected to engage in the organizational, personal and social dimensions of their role, but differences in thinking occur when it comes to their providing for a formal religious formation program.

415. McBride, Alfred A. *The Christian Formation of Catholic Educators*. Washington, DC: The Chief Administrators of Catholic Education (CACE) Department of the National Catholic Educational Association (NCEA), 1979.

Serves as a guide for all Catholic education offices providing a framework for the adaptation and development of local programs of Christian teacher formation. Addresses the on-going formation of Catholic educators after beginning work in the schools and in parish religion education centers. Reflects on the Church's methods with a call to faith through evangelization, the deepening of the call in catechesis, the commitment to the Church as a community and institution, commitment to prayer and the sacraments, the need for social awareness, and the fostering of the educator's personal fulfillment. Sees these guidelines as a vision for the formation of Catholic educators.

416. McCann, Mary Beatrice. "A Description of Social Studies in the Catholic Secondary Schools of the Archdiocese of Philadelphia, 1890-1976." (item 166).

417. McCann, Mary M. "Catholic Schools and a Democratic Model of Administration." *Notre Dame Journal of Education* 3 (Winter 1973): 318-23.

Investigates the administration of the Catholic schools in the 70's, noting the complexity of the structure and the unclear delineation of power and responsibility. Reviews the bureaucratic tradition of the American Catholic schools and addresses the need to look to a flexible adaptive structure that evolves in response to solving problems. Turns to a democratic model of organization and leadership. Holds that when the Christian educators internalize democratic values and attitudes, the Church, as well as the schools and society, will be better served.

418. Malone, Richard Joseph. "The Roman Catholic Secondary School As Faith Community: Educational, Developmental and Theological Considerations." S.T.D. dissertation. Boston University, 1981.

Outlines a model of the Catholic secondary school as faith community developed in response to *To Teach As Jesus Did* and other post-Vatican II documents. Surveys recent theory in religious education, and studies the implications of adolescent development for the high school faith community model. Discusses Karl Rahner's theology of the human person in the faith community and presents a case study of a Catholic high school for boys which has been involved in self-evaluation and redefinition in the light of the challenge to form a faith community. Sees the need to study factors that could limit the potential effectiveness of a Catholic secondary faith community.

419. Maltby, Gregory P. "The Organization of Catholic Secondary Schools: A Preliminary Statement on Catholic School Governance." Paper Presented at the Annual Meeting of the American Educational Research Association (Washington DC, March 30-April 3, 1975).

Studies the related issues and differences among Catholic high schools, and local control evaluating how centralization impacts on the perceptions of parents who support the schools. Finds that centralized control of the Catholic high school diminishes the difference in the mind of the Catholic parent and may result in a loss of support since the parent and student in selecting a Catholic high school to attend look for a "distinctive atmosphere" which influences them in their choice.

420. Marmion, John P. "Catholic Education: The Changing Scene in America." *Clergy Review* 62 (July 1977): 285-88.

Gives a commentary on the sociological reports of Greeley and Rossi focusing on the study *Catholic Schools in a Declining Church* (item 406) and considers that the statistics and conclusions point to the wisdom of increased support for Catholic schools. States that it is compelling reading and that those interested in Catholic schools should take note.

421. Mayock, Louise A. "The Influence of the Second Vatican Council on the American Catholic School." Ed.D. dissertation. University of Pennsylvania, 1979.

Studies the themes in the Vatican II Council documents that characterized new directions for Catholicism investigating whether or not the new directions influenced the American Catholic school, the teachers and administrators who implement the instructional programs. Examines the research of the National Catholic Educational Association (NCEA) activities and the periodical literature, and surveys forty diocesan superintendents of schools. Traces the movement of the periodical literature finding that it reflects the council documents and activities of NCEA. Notes that the superintendents' survey reflects the effects of the searching and growth of the Catholic school system in the post-conciliar years and culminates in delineation of the superintendents' role expectations. Reports that the most important factor in each set of outcomes is the impact of the bishops' pastoral, *To Teach As Jesus Did.*

422. Metzcus, Richard H., Gregory M. Holtz, and Jerry Florent. "New Directions in Catholic Education: An Empirical Approach." *Notre Dame Journal of Education* 6 (Spring 1975): 5-12.

Discusses alternative directions for Catholic schooling and explains each within the framework of empirical research and theory. Rejects the first alternative to continue mindlessly, but finds positive elements in seven others: High School Concentration; Early Childhood "Mothering" Education; Critical Period Religious Education; Adult Religious Education; Moral and Value Education; Urban Education Concentration; and Educating for Human Development. Advocates the last alternative believing that the curriculum which focuses on growing relationships with others, the environment and institutions is a sound academic and interpersonal program. Sees it as an opportunity for the Catholic school to develop a program to help remedy social problems.

423. Miller, Steven I. and Jack Kavanaugh. "Catholic School Integration and Social Policy: A Case Study." *The Journal of Negro Education* 44 (1975): 482-92.

Addresses the trend of increasing social segregation of urban Catholic schools when upper middle-class families migrate to the suburbs resulting in policy and social consequences. Recognizes the dilemma of the Catholic Church committed to an open, integrated education grounded in Christian principles. Researches an all-girls Catholic high school with a racial balance to determine the socioeconomic implications of re-segregation and how both black and white parents view crucial education variables. Notes that both black and white parents favor integrated schooling, and are concerned with quality education, but the motivations differ.

424. Moynihan, Daniel Patrick. "A Matter of Justice." *Catholic Mind* 79 (December 1981): 22-32.

Advocates tuition tax credits for families with children in private elementary and secondary schools in a speech delivered at a Catholic high school in New York. Describes the background of aid to nonpublic education and the views and intentions of American administrations from John F. Kennedy to Ronald Reagan. Describes the author's part in the campaign for tuition tax credits and the introduction of the Packard-Moynihan bill in February 1981. Shares perceptions concerning federal aid to education in the present climate indicating that circumstances have changed the prospects for aid to private and nonpublic schools. Reaffirms support for aid for all students and all schools on an equitable basis.

425. Mugavero, Francis J. "Pastoral Letter on Education." *Catholic Mind* 71 (May 1973): 10-14.

Records the pastoral letter issued by the Bishop of Brooklyn on January 23, 1973 reflecting on the importance of the teaching mission of the Church and citing some difficulties facing the Catholic schools. Proposes a new approach for renewal that would organize parishes in clusters within given geographical areas in order to work together towards consolidation of schools. Exhorts the parishes to promote programs for Catholic students attending public schools and to meet the needs of handicapped or retarded young people. Calls on pastors and their associate priests to provide leadership in the implementation of educational programs.

426. Murdick, Olin J. "Catholic Schools in American Society: A New Look," pp. 57-68. (item 403).

Reviews the idea of religious freedom in America and discusses thirteen principles contained in the Vatican II documents, *Declaration on Religious Freedom*, in the historical and present context of the American experience. Explains how the image of the Catholic school as an ecclesiastical enterprise rather than a parental one contributed to the development of a national policy on nonpublic school aid. Faults the courts and the makers of American public opinion for violating the right of parents to determine and select the kind of education for their children that their consciences dictate. Suggests a new beginning, a rethinking of the problem of freedom, and a new effort to solve it.

427. Murdick, Olin J. "Who Runs Catholic Schools? A Model for Shared Responsibility." *Notre Dame Journal of Education* 6 (Summer 1975): 103-90.

Articulates a theory regarding the functions, structures and roles that characterize the policy process of the local Church's educational mission and develops a model based on the theory. Identifies three structures and agencies that are essential to the policy process: 1) the parish council; 2) the parish board of education; and 3) the school administrator. Presents a primer of guidelines for implementing the shared leadership ideal urged by the American bishops.

428. Murray, Michael Sanders. "Negotiated Contracts in Catholic Elementary and Secondary Schools." Ed.D. dissertation. Rutgers University, 1977.

Studies the evolution of collective bargaining in diocesan Catholic schools in America, analyzes negotiated contracts and explores the attitude of diocesan and church officials toward collective bargaining. Notes that attitudes of superintendents and school administrators run from a high degree of understanding of labor management to having no concept of any need for unionization and collective bargaining. Cites the problem peculiar to Catholic schools of whether religious teachers should be included in the bargaining unit, and states that the religious nature of the enterprise is reflected in contract language. Provides guidelines for collective bargaining in the Catholic school system.

429. National Conference of Catholic Bishops. *To Teach As Jesus Did: A Pastoral Message on Catholic Educations.* (item 30).

430. Newton, Robert R. "Educational Trends in Catholic Secondary Education." Paper presented at the Annual Meeting of the National Catholic Educational Association (New Orleans, LA, April 7-10, 1980).

Analyzes the educational trends of Catholic high schools in the 1970's indicating that the renewed interest in curriculum is due to the shift within the Church and to the increasing demand to demonstrate the difference, the distinctiveness, and the worth of the Catholic schools. Explores what is happening in the religious dimensions of the Catholic schools preparing students to make Christian responses to religious and moral challenges and emphasizes that all faculty members are responsible for the school's religious mission. Examines the personal dimensions of the Catholic schools and notes a return to traditional curriculum content and a development of self-initiation and self-direction in learning.

431. Newton, Robert R. "Lay Leadership in Catholic Schools: Dimensions and Dilemmas." Paper Presented at the Annual Convention of the Chief Administrators of Catholic Education (Albuquerque, New Mexico, October 1979).

Explores three ways to understand the concept of lay leadership in Catholic schools describing the challenges and problems they present: 1) a new vision of ministry of teaching in the Catholic Church which requires a significant change in roles and behavior by laity, religious and clerics; 2) the sharing of authority and responsibility for the direction of Catholic schools; 3) maintaining the Catholic school as a faith community. Poses possible problems and states that the Catholic schools must attempt to build community rather than assume that it exists. Says the emergence of lay leadership holds significant promise.

432. Rooney, Patrick C. "Religious Instruction in the Context of Catholic Schooling." *Notre Dame Journal of Education* 5 (Fall 1974): 259-74.

Speaks about the relationship between a Catholic school's religious education program and its daily operations describing the paradoxes between the "new" religion taught in the religion classes and the "regime" of the school. Discusses how the resultant tension develops and points out that the school as an institution cannot contradict what it is teaching in the classroom. Explains the mentality and attitude of contemporary American young people and the kind of culture in which the present American Catholic religious educators grew up. Presents the options open to Catholic school personnel toward a resolution of the tension between the school and the religion class.

433. The Sacred Congregation For Catholic Education. *The Catholic School*. Washington, DC: United States Catholic Conference, 1977.

Develops the idea of the Vatican II Declaration *Gravissimum Educationis* limiting it to a reflection on the Catholic school. Focuses on the nature and distinctive characteristics of a school that calls itself Catholic and re-emphasizes the educational value of a Catholic school. Discusses the Catholic school and the salvific mission of the Church, the present difficulties, the school as a center of human formation, its educational work and responsibility today. Provides practical directions for organization and planning and extends encouragement to all who work in the Catholic school.

434. Schillo, Genevieve. "Non-Catholics in Catholic Schools: A Challenge to Evangelization." Paper presented at the Annual Meeting of the National Educational Association (New Orleans, LA, April 7-10, 1980).

Reports on the increase in enrollment of non-Catholic students in Catholic schools in the United States focusing on the schools in the Archdiocese of Omaha. Finds that the largest number of non-Catholic students are from families living in inner-city or changing neighborhoods and discusses why non-Catholic parents send their children to Catholic schools. Believes that non-Catholic admissions may be eroded if the educational mission policy is not clearly expressed, requests for resources for special needs are not made, and the true value and true cost of Catholic school education are not publicized.

435. Sheehan, M. Lourdes. "A Study of the Functions of School Boards in the Educational System of the Roman Catholic Church in the United States." Ed.D. dissertation. Virginia Polytechnic Institute and State University, 1981.

Researches parish, interparish, and diocesan school boards that are under the direct authority of the bishop of the diocese. Discusses the history of Catholic school boards in the United States and the development of Catholic schools. Finds that many Catholic school boards have not functioned effectively because the organizational system under which they operate is not consistent with the authority structure of the Catholic Church. Shows that the way boards relate to Catholic schools is dependent on the organization of the school and describes models for school organization consistent with the authority of the Church. Makes recommendations establishing lines of accountability and responsibility for all Catholic schools.

436. Shuda, Robert J. "The Future of the Catholic Elementary Schools: Some Thoughts." *Religious Education* 73 (January-February 1978): 13-21.

Reflects on the future of the Catholic elementary schools which are supported by parents who want quality education in an atmosphere of religious orientation and order, and expresses the belief that this will continue if there is a shared commitment by hierarchy, educators and laity. Discusses three models of the Catholic elementary school: the traditional parochial school; the ecumenical school; and the special-need model such as inner-city schools for minorities and schools of special education. Believes there may be fewer Catholic schools in the future but those that continue or begin will be good contemporary schools providing quality education.

437. Sullivan, Gertrude Ann. "A Planning Process to Establish Regionally Organized Catholic Elementary Schools." Ed.D. dissertation. Arizona State University, 1978.

Researches a planning process to establish a regionally organized Catholic elementary school and ascertains to what extent Catholic educational leaders agree on the critical tasks involved in the planning process and in the areas of responsibility for those tasks. Surveys bishops, diocesan superintendents, diocesan board presidents, and Catholic leaders in the National Educational Association and the United States Catholic Conference and finds they agree that all but three tasks specified in the planning process are essential, but they lack agreement in assigning responsibility. Recommends that a procedural handbook be formulated and a study be made of role descriptions in each diocese.

438. "Superintendent's Vision of Catholic Schools." *New Catholic World* 224 (March-April 1981): 77-87.

Expresses the vision of Catholic schools held by superintendents of schools of four archdioceses and three dioceses in the United States. Relates a renewed confidence in Catholic schools as a valuable and visible part of the educational ministry of the Church. Discovers mutual visions concerning Catholic education as it faces the challenges of the 80's including its availability to the poor and the Catholic school as a center of faith life. Notes the view that future new Catholic schools should be built in the suburbs and ways need to be found to evoke interest and commitment of suburban Catholics to Catholic education.

439. *Teach Them: Statement on Catholic Schools.* Washington,
     DC: United States Catholic Conference, 1976.

     Contains the message of the American Catholic Bishops
     concerning Catholic schools issued May 6, 1976. Reaffirms
     commitment to the Catholic schools which grow in effective-
     ness as determined by educational and religious measures.
     Recognizes the role of parents, teachers, administrators, pa-
     stors and the community. Asks the Committee on Education
     and the Department of Education to pursue certain steps for
     the maintaining and strengthening of the Catholic schools in
     their commitment to teach as Jesus did. Urges the nation to
     acknowledge the contributions that Catholics and other non-
     public schools make to the total educational effort in the
     United States.

440. Toale, Thomas E. "An Evaluation of Catholic Secondary
     Schools Within the Archiocese of Dubuque, Iowa and
     Throughout the United States on Selected Quality and Quan-
     tity Indicators From 1966 to 1986." (item 381).

441. Vaughan, Sister Kieran. "Catholicity and Goal Agreement in
     Catholic Elementary Schools Having Lay Faculties and Lay
     Principals." Ed.D. dissertation. University of California, Los
     Angeles, 1978.

     Determines the continuity of Catholicity in Catholic ele-
     mentary schools having lay faculties and lay principals within
     the Archdiocese of Los Angeles and the Diocese of Orange,
     and the extent of goal agreement among parents, teachers,
     principals, and priests within a school community. Analyzes
     specific practices that exemplify the continuity of Catholicity
     and identifies the degree of acceptance and satisfaction ex-
     pressed by parents.

442. Vitullo-Martin, Thomas. *Catholic Inner-City Schools: The
     Future.* Washington, DC: United States Catholic Conference,
     1979.

Attempts to determine the needs of the inner-city schools which have been closing as part of the general pattern of Catholic school reductions. Sees the decline resulting from a decrease in minority enrollments because schools could not or did not adapt to changing neighborhoods. Discusses the problem of decreased income in the inner-city schools and how the territorial organization of the Church limits diocesan officials' ability to redistribute Church income. Explains the public benefits of inner-city Catholic schools and considers several approaches for assisting them, realizing that each inner-city school requires some organizational changes.

443. Walton, Priscilla Ann Helm. "Community and the Parochial School in the Inner City." Ph.D. dissertation. Northwestern University, 1981.

Examines a Catholic parochial school in a large metropolitan center of the Midwest in a neighborhood of ethnic transition focusing on the social characteristics of the population that uses the school and on how ethnic groups relate within the school setting and within the community. Attempts to understand the relationship of the school to the larger Archdiocesan system and to the Catholic Church's commitment to education in the inner-city. Interprets the findings which confirm the importance of the parochial school in the inner-city, noting how the school links the parents in the neighborhoods. Indicates the need for small responsive parochial schools to provide quality education and for more creative use of existing structures.

CHAPTER 9
Current Concerns
1982-1991

The era 1982 to 1991 began with a tentativeness and mixed messages from Church leadership but moved toward plans to remedy the confusion and give hope for a strengthened future. The major concerns stated by Alfred McBride at the NCEA 1982 convention[1] are still predominant themes of this decade. Catholic schools' leaders are concerned with Catholic identity and establishing secure financial bases for the schools. Academic excellence of the schools seems present in many places. The concern now is the role of theology, global awareness and cultural diversity. Much of the activity during this time focuses on these issues.

Demographics

In 1989-90, there were 8,719 Catholic schools in this country (7,395 elementary and 1,324 secondary). According to The National Center for Education Statistics in *Projections of Education Statistics to 2001 -- An Update*,[2] this may reflect the demographic movements throughout the country in this period.

Exhibit 3
Elementary and Secondary Schools by Region

	1982-83	1988-89	1989-90
All Schools			
New England	668	608	598
Mideast	2,730	2,535	2,467
Great Lakes	2,429	2,266	2,245
Plains	1,065	1,026	997
Southeast	1,041	996	985
West/Far West	1,499	1,436	1,427
United States	9,432	8,867	8,719

There are interesting new trends on the other hand. Enroll-ment in preschool increased by 187% and kindergarten numbers grew by 16.4%. A greater number of ethnic minority students are presently being served by the Catholic schools. In 1989-90, 23% of the students came from minority families. Hispanic students in the schools are 97% Catholic, while 64% of black students are non-Catholic.[4]

Research

Several important research studies in this era gave positive at-tention to the schools. The three most notable studies are High School and Beyond,[5] The National Assessment of Educational Progress, and the National Education Longitudinal Studies.[6]

Academic Achievement

The general results of these national and regional studies de-monstrate that students in Catholic elementary and secondary schools, on the average, score better on tests of achievement than do children in public schools. Catholic school students achieved higher average scores than the sample of students used to derive national standards. The research reports also found substantially lower dropout rates and a higher percentage of college-bound graduates than in public schools.

One important finding reported first by Coleman in 1982[7] and strengthened by his research in 1987 became a source of controversy. Coleman defined a "Catholic Effect" which showed a distinct school influence beyond socioeconomic status, family, race and ethnicity. Coleman pointed out the achievement differences between Catholic school students and public schools are greatest for students who come from families with lower levels of parental education or income and those who are members of minorities. The research also showed there is less difference in achievement between minority students and others. This result led Coleman and his associates to claim Catholic schools are better examples of the traditional American "common school" ideal than the public schools. Critics of the Coleman report criticized the research methodologies.[8]

Religious Attitudes

Andrew Greeley's research on religious outcomes continued into the 1980's.[9] Research was also done in this dimension as well by Guerra, Donahue and Benson[10] and Convey.[11] All the research points to the strong contribution Catholic schools make to the life of the student and to the student's adult life compared to Catholic students who did not attend Catholic schools. Catholic school students have increased knowledge, understanding and demonstrate a closeness to the Church. More than Catholic public school students, Catholic school students are more likely to attend Mass, view religion as important in their lives and reject self-centered and selfish viewpoints. Further, Greeley's studies suggest attending a Catholic school has a measurable effect on behaviors and values over and above the influence of parents. (A very concise summary of the major research done on the effectiveness of Catholic schools can be found in Convey, John J. "Catholic Schools in a Changing Society: Past Accomplishments and Future Challenges," in *The Catholic School and Society*, Washington, DC. National Catholic Educational Association, 1990.)

Examples for Other Schools

Researchers, most notably Chubb and Moe of the Brookings Institute[12] and Patricia Bauch OP,[13] have matched the characteristics found in many Catholic schools with the conventional wisdom known as the "effective schools literature." Much of what is effective in the Catholic schools has been held up to public educators as examples for school improvement. The characteristics found in many Catholic schools are agreement about the school's purpose, committed teachers, responsiveness to the needs of the students and their parents, substantial freedom for principals and teachers at the school level to exercise creativity and leadership and an efficiency born of decentralization. These characteristics are strikingly present in the present public school call for restructuring.

Despite these many favorable findings, and the importance of them to American education, Catholic educators are left feeling they still face an uneasy future unless problems of identity and finance are solved.

Development Efforts

Finding the Catholic school system challenged by a shift away from the traditional financial support structure (tuition and parish subsidy) there has been a move toward sound business practice, development efforts and the necessity for public relations. Early efforts to move the schools in this direction came from John Flynn, Diocese of Omaha; Jerry Jarc, presently in Cleveland; and Richard Burke working originally with the Diocese of Hartford. From 1985 on, the development and public relations effort has been in full bloom. Evidence of this has been the expansion of single convention sessions on development to a full track of meetings on this topic at the National Catholic Educational Association Annual Convention. Large numbers of members are attending sessions on development exclusively.[14] Development offices and directors, once found mostly in higher education, are now at work in high schools, elementary schools, as well as in some parishes. Development programs require educators to assess the quality of the school and the service it provides, study and evaluate how the school is managed, understand the public's perceptions of the school and define the receptiveness of investment of both human and financial resources. The importance of development efforts is stressed as recently as 1990 in the bishops' letter of support for schools (see "A Long-Awaited Voice" in this chapter).

The Catholic Education Futures Project

In order to address the profound changes predicted by futurists, Catholic educators across the nation participated in the Catholic Education Futures Project. Representatives from 22 organizations were invited to engage in a process of planning, reflection, discussion and implementation by staff members of the National Catholic Educational Association and the department of education of the United States Catholic Conference, initiators of the project. Planning began in 1986, followed by a period of study and reflection during which participants read common texts on such topics as spirituality, technology, science, education, economics, history and selected church documents to prepare for the symposium held at the University of Dayton in May of 1988.

More than 300 educators from across the nation and from the 22 national organizations then gathered in May (19-26, 1988) to explore ways of thinking about the future of Catholic education in its broadest sense and to promote greater unity in carrying out the mission of education within the Church. The goals of the symposium were:

- Increased understanding between and among national organizations about their ministries and missions
- Agreement on the ingredients for a common vision statement for Catholic education in the U.S.
- Consensus of a broad agenda for the future of Catholic education
- Development of specific action plans for each of the sponsoring organizations. (For information about Catholic schools specifically, see the section of this chapter entitled, National Congress Catholic Schools for the 21st Century.)

- Determination of a date to reconvene within two to four years to reflect on the progress of the action plan.[15]

During the symposium phase of the project, participants produced directional statements. Following are the 14 statements which received the highest degree of consensus.

1. Catholic education exists to proclaim the Gospel, to promote lifelong personal growth and faith formation of all peoples, and to support the mission of the Church.
2. Catholic education promotes respect for all cultures which make up our pluralistic society.
3. Catholic education embraces a global perspective that reverences the dignity of the people of the earth, and attends to the economic, ecological, cultural and political interdependence of the world.
4. Catholic education brings together people from diverse educational settings to explore new ways of moving to the future.
5. Catholic education works toward the elimination of sexism and racism in its own structures and curricula, in the Church and in society.
6. In its institutions, structures, and programs, Catholic education promotes the Church's social teachings and educates for peace, justice and service.
7. Catholic education nurtures and fosters the formation of family, of parish community, and of broader communities in which people live.
8. Catholic education is conscious of and interactive with societal trends.
9. Catholic education needs to develop more effective uses of our changing resources.
10. We also need to renew existing structures and to create new ones for the delivery of education to all people, but with particular concern for the poor.
11. At all levels Catholic education includes participative and collaborative planning processes that involve those who will be affected.

12. Catholic education enables people to work for the elimination of poverty and injustice in all its forms.
13. Catholic education develops an understanding of the positive and negative impacts of science and technology on human life and faith.
14. The Catholic school community collaborates with other elements of the Church's educational mission and commits itself to promote lifelong learning through a sharing of resources, facilities and personnel.[16]

Designers of the Futures Project hope to facilitate collaboration among the participating organizations and reconvene the symposium members in 1992 to assess the development and implementation of the directional statements by the individual organizations. Boosters of the project were pleased with the process and the possibility of further discussion beyond the symposium. Detractors, however, expected that a very clear direction for education and for Catholic schools particularly would be set. Others hoped for more radical directional statements. Whether viewed positively or negatively, the symposium in itself was a remarkable gathering of people in Catholic education in its many forms. The outcomes of the project are not fully known at the time of this writing.

A Long-Awaited Voice of Support: November 1990 A Statement from the U.S. Bishops

In preparation for the 25th anniversary of their pastoral letter, "To Teach as Jesus Did," in 1997, the U.S. bishops delivered a letter of support for elementary and secondary schools and committed themselves "to certain seven-year goals as a sign of our affirmation laid down in that pastoral."[17] Voicing both affirmation and support, the bishops acknowledged a deep conviction that "Catholic schools must exist for the good of the church;" that "Catholic schools have provided and will continue to provide an excellent total education;" and "our church and nation have been enriched because of the quality of education provided in Catholic schools over the last 300 years." The bishops, in a hope to "sustain and expand this vitally important mission," outined the following goals:

a) Catholic schools will continue to provide high quality education for all their students in a context inflused with Gospel values.

b) Serious efforts will be made to ensure that Catholic schools are available for Catholic parents who wish to send their children to them.

c) New initiatives will be launched to secure sufficient financial assistance from both private and public sectors for Catholic parents to exercise this right.

d) That the salaries and benefits of Catholic schoolteachers and administrators will reflect the teaching as expressed in "Economic Justice for All."

Further, in order to achieve these goals, the bishops will initiate the following actions:

1. Teach practical aspects of stewardship by all Catholics for support of the apostolate of Catholic education.

2. Establish a national development office by January of 1992, which will assist the establishment and efforts of diocesan development offices. This national office will assume a responsibility for ethical practices, offer education and study national funding efforts for the schools.

3. Support federal and state legislation efforts aimed at providing financial assistance to all parents so they can afford to choose the schooling they desire for their children.

   Encourage the Catholic community to enter the discussion about school choice and form parent organizations at local, state and national levels to join a proposed national parent organization which would work toward choice as well as provide financial support for that choice. Two million dollars, an additional staff position in the

United States Catholic Conference Department of Education, and one additional staff person in the Office of Government Liaison will be designated to the resolution on parental rights.

And finally,

4. Develop a strategic plan for Catholic schools. This work will be done by the USCC Committee on Education. A preliminary plan is scheduled for 1995.

Planning for the Future: National Congress on Catholic Schools for the 21st Century

Aware that while research shows Catholic schools to be very effective, yet enrollment and support for the schools seem to be decreasing, the National Catholic Educational Association has planned a national congress "to revitalize and renew the climate of opinion and commitment to the future of Catholic schooling in the United States."[18] The gathering has three goals and will address five themes. A review of the purposes and especially of the themes will give the reader a clear picture of the present Catholic education concerns.

The main goals of the Congress are:

1. To communicate the story of academic and religious effectiveness of Catholic schools to a national audience that includes the whole Catholic community, as well as the broader social and political community.
2. To celebrate the success of Catholic schools in the United States and broaden support for the continuation and expansion of Catholic schooling in the culture.
3. To convene an assembly of key leaders in Catholic schooling as well as appropriate representatives of researchers, business and public officials in order to create strategies for the future of the schools.[19]

Eleven papers have been commissioned around the five central themes of the Congress. They will serve as a conversational starting point for the Congress and also for the regional meetings being held around the United States prior to the Congress itself. A brief summary of these papers follows:[20]

1. Catholic Identity of Catholic Schools (papers written by James Heft SM and Carleen Reck SSND). These two papers address the Catholic schools' involvement in the mission of the Church and how well they institutionalize characteristically Catholic traditions and emphases. They remind readers that Catholic schools must concern themselves with teaching all subjects well, the religious formation of students, the inclusion of gospel values, the building of a community of faith-filled people, and serving others after the example of Jesus. Catholic educators need to help others discover the unique treasure of the Catholic tradition found in educational institutions as well as manage the schools to be productive and cost-effective. While there is a need for the civic community to understand the value of Catholic education, it is important that the Catholic community, led by the bishops, provide economic support for the schools and most importantly reaffirm the unique vision of excellent education that is truly Catholic.

2. Leadership of and on behalf of Catholic Schools (papers written by Karen Ristau and Joseph Rogus). Both papers agree that Catholic schools do a good job and both papers agree that strong leadership has been available to the schools in the past. Both writers express concern for the number and quality of leaders for education in the future. The uncertainty about leadership is a dimension contributing to the current "endangered" status of the schools. The need for effective leaders is a concern for American society in general and within education as well. The new leaders in Catholic schools must be prepared well in theology, scripture, church teachings, and the role of the school in the Church's mission as were their predecessors,

members of religious orders. The new leaders also will need to understand their role in a dynamic, circular system; one no longer hierarchical. A decided agenda should be established for the recruitment, professional preparation and support of effective leaders. The resources of the entire Catholic community should be put at the service of leadership development.

3. The Catholic School and Society (papers by Frederick Brigham, John Convey and John Cummins). The first paper addressing this theme presents a summary of the demographic, statistical and financial profile of Catholic education in 1990. It is presented as a background for informed discussion of the topic, the Catholic school and society. The two remaining writers in this section review again the favorable findings concerning the effectiveness of Catholic schools. The challenges remain nonetheless. Catholic schools must find additional sources of revenue. Serious attention must be paid to the educational needs in the urban setting. Schools must continue to offer a strong academic program but must not neglect religious education and the faith community in the school. This dimension becomes even more important as the breakdown of the family unit continues. While schools will continue to prepare students for responsibility as world citizens, they should also be ready to assume new configurations in the future. There is now an urgent need for discussion of these points beyond the Catholic community. This discussion needs to move into the public square for discussion and policy debate.

4. Catholic School Governance and Finance (papers by Rosemary Hocevar, OSU and Lourdes Sheehan, RSM). New directions and forms of governance will need to be developed in the future. While there still are parish or diocesan schools and schools "owned" by religious congregations, changing demographic patterns forced consolidation of parish schools into regional or inter-parish ones demanding new models. The public school board

model is not appropriate for a Catholic school and neither are former ownership ones -- the pastor, bishop, religious congregation leaders owned the school and were the decision makers. Some suggestions have been made for boards based on sponsorship, colleagueship or partnerships offering a power-sharing approach. The essential question to be answered is what is the Church's understanding of decision making in the operation of schools? Boards will have to be accountable for the finances of schools and should influence the entire Catholic community to accept responsibility for the future of the schools. It is hoped that the steps outlined in the bishops' "Statement in Support of Catholic and Elementary Schools" (see "A Long Awaited Voice of Support" in this chapter) if implemented, will help the challenges which the schools face.

5. Political Action, Public Policy and Catholic Schools (papers by John E. Coons and Frank Monahan). Since Catholic schools have clearly demonstrated their contribution to the public good, it is time for the Catholic school community to move into the political arena. The record of support for private schools in the United States is mixed. The political barriers are real but not formidable. The school community should engage in public policy debates at all levels, define its own policy goals and work at the grass roots level to develop a consensus of support. The broader world of private schools and the constituent parents' groups should take an active part to effect favorable treatment. There are strong advocates for choice as an instrument of school reform and also as a way to make all education more democratic. The role of the Church in this movement can be a very important one.

This national congress will be held in Washington, D.C., in November of 1991. The theme paper topics reflect the current status of Catholic Schools in the United States. Many of these concerns are not new. The continued success of the schools depends on the answers posed and the strategies developed at the Congress.

Summary

In 1991, there are serious concerns about the future of Catholic schools on one hand and on the other, "good news" about their success academically and in the religious formation of the students. The most serious issues are about finances and Catholic identity both of which call for creative and collaborative leadership.

The literature during the years 1982 to 1991 (see annotated bibliography, chapter 9) points out that the schools are carrying out the Church's mission of evangelization. They integrate Gospel values in solid academic programs. Greeley[21] says Catholic schools are an "example par excellence of the Catholic communal ethos and the Sacramental Imagination at work." Yet the call for clear Catholic identity still resounds. Joseph Cardinal Bernardin of Chicago calls for the school community to once again articulate the unique purpose of the schools and challenges the Church to reaffirm the need for Catholic education.[22] Jack Calareso[23] asks superintendents to recapture the Catholic identity of the schools. O'Gorman[24] suggests a need for criteria to evaluate the Catholic identity. The discussion of Catholic identity is one of the five major topics planned for the National Congress on Catholic Schools for the 21st Century. The mixed reviews about the viability of Catholic identity suggest the problem may well rest beyond the schools. The question of what it means to be Catholic twenty-five years after Vatican II has diverse answers. Catholic identity in the broader Catholic community is an issue which affects the schools but one which may not be able to be solved by the schools alone.

The other area of serious concern is one of financing the schools. The challenge is multifaceted. More money is needed; much of it to assure a just wage for the teaching staff. Yet raising tuition brings the problem of affordability and availability for low and moderate income families. Development programs promising financial aid seem like one answer. The bishops' hope to establish a national development office could help overcome the difficulties small and/or poor schools would have to generate the human resources and capital needed to start such efforts. Schools will have to study governance issues very carefully when money is given from new kinds of donors.

There are other questions. Staffing, leadership, support (which was not missing in an earlier, poorer time), and governance for new configurations are also serious subject matter. Not content to suffer problems, national leaders are addressing the issues in forums which include educators across the nation. In sum, an accurate and hopeful assessment of Catholic education is offered by Michael J. Guerra,

> A realistic appraisal of the current status of Catholic schools must acknowledge the presence of both darkness and light, but their future can still be shaped by the wisdom, courage and capacity for collaboration that the present leadership brings to its work. Some look at today's dim light and call it twilight, but others see it as dawn. In either case, this is a good time to light new fires.[25]

Endnotes

1. McBride, "Major Challenges Facing Catholic Education in the 1980's." *Momentum* 13 (December 1982): 10-11.

2. U.S. Department of Education, Office of Educational Research and Improvement, *Projection of Education Statistics to 2001 An Update*. Washington DC, December 1990, pp. 119-20.

3. Brigham, F. H., *United States Catholic Elementary and Secondary Schools 1990-91. Annual Statistical Report on Schools, Enrollment and Staffing*. Washington, DC: National Catholic Educational Association 1991. p. 10.

4. *Ibid.*, pp. 14-20.

5. Coleman, J. S., Hoffer, T., and Kilgore, S. *High School Achievement: Public, Catholic, and Private Schools Compared.* New York: Basic Books, 1982.

6. Lee, V. E. 1983-84 *National Assessment of Educational Progress Reading Proficiency: Catholic School Results and National Averages.* Washington DC: National Catholic Educational Association, 1985.
    Lee, V. E. 1983-84 *National Assessment of Educational Progress Writing Proficiency: Catholic School Results and National Averages.* Washington DC: National Catholic Educational Association, 1987.
    Lee, V. E. and Stewart, C. *National Assessment of Educational Progress Proficiency in Mathematics and Science* 1985-86: *Catholic and Public Schools Compared.* Washington, DC: National Catholic Educational Association, 1989.
    Marks, H. M. and Lee, V. E., *National Assessment of Educational Progress Proficiency in Reading* 1985-86: *Catholic and Public Schools Compared.* Washington, DC: National Catholic Educational Association, 1989.

7. Coleman and Kilgore, *High School Achievement.*
    Coleman, J. S. and Hoffer, T. *Public and Private High Schools: The Impact of Communities.* New York: Basic Books, 1987, pp. 199-208, 118-49.

8. The National Center for Educational Statistics commissioned five papers on the data produced by the longitudinal study *High School and Beyond* in 1980. *Public, Catholic and Private Schools* by Coleman, Hoffer and Kilgore (see endnote 5) was available in draft form in 1981. The editorial board of the *Harvard Educational Review* sponsored a colloquium on this paper. The entire issue of the November 1981 *Harvard Educational Review* presented the critique of the research. *Harvard Educational Review*, Vol. 51, No. 4, November 1981.

9. Greeley, A. M. *Catholic High Schools and Minority Students.* New Brunswick, N.J.: Transaction Books, 1982, pp. 53-56.

10. Guerra, M. J., Donahue, M. J. and Benson, P., *The Heart of the Matter: Effects of Catholic High Schools on Student Values, Beliefs and Behaviors.* Washington, DC: National Catholic Educational Association, 1990.

11. Convey, J. J. "Encouraging Findings about Students' Religious Values." *Momentum* 15 (February 1984): 47-49.

12. Chubb, J. E. and Moe, T. M. *Politics, Markets and America's Schools.* Washington, DC: The Brookings Institute, 1990, pp. 26-68.

13. Bauch, P. A. "Can Poor Parents Make Wise Educational Choices?" in Boyd, W. L. and Cibulka, J. G. (Eds.) *Private Schools and Public Policy: International Perspectives.* Philadelphia, PA. Falmer Press, 1989, pp. 285-313.

14. Evidence of this trend can be found in the convention program for the annual National Catholic Educational Association conventions starting in 1985.

15. Hall, Suzanne E., "The dangerous journey through opportunity to transformation." *Momentum* 19 (September 1988): 12.

16. *Ibid.*

17. All references to the U.S. Bishops letter are from "U.S. Bishops' Meeting, Support for Catholic Schools." *Origins*, 29 November 1990, pp. 401-04.

18. Seadler, P. *National Congress for Catholic Schools for the 21st Century; An Overview.* Washington, DC: National Catholic Educational Association, 1990, p. 1.

19. *Ibid.*, p. 1.

20. The full text of all the papers are available from the National Catholic Educational Association. Washington, D.C.

21. Greeley, Andrew M. "The Touchstone: Catholic Schools." *The Catholic Myth: The Behavior and Beliefs of American*

Catholics. New York: Charles Scribner's Sons, 1990, pp. 162-81.

22. Bernardin, Joseph Cardinal. "Catholic Schools: Opportunities and Challenges." *Chicago Studies* 28 (November 1989): 211-16.

23. Calareso, Jack P. "Only If Superintendents Exert Strong Leadership in the 1990s Will Catholic Schools Realize Their Promise in the 21st Century," *Momentum* 20 (April 1989): 14-17.

24. O'Gorman, Robert T. "Catholic Education and Identity: The Future in LIght of the Past." *Momentum* 19 (September 1988): 18-21.

25. Guerra, Michael J., *Lighting New Fires: Catholic Schooling in America 25 Years After Vatican II.* Washington, DC: National Catholic Educational Association, 1991, p. 30.

Bibliographic Entries

444. "The Answers to Your Textbook Questions: A Dialogue Between Educators & Publishers," *Today's Catholic Teacher*, 24 January 1991, pp. 12-14, 16, 18.

Records questions and answers between Catholic school educators and publishers discussing the development of a basic textbook series and why it is a lengthy and expensive process. Talks about research of content, the current state and local curriculum guidelines, and the market-response. Notes the contemporary teachers' ability to evaluate textbooks and their role in textbook selection. Observes that the principal has the responsibility to make or cause decisions to be made, but it is the teacher who uses the book. States that the content of the series must reflect the values of the Catholic school.

445. Bauch, Patricia A. "Legacy of the 'Sister's Schools," *Momentum* 21 (September 1990): 23-27.

Recounts the emergence of recent scholarship concerning the role of women religious in the development of Catholic schools drawn from the chronicles and archives of their religious communities. Describes how the Sisters shaped a dynamic institutional force and discusses the characteristics they displayed -- a democratic pluralism, community and autonomy. States that these qualities and the Sisters' ethos of caring which became the context of Catholic schools distinguish the Catholic schools today.

446. Beaudoin, David M. "Catholic Identity of Elementary Schools in the United States." *Chicago Studies* 28 (November 1989): 303-19.

Focuses on the Catholic identity of elementary schools in the United States in relation to American cultural diversity. States that the Catholic school community discovers and creates its identity in carrying out the Church's mission of evangelization and in the process of integrating education and the Gospel values. Discusses cultural diversity and the Catholic Church in the United States, American culture and Catholic schools, and believes that the American and Catholic values which foster the dignity of the person and community must be experienced in the life of the Catholic schools in order for them to survive.

447. Bernardin, Joseph Cardinal. "Catholic Schools: Opportunities and Challenges." *Chicago Studies* 28 (November 1989): 211-16.

Reflects on Catholic education in the Archdiocese of Chicago listing the necessary ingredients for success and identifies three challenges to Catholic education in the United States as it enters the 1990's. Puts forth the challenge of articulating the unique purpose of Catholic schools, the challenge to the Church to reaffirm the need for Catholic education which will require experimenting with models of Catholic schools, and the final challenge of making sacrifices necessary to preserve Catholic schools that are helping young people choose values that are for life. Describes the visionary leadership, effective marketing, and recruitment as necessary components for the continuance of strong and viable Catholic schools.

448. Bernardin, Joseph Cardinal. "Chicago Parish and School Closing/Consolidations Announced," *Origins*, 19, 1 February 1990, pp. 565, 567-71.

Gives the text of Cardinal Bernardin's address on January 22, 1990, to the pastors of the Chicago Archdiocese and the directors of archdiocesan agencies concerning the plan to ensure greater financial stability and to "reshape the Church in Chicago to meet the needs of a new decade and, indeed, a new millenium." Reflects on the decisions to close parishes, missions and schools touching on the areas of parish revenues and money management, Catholic grammar schools, parish assessments, parish consolidations and closures. Exhorts his people to join with him in enduring "today's pain for a better tomorrow..." and notes that change is a sign of life.

449. Berninger, Joan M. and Roy C. Rodriguez. "The Principal as Catalyst in Parental Involvement," *Momentum* 20 (April 1989): 32-34.

Advocates the expansion of the traditional role of the parents in the Catholic school to include citizen advocacy and shared decision making. Regards the principal as the leader who must integrate parents into the school's educational task pointing out that parent involvement is recognized as a primary educational ingredient of effective schools. Demonstrates the ways that the principal can help parents participate in an effective partnership and help teachers involve parents in the education of their children.

450. Bevilacqua, Anthony. "Catholic Schools in the 21st Century," *Origins*, 19, 16 November 1989, pp. 396-400.

Addresses Catholic educators concerning Catholic schools and their leadership role in American society. Delineates five challenges Catholic educators face as they prepare for the 21st century: 1) believing in the resurrection of the Catholic schools after the dying; 2) the cultivating of leadership in young people; 3) having the courage to believe in the value of Catholic schools; 4) achieving an interdependence working with parents, the wider Catholic community and corporate communities; and 5) becoming more effective Catholic communities of lived faith.

451. Brittan, Steve and Marie Chaminade. "Educational Funding: Are You Getting Your Fair Share? Funding for Teachers, Students, & Parents," *Today's Catholic Teacher*, 23, May/June 1990, pp. 20-29.

Puts together a special educational funding section which provides basic information about the federal, state, and local programs that are available. Notes that it is a long-time process to get the funding and it requires persistence and expertise. Explains Chapter 1 funding of the reauthorized Educational Consolidation and Improvement Act (ECIA), Chapter II of the Elementary Secondary Education Act of 1988 and Title II which provides funds for enhancing math and science education. Includes sources of help and a chart of state benefits showing materials, funds, and services that each state makes available to students attending nonpublic schools.

452. Buetow, Harold A. *The Catholic School: Its Roots, Identity, and Future.* (item 2).

453. Buetow, Harold A. *A History of United States Catholic Schooling.* (item 46).

454. Byron, William J. "Needed: A New Educational Partnership Between Government and Families." Paper Presented at the Annual Meeting of the National Catholic Educational Association (New Orleans, LA, April 20-23, 1987).

Declares that Catholic schools serve both Church and state and they deserve support from both. Enjoins Catholic families to exercise their rights as citizens to influence their government's education policies and proposes financial options: 1) educational savings accounts with tax advantages; 2) IRAs modified by law to permit early spending without penalty; 3) education vouchers; 4) tuition tax credits; 5) teacher tax credits; 6) family credits when one spouse stays home to assist in the children's education; 7) improved student financial aid; and 8) double tax deductibility for donations to private schools. Expresses the need for a new educational partnership between government and families.

455. Calareso, Jack P. (John Peter). "Only If Superintendents Exert Strong Leadership in the 1990s Will Catholic Schools Realize Their Promise in the 21st Century." *Momentum* 20 (April 1989): 14-17.

Calls for the superintendents of Catholic school systems to exert the leadership needed in addressing the vital issues facing Catholic education. Declares the challenges for superintendents are: to be concerned about recapturing the Catholic identity of the schools, to be willing to invest in future leaders and work with leaders in higher education, to foster a spirit of cooperation and collaboration, and to lead Catholic schools in global awareness. Comments that the superintendents must be the leaders of leaders.

456. Calareso, John Peter. "The Rationale for the Choice of Catholic Elementary and Secondary Schools by Administrators, Teachers and Parents." Ph.D. dissertation. Marquette University, 1989.

Delineates why administrators and teachers minister in Catholic schools and why parents send their children to Catholic schools in today's world. Analyzes research findings which indicate that for administrators the most important factor for choice of Catholic schools is a combination of quality of academic education and faith formation; for teachers

and parents quality of academic education is the most important factor. Concludes that Catholic schools are more highly
valued for their academic excellence; lay teachers with no or
little Catholic school experience are increasing; and there is a
dichotomy of values and understanding relative to the mission
or purpose of Catholic schools.

457. Campbell, James R. and Thomas Carney. "The Achilles Heel
of Catholic Education," *Momentum* 18 (November 1987):
24-26.

Comments on the failure of Catholic educators to use the
data available to them from recent studies to develop programs for the gifted and talented in Catholic schools. Examines the underlying issues that precluded such programs in the
past. Rejects the idea that they are expensive and believes the
compelling reason is the traditional one of not making too
much of oneself. Contends that goal-orientation and self-ac-
tualization are ideas appropriate today and critical thinking
strategies are essential.

458. *The Catholic High School: A National Portrait*. Washington,
DC: National Catholic Educational Association, 1985.

Presents the data obtained from the responses of American Catholic high school principals surveyed in 1983 by the
National Catholic Educational Association. Creates a com-
posite of the resources, programs, facilities, personnel, and
policies of Catholic high schools and examines how they may
vary by gender, composition, size, governance and percentage
of students from low-income families. Describes the study as
a unique, quantitative, national sample of Catholic high
schools. Includes appendices containing a list of project con-
sultants, a survey instrument and national data, as well as significant achievements in Catholic schools.

459. *The Catholic High School Teacher: Building on Research*.
Washington, DC: National Catholic Educational Association,
1987.

Contains the proceedings of a symposium based upon the study "Sharing the Faith: the Beliefs and Values of Catholic High School Teachers," held at Fordham University at Lincoln Center, March 5-7, 1987. Includes a consensus statement that comprises assumptions, issues concerning the purpose of the Catholic high school, staffing, and recommendations. Provides the texts of three major papers: "Mindsets: A Way of Talking About Catholic High School Teachers" by John S. Nelson; "The Self-Understanding of Catholic Secondary Teachers" by Zeni Fox; and "Building Responsive Catholic Schools: The Need for a Comprehensive, Long Range Diocesan Effort in the Religious Development of Catholic High School Teachers and Administrators" by Robert J. Starratt. Includes responses from four Catholic high school teachers.

460. *Catholic High Schools: Their Impact on Low-Income Students.* Washington, DC: National Catholic Educational Association, 1986.

Continues the study of Catholic high schools in the United States (item 458) surveying low-income students and their teachers. Gives a background to the Church's commitment to educating the poor and profiles five low-income serving schools comparing them to other Catholic schools and finding them comparable in the four areas of school climate: dimensions of faith community, morals, academic emphasis, and discipline. Discusses students' views of family, school and use of time, their religious beliefs, attitudes, and behaviors. Examines students' life skills and teachers' perspectives on teaching in low-income schools. Addresses the educational outcomes and makes recommendations that would strengthen and preserve low-income Catholic schools.

461. "Catholic Schools: Confronting Challenges of the Future," *Origins,* 20, 27 September 1990, pp. 260-63.

Comprises the pastoral statement of the Ohio bishops of the Latin and Eastern rites reflecting on the history of the Catholic schools and the present challenges facing them. Focuses on the agenda for future action and states that Catholic schools must remain among the poor and remain available to middle-class and prosperous Catholics. Discusses the need for restructuring and for finding new resources for the schools in order to keep pace academically, to build, and to compensate teachers and administrators adequately. Places responsibility for the Catholic schools on all Catholics noting that they are a heritage and must remain a legacy for future generations.

462. *Catholic Secondary Education: Now and in the Future. A Seminar.* Washington, DC: National Catholic Educational Association, 1982.

Records the keynote and major addresses of a seminar on Catholic secondary education held at the University of Dayton in June 1982. Centers around the topics concerning what makes Catholic schools Catholic, collection and data sharing, new educational technologies, the curriculum, teacher and administrator development, the Catholic high schools relationship to the larger Church structure, and assessment of the effectiveness of the religious education programs.

463. *Catholic Secondary Schools and Colleges: Renewing the Partnership.* Proceedings of the Symposium on Secondary School-College Collaboration, Anaheim, California, April 3-5, 1986. Washington, DC: National Catholic Educational Association, 1987.

Explains the history and process which culminated in the symposium on the collaborative partnership of Catholic secondary schools and Catholic colleges and universities. Incorporates the four papers presented at the conference reflecting mission, vision, leadership, and curriculum: 1) "The Mission of the Catholic High School and the Catholic College, 1986" by the Bishop of Oakland, John S. Cummins; 2) "Catholic Secondary Schools and Colleges: Renewing the Vision" by Michael J. Guerra; 3) "Leadership: Twenty-First Century Style" by Mary D. Griffin, Christine Fritz, Marla Loehr, and August Rakoczy; and 4) "Catholic Secondary Schools and

Colleges: Partnership in a Continuous Curriculum" by Sister
Mary Peter Traviss.

464. Coleman, James S. "Social Capital and the Development of
Youth." *Momentum* 18 (November 1987): 6-8.

Discusses the major points of the research conducted and
published in *Public and Private High Schools: The Impact of
Communities* (item 465) and examines the effects of communities constituting "social capital" which supports and con-
strains young people in high school. Indicates that the
Catholic schools have a body of social capital that is a natural
support community and believes that Catholic school students
take more standard math, English, and history courses because
of the social capital presence.

465. Coleman, James S. and Thomas Hoffer. *Public and Private
High Schools: The Impact of Communities.* New York: Basic
Books, Inc., 1987.

Extends the research on achievement published in 1982 in
*High School Achievement: Public, Catholic, and Private
Schools Compared* and studies the functioning of the school
as an institution in a changing social structure. Examines the
educational institutions of the public and the private schools
which have different goals and are designed differently. Shows
how these different orientations have implications for the effect of schools on young people. Discusses the concept of social capital in school and communities and how it affects
school functioning. Finds that the results of the study have
implications related to the social context of the schools.

466. Convey, John J. "Implications of the Functional Community
for Catholic School Parents." *Momentum* 18 (November
1987): 14-15.

Agrees with the findings of the Coleman and Hoffer study
that it is the community of the Catholic school that makes it
effective, expanding on the school as a functional community

which provides norms and values and facilitates social relations. Explains how a strong functional community is formed from the religious nature of the school, the commitment of the teachers, and the values of the parents under the leadership of an effective principal. Demonstrates that the parents' full involvement in the functioning community of the school contributes to the greatest good of their children.

467. Coreil, Judith. "AIDS: A Catholic Educational Approach," *Today's Catholic Teacher*, 23, September 1989, pp. 52-53.

Recommends the NCEA teaching manual on AIDS (item 502) and discusses what teachers in Catholic schools or parish religious centers should consider as they prepare to instruct students about AIDS. Outlines concepts to be lived and developed by the teacher and addresses the objectives of a lesson: correct knowledge of the Church's teaching; skills for decision-making and handling peer pressure; and attitudes and values. States the importance of using a collaborative approach with parents noting that the NCEA manual advises asking parent approval before instruction is given.

468. Daues, Margaret A. "The Modern Catholic Teacher: A Role Analysis in the Post-Vatican Schools." Ph.D. dissertation. Fordham University, 1983.

Defines the role of the teacher in the contemporary Catholic school identifying and analyzing the expectations held for the Catholic school teacher by educators, parish clergy, board members, and parents. Attempts to determine any differences between and among the respondent group regarding three teacher roles: traditional, emergent, and enduring. Finds that educators identify with the emergent teacher role indicating assimilation of Vatican II directives. Explains how parents relate to the traditional teacher role and how the clergy identifies with both the pre-Vatican II and the post-Vatican II teacher roles. Makes recommendations for staff development, the total school community, the pastor's role, non-Catholic families, the contemporary teacher role, and for further research.

469. Deedy, John. "Are Catholic-School Days Numbered?" *U.S. Catholic* 53 (September 1988): 6-13.

Describes the state of the Catholic schools in the United States noting the lack of new schools and discusses the reasons ranging from demographics to faculties to money and defeatist attitudes. Discusses how Catholics perceive the Catholic schools' effectiveness and importance and their willingness to make sacrifices to enroll their children in a Catholic school. Tells of the construction of two new parish schools in the Diocese of Orlando, Florida, citing four elements involved: growth, demand, enthusiasm and support. States that the ultimate issue may be to believe that Catholics can build new schools if they really want to.

470. Dolan, Jay P. "Schools." (item 55).

471. Doyle, Michelle L. "To the 'Kids Who Are Different'." 21 *Momentum* (April 1990): 64-67.

Speaks to the needs of the disabled learners in the classroom. Develops a process for defining the problems of learning disabled students and for finding solutions that will allow the child to continue in Catholic education. Examines the role of the classroom teacher whose understanding and commitment are key to the effectiveness of the process. Recognizes the feelings and needs of the parents and the necessity to work cooperatively with them.

472. Dunlap, Jan. "Catholic Schools: The Shape of Things to Come," *St. Anthony Messenger*, 96, April 1989, pp. 8-13.

Examines what is happening today in Catholic schools as they seek to respond to the changing needs and circumstances of the American Catholic community. Sees the need to examine purpose and goals which shape the identity and functions of the school and the need to evaluate the way in which the Catholic schools are structured and financed. Discusses the components of development, the importance of the mission statement and explains how changing demographics add to planning problems. Asserts that creative leadership is the key to any successful school strategy and that Catholic schools must reshape themselves in order to remain viable in the twenty-first century.

473. Finley, Mitch. "Catholics Should Demand Tuition Vouchers." *U.S. Catholic* 56 (March 1991): 14-19.

Advocates that Catholics be willing to fight for tuition vouchers if they believe in their basic fairness. Confronts the opposition and maintains that the idea behind tuition vouchers is widespread throughout American society since it is third-party payment for social services. Provides a "Feedback" section which gives the comments of a representative sample of subscribers. Shows that a decided majority of readers believe that tuition vouchers do not violate the principle of separation of church and state, that they would eventually improve education for all, and that Catholics have a duty to fight for tuition vouchers.

474. Gary, Barbara Stewart. *Seeking Foundation Grants*. Washington, DC: National Catholic Educational Association, 1985.

Explains the process for seeking grants from foundations providing step-by-step suggestions for Catholic school administrators and development directors. Explains the types of foundations, how to approach them, and how to write a proposal and package it. Includes appendices with two sample proposals and information on the Foundation Center.

475. Gilbert, John R. *Pastor as Shepherd of the School Community*. Washington, DC: National Catholic Educational Association, 1983.

Reflects on the image of the American Catholic pastor as the shepherd, the person who cares for his school community, and focuses on concerns about this aspect of the pastoral ministry. Discusses consulting with the parishioners, shared ministry and decision-making, and outlines the respective roles of pastor and principal. Treats the relationship of the school to the total parish community working with parental groups and school boards. Expresses as important concerns the quality in worship with children and keeping up with the current research on Catholic education and religious educational trends. Places finances at the end believing that they must follow other concerns, not precede them.

476. Glatthorn, Allan A. and Carmel Regina Shields. *Differentiated Supervision for Catholic Schools.* Washington, DC: National Catholic Educational Association, 1983.

Presents an approach to supervision of classroom instruction in Catholic schools offering four supervisory options predicated on a special Christian vision of the child, the school, the curriculum, the teacher and the supervisory relationship. Discusses the clinical supervision for beginning teachers; collaborative professional development in which teachers work together for mutual improvement; self-directed development for mature, autonomous teachers; and administrative monitoring, an informal supervision of the instructional staff. Describes strategies for implementing the differentiated program.

477. Gnirk, Lloyd A. "The Role of the Chief Administrator in Development." Paper Presented at the 83rd Annual Convention, Exposition, and Religious Education Congress (March 31-April 3, 1986).

Sees development as a vital ministry of the Catholic Church and an integral part of the ministry of Catholic education developing people and helping them to grow. Discusses the qualities of a successful development program: quality Catholic education, sound business management, and effective public relations -- and explains how these characteristics attract people and funds. Demonstrates the importance of the chief administrator responsible for the development program both internally within the school community and externally involving alumni, business corporations, foundations and individuals who perceive a positive image of the school. Emphasizes the goal of the ministry of development to bring Christ to people and people to Christ.

478. Greeley, Andrew M. *Catholic High Schools and Minority Students.* (item 405).

479. Greeley, Andrew M. "The Touchstone: Catholic Schools." *The Catholic Myth: The Behavior and Beliefs of American Catholics.* New York: Charles Scribner's Sons, 1990, pp. 162-81.

Looks at the evidence in six projects and many books that show the success and worth of Catholic schools and recounts the opposition to them despite the evidence. Describes the effectiveness of Catholic schools but considers them a casualty of the era following the Vatican II Council. Discusses the findings of the 1988 General Social Survey of the National Opinion Research Center (NORC) and claims that all criticisms aimed at the Catholic schools are an "...example par excellence of the Catholic communal ethos and the Sacramental Imagination at work." States that the Catholic leadership does not appear to be as committed to Catholic schools as it was before the Council.

480. Hall, Suzanne E., ed. *Challenging Gifted Students in the Catholic Schools.* Washington, DC: National Catholic Education Association, 1985.

Offers Catholic educators information, curricular ideas and resources to enable them to reach out to gifted children in Catholic schools responding to their needs with understanding and commitment. Explains the meanings of "giftedness" through a matching chart and develops goals for the school, classroom, person, and the community. Discusses the assessment process of referral, screening, and identification and stresses that the evaluation of the gifted must address high levels of development rather than acquisition of skills.

481. Hall, Suzanne (E) and Carleen Reck, editors. *Integral Education: A Response to the Hispanic Presence.* Washington, DC: National Catholic Educational Association, 1987.

Assists Catholic ministers and educators in understanding and responding to the needs of their Hispanic students and families and is the result of a series of hearings sponsored by NCEA which revealed that the Hispanic people want to have their children educated in Catholic schools but cannot pay the tuition and do not experience acceptance of their culture, language, and religious expression. Sets forth a model of education that not only fulfills the five purposes of bilingual education but also offers an "Integral Education," a term coined by the Hispanic Encuentro. Concludes that American Catholic schools are in a position to expand programs that would respond to Hispanic students in teaching methodology, personal/cultural support, language assistance and administrative awareness.

482. Hawker, James and Thea Bowman. *The Non-Catholic in the Catholic School.* Washington, DC: National Educational Association, 1984.

Considers in two articles the nature, mission and responsibility of the Catholic school which must be viewed in its relation to the Church. Discusses in "Schools as an Evangelizing Community: Guidelines Regarding Teacher, Pupils, Parents" by James Hawker, principles concerning the non-Catholic teacher in the Catholic school, the non-Catholic pupil in the Catholic school, and the non-Catholic parents and the Catholic school. States that the school must be a community of faith where an evangelizing and catechizing ministry is being fulfilled. Contains in the second article "Religious and Cultural Variety: Gift to Catholic Schools" by Sister Thea Bowman, a personal reflection on attending a Catholic school as a non-Catholic and stresses how the presence of a non-Catholic in Catholic schools can help children to learn and appreciate other religions and cultures.

483. Hennessy, Rose Marie, edited by Thomas C. O'Brien. *Principal as Prophet*. Washington, DC: National Catholic Educational Association, 1983.

Presents four papers supporting the prophetic concept of the Catholic school principal's leadership in the Church: "Principal as Prophet" by Sister Rose Marie Hennessy, "Guidelines for Reflection for Catholic School Principals" by Sister Mary James Merrick, "Guidelines for Diocesan Office Personnel" by Brother Dominic Berardelli, and "Guidelines for Parish Directors of Religious Education" by Thomas Smith. Suggests the special calling for the principal citing Old and New Testament passages in support of the concepts. Relates how the diocesan office personnel can help the principal spread the Christian message and discusses the role of the DRE (Director of Religious Education) whose work is also that of a prophet.

484. Hughes, Jane Wolford and Mary Lynch Barnds. *Partners in Catholic Education: Pastor, Professional, Parent: A Workbook for Leaders in Education*. Washington, DC: National Catholic Educational Association, 1989.

Develops a workshop format designed to help those who have a direct leadership role in the educational life of the parish. Describes and analyzes the present situation developing workable strategies for future planning. Provides readings on change, partnership/collaboration, community, and values. Maintains that the philosophy and methods of the workbook will help to bring about organizational changes that will increase effectiveness through partnership and collaboration.

485. Hunt, Thomas C. and Norlene M. Kunkel. (item 65).

486. *In Support of Catholic Elementary and Secondary Schools*. Statement of the United States Catholic Bishops. Washington, DC: United States Catholic Conference, November 1990.

Affirms the principles set forth in the pastoral letter of 1972, *To Teach as Jesus Did*, and commits to goals for 1997, the pastoral's twenty-fifth anniversary: 1) to continue the high quality of education in Catholic schools; 2) to ensure the availability of Catholic schools; 3) to undertake new initiatives for securing sufficient financial assistance; and 4) to assure that the salaries and benefits of Catholic teachers and administrators reflect the teachings expressed in *Economic Justice for All*. Expresses commitment to the accomplishment of the goals and acknowledges and affirms the total education provided by Catholic schools. Calls upon all to sustain and expand this ministry of the Church.

487. Janosik, Maryann Kathleen. "Propagating the Faith: Catholic Educational Policy Making in Post-Vatican II Cleveland." Ph.D. dissertation. Case Western Reserve University, 1989.

Examines the impact of Vatican II on education policymakers in Cleveland considering the Cleveland diocesan school system as representative of the larger issues and conflicts facing Catholic schools in the United States. Divides the study into two parts identifying national issues of concern to Catholic schools in Part One -- lay teacher status, racism, and human rights. Explores in Part Two how Cleveland's Catholic educational leaders addressed the issues of larger lay staff, black students enrolled in Catholic schools, and the human relations policy which solidified the post-Vatican II movement toward ecumenism.

488. John Paul II, Pope. "The Pope's Address to Teachers," *Origins*, 17, 8 October 1987, pp. 279-81.

Records the words of Pope John Paul II addressed to Catholic educators in New Orleans on September 12, 1987 during his pilgrimage to the United States. Speaks of the rights and duties of parents in the education of their children and the increasing role of lay people as administrators and teachers in Catholic schools. Encourages Catholic teachers to continue providing quality Catholic education to the poor and calls for justice and fairness in all matters. Points out the challenge of understanding Catholic identity in education and discusses the opportunity open to educators to inculcate correct ethical attitudes and values in young people. Exhorts Catholic educators to take Jesus Christ the teacher as their model.

489. Kealey, Robert J. "Collision Course: Clergy and Laity on Catholic Schools." *Chicago Studies* 28 (November 1989): 277-91.

Contrasts the views of clergy and laity concerning Catholic schools placing them in an historical context and within the framework of the pronouncements of the Vatican and the American hierarchy. Ascertains clerical attitudes from informal observations reported by Catholic school principals who indicate that many priests are unfavorably inclined toward Catholic schools, and from formal research studies that show clergy to be in favor of Catholic schools on a theoretical level but their support wanes when finances are the issue. Considers the current trends that indicate renewed interest by the laity in Catholic schools and discusses a parallel rather than collision course with priests and laity working together as partners sharing decision-making responsibilities.

490. Kealey, Robert J. *Curriculum in the Catholic School.* Washington, DC: National Catholic Educational Association, 1985.

Explains the instructional program of a Catholic school describing the learning process and all aspects of the curriculum from the content to the personnel who implement it. Discusses the characteristics of a Catholic school that shape curriculum development: sponsorship, philosophy of education, goals, total educational programs, academic quality, and values development. Details practical steps for developing the curriculum and examines the role of the teacher in implementing it. Reviews the principal's responsibilities in developing and implementing the curriculum and taking care of the needs of the personnel involved. Appends a textbook evaluation instrument and provides suggestions for study.

491. Kealey, Robert J., and Carleen Reck, editors. *Directions for Justice/Peace Education in the Catholic Elementary School.* Washington, DC: National Catholic Educational Association, 1985.

   Clarifies approaches for integrating the teaching of justice and peace education into the Catholic elementary school curriculum, attempts to increase understanding and to implement faculty development for teaching justice/peace education. Outlines options appropriate for the Catholic elementary school in deciding the school's direction toward justice/peace education. Sets forth principles for assessing a school's progress as a peaceful and just institution and provides questions and references for educators who wish to work toward a social analysis of the Catholic school.

492. Lynch, Robert. "The Climate of Choice in American Education," *Origins*, 20, 15 November 1990, pp. 373-77.

   Analyzes the climate in America today for choice in education and the chances such choice would have for legislative success. Discusses four constitutional considerations: 1) We live in litigious times; 2) The Aguilar vs. Felton opinion has precluded private school students from receiving equitable statutory benefits from Chapter 1 programs; 3) There are state constitutional issues to be confronted; and 4) Changes in membership of the Supreme Court over recent years are important. Emphasizes the necessity for new approaches that will win public support and judicial approval and believes that the state legislature holds more promise than Washington.

493. McCready, William C. "Catholic Schools and Catholic Identity: 'Stretching the Vital Connection'." *Chicago Studies* 28 (November 1989): 217-31.

   Examines "Catholic identity," its development and two most important supports, the parochial school system and the Catholic family. Describes the questionable strength of these supports today stating that Catholic identity is no longer tied to an institution but to a Catholic culture. Shows that the parochial schools help to maintain functional communities which address issues having cultural meaning and states that without Catholic schools the collective ability to address important value-oriented issues is impaired. Finds no strong Church leadership supporting the rationale for Catholic schools and contends that failure to meet the challenge of their growth and survival will severely handicap generations to come.

494. McDermott, Edwin J. *Distinctive Qualities of the Catholic School.* (item 23).

495. Mahany, Barbara. "The Rugged Devotion of Teachers in Catholic Schools." *U.S. Catholic* 49 (September 1984): 30-35.

Recounts stories of commitment and dedication of parochial school teachers despite the low pay and extracurricular loads noting that love, religious commitment and academic excellence are the characteristics that motivate them. Relates how some Catholic school teachers could not afford to stay and says that if teachers must leave the Catholic schools because of financial circumstances, excellent veteran educators will continue to be lost to the Catholic school system.

496. Malone, James. "Hopes for Catholic Schools in the '90s," *Origins*, 20, 27 December 1990, pp. 468-71.

States in an address by the Bishop of Youngstown, Ohio, that Catholic education must be continued and must be strengthened. Examines the intangible decision made within the Church that Catholic education is no longer as high a priority as it was in the past. Focuses on the future of Catholic education voicing the hope that the community of faith will support Church ministries more adequately and discusses ways to realize this hope. Regards the rediscovery of Christian enthusiasm about the faith to be most important.

497. Malone, James. "The Religious Dimension of Catholic Education." *Chicago Studies* 28 (November 1989): 264-76.

Meditates on the meaning of *The Religious Dimension of Education in a Catholic School* (item 515) reflecting on Catholic education in the United States in the light of the challenges posed by the Vatican document. Addresses two problematic areas which compromise the Catholic schools' ability to achieve the objectives discussed: parental insecurity regarding their role as the primary religious educators of their children; and teachers in Catholic schools who are either not Catholics or are not active Catholics. Mentions ways to assist parents to assume their proper role and maintains that there must be criteria for hiring faculty to ensure that the religious dimension of the Catholic schools can be effectively carried out. Says it is time to make a decision about the future of Catholic education in the United States.

498. Manno, Bruno V. "Catholic School Educators: Providing Leadership for the Education Reform Movement." *The Living Light* 25 (October 1988): 7-12.

Contends that Catholic school educators should be involved in the current education reform movement and discusses the seven major issues on the reform agenda: choice and diversity, school organization, productivity and accountability, the curricula of the home, the teaching of content, development of character and democratic values, and improving and enhancing the profession. Considers the educational reform movement to be a special opportunity for Catholic school educators to learn from the reform discussions and to contribute to its continuing development.

499. Manno, Bruno V. "The Need to Share the Lessons of Social Capital." *Momentum* 18 (November 1987): 9-10.

Discusses the Coleman report *Public and Private High Schools: The Impact of Communities* with regard to educational reform examining the implications of the research on four elements of education: the choice of schooling in the best interest of the child; school organization with more decentralization and local autonomy; parent involvement in the education of their children; and teaching values and setting standards. Points out how Catholic school philosophy and practice are supported by the Coleman study and have much to contribute to the education reform movement.

500. Moran, Mary Louise. "Diocesan Policy for Catholic Schools in the Light of Catholic Social Teaching." Ph.D. dissertation. Fordham University, 1986.

Examines seven Catholic school policy manuals from dioceses covering various areas of the United States in order to determine the extent to which they correspond to three concepts of the Church's social teaching as expressed in contemporary Catholic social documents. Delineates the concepts: 1) that persons are central to an institution; 2) that persons have a right to integral development; and 3) that persons need to participate responsibly in the decisions that affect their lives. Finds that little clarity is shown about mission or objectives, community relations policies do not match the concept of faith community, and few provisions are made for co-responsibility and co-participation. Calls for the development of new policy strategies to institutionalize the Catholic social teaching on person, development, and participation.

501. Mutschler, Mary Jo. "Effective Catholic Schooling: An Organizational Analysis." Ph.D. dissertation, Fordham University, 1985.

Identifies characteristics of highly effective Catholic schools as the organizational system, the religious atmosphere, and the academic performance. Finds the principal's consultative-participative administrative style, team cooperation, decision making, goal emphasis, teachers' support and implementation, and communication with students are characteristics that differentiate the highly effective school from the effective school. Studies the perceptions of religious atmosphere noting that Church attendance influences the teachers, parents and students but religious affiliation does not. Indicates that in the highly effective Catholic school there is a strong correlation between principal and teacher perceptions of the organizational system of the school.

502. NCEA AIDS Education Task Force. *AIDS: A Catholic Educational Approach.* Washington, DC: National Catholic Educational Association, 1988.

Provides Catholic school teachers with educational tools needed for AIDS education addressing primarily the issues of HIV infection. Suggests lessons designed for use in Catholic schools as well as in parish catechetical programs and for developing attitudes, values, and skills through a planned sequence of learning opportunities. Includes a teacher's manual and a leader's guide.

503. National Center for Research in Total Catholic Education. *Effective Catholic Schools: An Exploration With a Special Focus on Catholic Secondary Schools.* Washington, DC: National Catholic Educational Association, 1984.

Summarizes the results of research into the effectiveness of Catholic Schools focusing on Catholic secondary schools with a substudy of the relationships between Catholic secondary and elementary schools. Analyzes the secondary schools in sections 1 through 5 describing their Catholic character, the curriculum and academic organization, the quality of the instruction, faculty roles and concerns, and student life. Reports on the elementary school in section 6 and devotes sections 7 and 8 to two major problems: finance and governance. Sees teachers as the strength of Catholic secondary schools and finds that the Catholic schools accomplish much with modest resources. Urges continuation of adaptation to change while maintaining a commitment to spiritual traditions.

504. O'Brien, John Stephen. *Mixed Messages: What Bishops & Priests Say About Catholic Schools.* Washington, DC: National Catholic Educational Association, 1987.

Presents the findings of the dissertation study in item 505 in a readable format with some screened sections in Chapters 3 through 7 that have information not related to all of the bishops and priests. Notes that the reader can skip these screened sections if interest is only in the major findings.

505. O'Brien, John Stephen. "A Study of the Perceptions of Bishops, Pastors, and Future Pastors Toward Catholic Schools." Ed.D. dissertation. Virginia Polytechnic Institute and State University, 1986.

Investigates how Roman Catholic bishops and priests perceive the value, effectiveness, funding practices and future structure of Catholic schools. Finds the majority of bishops and priests agree that Catholic schools play an essential role in the Church's mission and shows that the majority of both groups see them as generally satisfactory. Notes divergent views on financing the Catholic schools with more bishops than priests saying they should continue to be financed by the parish. Discovers that a large majority of the bishops think the Church should build new Catholic schools in the suburbs even if the schools have lay faculties, but priests are less interested in building new schools, especially with lay faculty. Makes suggestions for possible action that will help Catholic education.

506. O'Gorman, Robert T. "Catholic Education and Identity: The Future in Light of the Past." *Momentum* 19 (September 1988): 18-21.

Shows how a particular Catholic ethos in each of three historical periods affected the content and structure of Catholic education and explains the relationship between educational forms and identity. Looks at the characteristics of contemporary Catholicism which has developed pluralism in its means of education and has changed its understanding about an ideal model of education. Stresses the need for criteria to evaluate Catholic identity in education and discusses five characteristics or norms to guide the formation of identity:

sacramentality, critical awareness, tradition, authority, and community.

507. O'Neill, Michael. "An Agenda for the Future." *Momentum* 18 (May 1987): 55-58.

Advocates a consideration of the ownership and gover-nance of Catholic schools from professional religion to the total Catholic community and advances three arguments for change in the ownership structure of Catholic schools: a the-ological argument, a sociological or political argument, and a management effectiveness argument. Discusses each argument and points out that three happenings -- the new lay dominance in Catholic education, the renewed theology, and the new so-cioeconomic status of Catholics have changed the sociological and political scene. Asserts that the question of governance cannot be addressed without addressing ownership.

508. Parise, Michael. "Catholic Schools: Quo Vadis?" *The Priest*, 46, April 1990, pp. 31-34.

States that the identity of the Catholic school is found in the Church's mission to evangelize and as collaborators in evangelization, Catholic schools must become true settings for formation of Christian lives. Describes an eight-point plan of basic principles that can be implemented in Catholic parish schools: 1) Catholic schools must capitalize on their unique-ness; 2) The pastor is the director of Christian formation; 3) The principal is more than an administrator; 4) The principal is part of the leadership team of the parish; 5) Parish leaders need ongoing Christian formation; 6) Catholic schools need Christian formations groups; 7) The teacher is a key to the Christian formation of students' lives; 8) Formation for Christian life will lead to change.

509. Pejza, John P. "The Catholic School Principal: A Different Kind of Leader." Paper Presented at the Annual Meeting of the National Catholic Educational Association (St. Louis, MO, April 8-11, 1985).

Articulates the role of the Catholic high school principal who must provide both academic and religious leadership in order to have an effective Catholic school. Describes the challenge to establish unity among the faculty so that everyone works together without loose coupling and with commitment to the teaching apostolate of the Church. Shows how the Catholic principal must help to develop the school's distinctive Catholic culture and expands on the key elements to leadership of vision and inspiration. Notes that the Catholic high school principal's goal is to transform the school from an ordinary educational site into an effective faith community which is a center of Christian culture.

510. Perko, F. Michael. "Catholics and Their Schools From a Culturist Perspective." *New Catholic World* 230 (May-June 1987): 124-29.

Traces Catholic school development in an historical overview that shows how combining religion, ethnicity and culture provided the impetus for educational development. Describes the contemporary scene beginning with the decline of Catholic schooling from 1965 to 1975 and sees a disintegration in the ideology of American Catholicism in the form that it had from the 1950's to Vatican Council II. Raises questions about the future of Catholic schooling and finds the answers unclear. Looks at new markets for Catholic schools stating that for Catholic education to prosper it must also reflect the significant components of the culture. Believes that as long as American Catholics possess a "way of seeing" that differs from the mainstream, parochial schools will continue for the propagation of their culture.

511. Pitts, Arthur W. "What Would Mother Katharine Drexel Think of Pretty Eagle Catholic School's Evolution?" *Momentum* 20 (April 1989): 36-39.

Gives the personal account by the principal of Pretty Eagle Catholic elementary school located on an Indian reservation in Montana, of how he began to rebuild a Catholic identity by learning the Crow language and culture and thinking about the problems of Indian education. Talks of the school's history opening in 1887 as St. Xavier Mission School and becoming a public school during the mid 70's and early 80's. Describes what is happening in the school and the small successes with the track team that have given the students an opportunity to visit other schools off the reservation. States that people who believe in Catholic schools and those who believe in Native American Catholicism need each other.

512. Pollard, John E. "Government Funding: Whose Children Are They?" *Chicago Studies* 28 (November 1989): 292-302.

Summarizes the facts in the Aguilar v. Felton case (1985) in which the United States Supreme Court rendered a five-to-four decision holding unconstitutional the New York City program of educational assistance under Title I of the Elementary and Secondary Education Act of 1965 (ESEA) because it was provided to parochial school children on the premises of the parochial schools. Describes the effects of the decision on educationally deprived children from economically disadvantaged families. Regards the Court's perception of the religious identity of church-affiliated schools to be at issue and states that the Court consistently reduces religious identity to external, observable indications. Discusses how the fear of the government's excessive entanglement in the supervision of its own programs and personnel on church-sponsored school premises has severely limited the religious freedom of educationally deprived children.

513. *A Primer on Educational Governance in the Catholic Church.* (item 36).

514. Reck, Carleen and Judith Coreil. *Verifying the Vision: A Self-Evaluation Instrument for the Catholic Elementary School.* Washington, DC: National Catholic Educational Association, 1984.

Rates as a self-evaluation tool which provides for the assessment of a Catholic elementary school focusing on five major areas: philosophy, the Catholic school as community, the Catholic school in the community, the teaching/learning program and organizational services. Assists the school community to measure its growth towards its potential. Includes a guide for the coordinating consultant and for the visiting team, and discusses how to design and implement an improvement plan.

515. *The Religious Dimension of Education in a Catholic School: Guidelines for Reflection and Renewal.* Rome: The Congregation for Catholic Education, 1988.

Offers general guidelines to bishops, religious superiors and those in charge of Catholic schools to assist them in examining whether or not the *Declaration on Christian Education* promulgated by the Vatican Council in 1965 has become a reality. Explores the religious dimension of the school climate and school life and work. Discusses religious instruction in the classroom and the importance of the religion teacher, and states the need to promote the establishment of formation centers for lay teachers. Summarizes the religious dimension of the formation process as a whole and suggests further study, research, and experimentation in all areas affecting the religious dimension of education in Catholic schools.

516. Russo, Charles J. with John Olsen. "Catholic School Collective Bargaining Revisited." *Momentum* 21 (February 1990): 62-64.

Analyzes attitudes towards collective bargaining in Catholic secondary schools in New York State and finds today a greater clarity as to the role of religious and lay faculty members, noting that their relationship has become more collaborative. Finds that Catholic high school personnel, administrators and teachers are contending with problem solving, setting objectives and salary considerations, and are looking for alternatives to the current collective bargaining models in American education.

517. Sass, Edmund, S. Linda Kulzer, and Deanna Lamb. "Facing the Challenges to Teacher Education for Catholic Schools." *Momentum* 19 (February 1988): 32-34.

Considers the implications for Catholic education of two reports: *A Nation Prepared: Teachers for the 21st Century* by the Carnegie Corporation's Task Force on Teaching as a Profession, and *Tomorrow's Teacher: A Report of the Holmes Group*. States that Catholic educators must be prepared to deal with the potential impact of the challenge posed by the reports which recommend restructuring of teacher education to increase licensure standards for beginning teachers. Points out that Catholic colleges and universities must continue to be involved in teacher education and urges dialogue between the higher education teachers and Catholic school administrators and teachers.

518. Seadler, Paul. "Soaring Above the Dilemma." *Momentum* 22 (February 1991): 14-16.

Relates the news of the convening of the "National Congress on Catholic Schools for the 21st Century" by the National Catholic Educational Association, to be held November 6-10, 1991 in Washington, DC, "to celebrate and communicate the good news of Catholic schools." States that the ultimate purpose is to develop strategies that will ensure the continuation and expansion of Catholic schooling into the 21st century. Explains the five issues that will be considered and discussed: Catholic identity, Leadership, School and society, Governance and finance, and Public purpose. Notes that two white papers have been commissioned for each issue and expresses the hope that they will serve as catalysts for thought and discussion at regional meetings. Perceives that now is the acceptable time to celebrate Catholic education as a great gift to the Church and the nation.

519. Shaughnessy, Mary Angela. *Catholic Schools and the Law: A Guide for Teachers.* New York: Paulist Press, 1990.

Provides Catholic school teachers with a practical guide to the principles of school law telling them what they ought to know and helping them to assess how much they know with a legal pre-test. Discusses the kinds of law that affect Catholic schools and offers helpful advice on how to avoid lawsuits. Explains the importance of the faculty handbook as part of the teacher's contract and presents a list of "Ten Commandments for Teachers" which, if followed, will insure avoidance of legal problems.

520. Smutny, Joan Franklin. "Gifted Children Who Are They? & What Can We Do For Them?" *Today's Catholic Teacher*, 23, September 1989, pp. 26-29.

Focuses on the gifted and talented children in Catholic schools explaining how to identify them and support them through appropriate curricula, programs, activities and materials. Voices the importance of understanding the creatively gifted, performance gifted, and the leadership gifted, as well as the intellectually gifted and describes the characteristics of each. Tells of summer programs for children ranging from age 4 to grade 11.

521. Sweeney, Patricia James. "The Catholic Schools of the '80s," *Origins*, 17, 8 October 1987, pp. 277-79.

Presents an address given during Pope John Paul II's meeting with representatives of Catholic schools and religious educators in New Orleans on September 12, 1987. Reflects on Catholic education as a gift given and shared and discusses the role of Catholic teachers in creating and sustaining community. Recognizes the financial problems but states that Catholic teachers of today are reaching out to the future, yet not forgetting they are touched by their past.

522. Sweeney, Patricia James. "Coleman Revisited: Policy Implications for Catholic Educators." *Momentum* 18 (November 1987): 11-13.

> Examines the study *Public and Private High Schools: The Impact of Communities* by Coleman and Hoffer and finds it is supportive yet challenging for Catholic high schools. Offers insight into the findings and believes the functional community of the Catholic schools and the keeping of curriculum requirements that public schools moved away from in the 1970's are important reasons for Catholic school achievements. Explains the concepts of human and social capital introduced in the report and prompts principals to provide a climate within the school that creates social capital and to develop it among the parents strengthening their relationship with each other and with the school.

523. Thompson, Larry A. and John A. Flynn. *Effective Funding of Catholic Schools*. Kansas City, MO: Sheed & Ward, 1988.

> Provides help for Catholic school leadership in establishing a background in development, identifying priorities, and taking the necessary steps to accomplish financial objectives. Describes development as long-range, continuous and characterized by many activities. Discusses the development program, development efforts and development activities and details the ingredients needed for a successful recruitment effort as well as a successful alumni program. Explains the work of Omaha Development Institute which teaches leaders of Catholic schools how to generate funding through developmental activities.

524. Toale, Thomas E. "An Evaluation of Catholic Secondary Schools Within the Archdiocese of Dubuque, Iowa and Throughout the United States on Selected Quality and Quantity Indicators From 1966 to 1986." (item 381).

525. Traviss, Mary Peter. *Student Moral Development in the Catholic School*. (item 41).

526. "Why Catholic Schools Outperform All Others." *U.S. Catholic* 54 (July 1989): 6-12.

Interviews James S. Coleman concerning his research on public and private schools and asks twenty-one questions about the findings which indicate the success of Catholic schools.

527. Wilson, Charles H. "School Aid: Constitutional Issues After *Aguilar* v. *Felton.*" *Catholic Lawyer* 31 (1987): 82-89.

Examines the cases of *Grand Rapids School District* v. *Ball* and *Aguilar* v. *Felton* issued on July 1, 1985, and regards the decisions as a severe blow against the concept of equity in education for all children. States that both decisions lack analytical coherence and seem to signal an end to the less hostile decisions of the Supreme Court from 1980 through 1984. Discusses the programs at issue in the *Grand Rapids* decision, the shared-time and after-hours instruction programs which were held unconstitutional because of the primary effect of advancing religion. Analyzes the *Aguilar* decision involving an establishment clause challenge to Title I of the Elementary and Secondary Education Act of 1965. Notes that by the time the Supreme Court ruled in the case Congress had re-enacted Title I as Chapter 1 of the Education Improvement and Consolidation Act of 1981.

CONTRIBUTORS

MARY A. GRANT is Director of the Health Education Resource Center, College of Pharmacy and Allied Health Professions, St. John's University, Jamaica, New York. She holds a B.S. in Education degree, a Master's degree in Library Science and a P.D. (Professional Diploma) degree in Educational Administration and Supervision from St. John's. In her professional career Ms. Grant has been a classroom teacher in Catholic elementary schools and a director of secondary school library media centers in the New York and Philadelphia areas. She has served as a library consultant for the Brooklyn diocesan schools. Her professional activities include having served on the board of the national Catholic Library Association for twelve years from 1977 to 1989 as board member, vice-president, president, and immediate past president. Ms. Grant continues to be active on the local and national levels of CLA.

THOMAS C. HUNT received the Ph.D. from the University of Wisconsin. He is Professor of Foundations of Education at Virginia Tech. His major interest is history of American education with an emphasis on religion and schooling. He is the co-editor of *Religion and Morality in American Schooling* (1981), and co-edited, with James C. Carper, *Religious Schooling in America* (1984), *Religious Colleges and Universities in America: A Selected Bibliography* (1989) and (with Carper and Charles S. Kniker) *Religious Schools in America: A Selected Bibliography* (1986). His articles have appeared in *Educational Forum, The Journal of Church and*

State, Momentum, The Catholic Historical Review, Paedogogica Historica, Journal of Presbyterian History, Religious Education, Methodist History, National Association of Episcopal Schools Journal, and *High School Journal.* He received the Thayer S. Warshaw award in 1986 for his essay on "Religion and Public Schooling: A Tale of Tempest."

KAREN M. RISTAU is an associate professor at the University of St. Thomas in St. Paul, Minnesota, where she directs degree programs in educational leadership. In addition to her administrative duties, Karen teaches organizational theory and leadership to students in graduate education and business programs. She earned her doctoral degree from the University of San Francisco and has thirteen years experience as an elementary school principal. She serves on the advisory committee for the National Catholic Educational Association department of supervision, personnel and curriculum.

AUTHOR INDEX

SUBJECT INDEX

SOURCE BOOKS ON EDUCATION